The HIDDEN PLACES *of* THE HIGHLANDS AND ISLANDS

Edited by
David Gerrard

Published by:
Travel Publishing Ltd
7a Apollo House, Calleva Park
Aldermaston, Berks, RG7 8TN

ISBN 1-902-00722-0

First Published: *1999*

Regional Titles in the Hidden Places Series:

Cambridgeshire & Lincolnshire	Channel Islands
Cheshire	Cornwall
Devon	Dorset, Hants & Isle of Wight
Essex	Gloucestershire
Heart of England	Highlands & Islands
Kent	Lake District & Cumbria
Lancashire	Norfolk
Northeast Yorkshire	Northumberland & Durham
North Wales	Nottinghamshire
Peak District	Potteries
Somerset	South Wales
Suffolk	Surrey
Sussex	Thames & Chilterns
Warwickshire & W Midlands	Welsh Borders
Wiltshire	Yorkshire Dales

National Titles in the Hidden Places Series:

England	Ireland
Scotland	Wales

Printing by: Nuffield Press, Abingdon

Maps by: © MAPS IN MINUTES ™ (1998)

Line Drawings: Michelle Pearce

Editor: David Gerrard

Cover : Clare Hackney

Born in 1961, Clare was educated at West Surrey College of Art and Design as well as studying at Kingston University. She runs her own private water-colour school based in Surrey and has exhibited both in the UK and internationally. The cover is taken from an original water-colour of Eilean Donan Castle in Ross-Shire

FOREWORD

The Hidden Places series is a collection of easy to use travel guides taking you, in this instance, on a relaxed but informative tour through the Highlands and Islands of Scotland, the last remote wilderness of Western Europe offering the visitor truly magnificent hills and mountains, impressive coastlines, an abundance of wildlife and a very colourful history. Our books contain a wealth of interesting information on the history, the countryside, the towns and villages and the more established places of interest in the area. But they also promote the more secluded and little known visitor attractions and places to stay, eat and drink many of which are easy to miss unless you know exactly where you are going.

We include hotels, inns, restaurants, public houses, teashops, various types of accommodation, historic houses, museums, gardens, garden centres, craft centres and many other attractions throughout the Highlands and Islands, all of which are comprehensively indexed. Most places have an attractive line drawing and are cross-referenced to coloured maps found at the rear of the book. We do not award merit marks or rankings but concentrate on describing the more interesting, unusual or unique features of each place with the aim of making the reader's stay in the local area an enjoyable and stimulating experience.

Whether you are visiting the area for business or pleasure or in fact are living in the locality we do hope that you enjoy reading and using this book. We are always interested in what readers think of places covered (or not covered) in our guides so please do not hesitate to use the reader reaction forms provided to give us your considered comments. We also welcome any general comments which will help us improve the guides themselves. Finally if you are planning to visit any other corner of the British Isles we would like to refer you to the list of other ***Hidden Places*** titles to be found at the rear of the book.

CONTENTS

1 Inverness and the Moray Coast

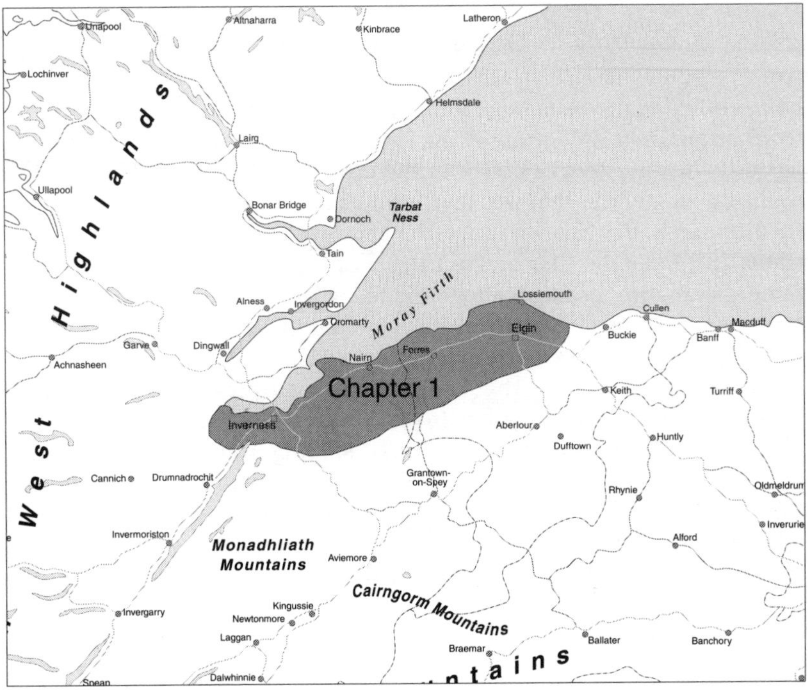

© MAPS IN MINUTES ™ (1998)

Covering some fourteen thousand square miles, (almost one-sixth of mainland Britain), the Highlands & Islands of Scotland can boast some of the most varied and spectacular scenery in Europe. There are huge tracts of territory such as the Monadhliath Mountains which are accessible only to the most determined, spellbindingly beautiful lochs and glens, stretches of fertile farmland, a coastline that ranges from the holiday beaches of the Moray Firth to the fearsome cliffs of northwest Sutherland, and a bewildering choice of literally hundreds of islands with scenery that varies from the dramatic hills of Arran and Skye, to the more gentle landscape of Bute and Caithness. Set within this scenic splendour are countless prehistoric ruins, a wealth of ruined castles and abbeys, some grand stately homes such as Dunrobin Castle and Ballindalloch Castle, appealing market towns, and unspoilt villages. The whole area is so sparsely inhabited that just minutes away from even the most popular tourist honeypots, the visitor can easily find peace and solitude. Throughout this vast region there is not a single mile of motorway, (although the main road artery, the A9, is dual carriageway for much of its length), not a single city, and only one really sizeable town, Inverness, with a population of some 40,000. It is here we begin our survey.

INVERNESS

Long known as the *"Capital of the Highlands"*, Inverness is a cosmopolitan town attractively sited around the River Ness where it flows into Beauly Firth. Its history stretches back to the 6th century when it developed as trading port serving what was then, and still is, the most populated part of the Highlands. In medieval times, David I elevated the town to royal burgh status and built the first of the three castles which were to occupy the same dominating position above the town. David's castle was destroyed by Robert the Bruce when he captured it from the English during the Wars of Independence. A second castle suffered a similar fate, being blown up by the Jacobites during the 1745 rebellion to prevent it falling into Hanoverian hands. The present **Inverness Castle** was erected in the mid 19th century, a striking mock-medieval building in red sandstone which today houses the Sheriff Court and during the season hosts the Castle Garrison Experience, a novel inter-active entertainment in which visitors take on the role of new recruits to the 18th century Hanoverian army. On the terrace outside the castle, the **Flora MacDonald Memorial** commemo-

Inverness Castle

rates the strong-charactered clanswoman who rowed Bonnie Prince Charlie over the sea to Skye after his defeat at Culloden.

Nearby, the **Town House** is another fine building in red sandstone, built in 1878 in the then- popular Victorian Gothic style and now used as council offices. In September 1921, the Town House was the venue for the first cabinet meeting ever held outside London when Prime Minister Lloyd George called an emergency meeting in response to the Irish crisis. In front of the Town House, the Mercat Cross stands above the ancient *clach-na-cuddain*, or **Stone of Tubs**, a rough block on which women carrying water from the River Ness would rest their buckets. A misty superstition asserts that the continued prosperity of Inverness depends on the stone never being moved.

Across the road from the Town House is the **Inverness Museum and Art Gallery**. The Museum concentrates on Highland and Jacobite history; the Art Gallery is largely devoted to images of old Inverness.

The oldest buildings in the town are to be found around Church Street where the **Steeple**, built in 1791, is notable for having had its spire straightened out after an earthquake in 1816. The most ancient structure is **Abertarff House** (National Trust for Scotland: NTS), a laird's town house dating from 1593 and distinguished by its round tower staircase and stepped gables.

Sombre memories are associated with the **Old High Church**, about a couple of hundred yards further north. After the battle of Culloden, any Jacobites who had survived that massacre were brought here and imprisoned before being taken into the churchyard and executed. Bullet marks left on the gravestones by the firing squads can still be seen. Around the corner from the Old High Church, a footbridge across the River Ness leads to **Balnain House**, an immaculately-restored Georgian house which is now home to an innovative, inter-active exhibition which traces the development of Highland music from heroic warrior songs to modern Gaelic folk-rock.

A little further out from the town centre, **Cromwell's Clock Tower** is all that remains of his garrison fort which was smartly demolished by Inverness townspeople at the Restoration. Many of the stones from the fort were used to build **Dunbar's Hospital** in Church Street. Founded by Alexander Dunbar in 1668 as an almshouse, it is one of the oldest buildings in Inverness, but it was used as a poor house, or Hospital, for only 16 years of its life. At various times it has been used as offices, workshops, schools and even the town's first fire station. This impressive building with its six dormer windows bearing scriptural quotes now houses an extensive selection of gifts and crafts, the vast majority of them made in Scotland. Anyone of Scottish descent will be interested in the **Clan Tartan Centre** at James Pringle's Holm Mills on Dores Road where traditional tartans and tweeds have been produced since 1798. Visitors can watch the centuries old art of tartan-weaving on impressive Hattersley power looms, trace their own links to a Scottish clan through a data base of more than 50,000 names all fully researched, browse in a shop stacked with a huge range of woollen clothes, and visit the welcoming restaurant. More information on 01463 223311. On a similar theme, the **Scottish Kiltmaker Visitor Centre** in Huntly Street is devoted entirely to the kilt and offers audio-visual displays on its history, the opportunity to watch kiltmakers at work, and there's even a Kilted Hall of Fame. Tel: 01463 222781.

As befits the Capital of the Highlands, Inverness is well-supplied with shops, restaurants and hotels. Of special note is the **Crown Court Hotel** which is located in a quiet residential area close to the town centre and has the ambience of a country house hotel in town. Awarded a 4-star rating by the Scottish Tourist Board, the hotel prides itself on its warm Highland welcome, its attention to detail and on making guests feel they are staying at somewhere "not a little out of the ordinary".

The Crown Court is immaculately furnished and decorated, its ten en suite bedrooms colour co-ordinated, extremely comfortable and fully equipped. Henderson's Bar provides an ideal setting for a sociable drink, and food is served either in the elegant main restaurant or in the intimate surroundings of the cosy brasserie. The Crown Court's chef has had wide experience at home and abroad, and enjoys exercising his skills with comprehensive menus containing a selection of Scottish and international

Crown Court Hotel, 25 Southside Road, Inverness IV2 3BG
Tel: 01463 234816

dishes. Whether you choose from the best of the marine harvest from sea or loch, venison and lamb from the hill, or beef from the plain, you will surely find something here to tempt your palate. The Crown Court is also the perfect location for weddings, functions, conferences and small business meetings with its spacious function suite and smaller Blue Room catering for any number of guests from 10 to 150.

A pleasant short walk from the town centre brings you to **Millwood House**, an admirable choice for a bed and breakfast stay. It stands in a quiet, exclusive area, surrounded by a large and beautifully maintained garden. Millwood House has been the home of Gillian and Bill Lee for many years and they welcome guests to share all the things they love about living here. Each guest bedroom has an individual charm, with every

Millwood House, 36, Old Mill Road, Inverness IV2 3HR
Tel: 01463 237254 Fax: 01463 719400

comfort supplied to make your stay a happy and memorable one. The peaceful sitting-room, with its cosy open fire and lots of books to browse through, is furnished with antiques and fresh with garden flowers. Breakfast, served in the old world dining-room overlooking the lovely garden, is really something special. The traditional Scottish breakfast includes a choice of haggis or black pudding, or you could select Scottish Kippers, Scottish Smoked Haddock, or a vegetarian option. Porridge, naturally, is also always available and so too is afternoon tea in the garden. Millwood House's attractions as a superior bed and breakfast establishment have also been recognised by the Scottish Tourist Board (5 star grading), the AA (a QQQQQ listing), and is also recommended by the Which? Good Bed & Breakfast Guide.

AROUND INVERNESS

Inverness stands at the hub of northeast Scotland's lines of communication, with a startling variety of landscapes within easy reach. To the north is the Black Isle, which is not black and not an island, but a promontory with the irresistible little town of Cromarty at its tip. To the northeast stretches the Moray Firth coastline with its sandy beaches and schools of dolphins; to the southeast, a 30 mile drive will bring you to the lovely valley of the Spey, Strathspey. Southwest of the town, the vast geological fault known as the Great Glen slices diagonally across the country, by way of fabled Loch Ness, to Fort William, while westwards rise the great hills of Easter Ross. We begin by visiting the Black Isle, and then travel more or less clockwise around the town.

A couple of miles north of Inverness, in the car park of the Tourist Information Centre on the A9, the **Dolphin and Seal Centre** offers a fascinating insight into the lives of these popular residents of the Moray Firth. The Centre has a magnificent view of the Firth, - just pick up a pair of binoculars and look out for one of the 130 individually identified dolphins which have made their home here. Measuring up to 4 metres in length, the Moray Firth dolphins are among the largest in the world, and since many of their favoured areas are close to the shore, this is one of the best places in Europe to see them at relatively close quarters. Underwater microphones pick up dolphin, seal and other underwater sounds and relay them to amplifiers in the Centre. Just put on a set of headphones and you can tune into this undiscovered world. From interactive computer displays and other exhibits, visitors can find out about the marine environment of the dolphins and discover how they use echo location to navigate and hunt for food. The Centre is open daily during the season.

Two miles north of the Dolphin Centre, the **Black Isle Wildlife and Country Park** is another excellent venue for a family outing. Wallabys, llamas, rare sheep and cattle are among the more unusual residents, but there are also plenty of cuddly smaller animals for children to handle. Other attractions include train rides, a picnic and play area, aviaries, a forest walk, gift shop and tearoom. The Park is open daily from March to November: for more details, telephone 01463 731656.

Northeast of the Wildlife Park, the A832 passes through **Fortrose**, with its ruined early 13th century Cathedral, and **Rosemarkie**, where the **Groam House Museum** displays a remarkable collection of Pictish sculptured stones, the most famous one dating from the 8th century and known as the "Soul of Rosemarkie". The museum also shows an interesting video which identifies the many Pictish sites in the area. Groam House Museum is open Monday to Saturday, and Sunday afternoons, during the season; weekend afternoons only from October to April.

CULLODEN MOOR

MAP 4 REF I6

4 miles E of Inverness off the B9006

At the Battle of Culloden, in August 1746, some 1500 Highlanders were slaughtered. A mere 76 English soldiers died. The casualty figures reflect how hopelessly outnumbered were the forces of Bonnie Prince Charlie against those of the Duke of Cumberland. Culloden became the graveyard for all the hopes of the Stuart dynasty of ever recovering the throne. Immediately after the battle, Cumberland ordered that none of the wounded should be spared, a brutal command that earned him the bitter nickname of "Butcher" Cumberland. Culloden was the last land battle of any significance to be fought in Britain and it marked the end of a distinctive Highland way of life. The clan leaders, forbidden to maintain private armies, became mere landlords, seeking rents rather than service. The English government passed a series of punitive laws designed to obliterate the Highlanders very culture: speaking Gaelic became a crime, wearing the tartan and playing the bagpipes were also banned.

The story of this turning-point in Scottish history is vividly presented at the **National Trust for Scotland's Visitor Centre** by an imaginative audio-visual and historical display. The Centre also houses a reference library and will check the records for you if you think that an ancestor of yours took part in the battle. Next door to the Centre is **Old Leanach Cottage**, outside which 30 Jacobite soldiers were burnt alive in the aftermath of the battle, and the **Well of the Dead** marks the spring where wounded Highlanders were killed as they tried to drink the water. Visitors can walk freely around the battlefield where flags show the position of the two armies, clan graves are marked by simple headstones, and the **Field of the English** marks the mass grave of the four-score English soldiers who died in the battle. Guided tours of the battlefield are available during the summer season and each year in April, on the Saturday closest to the date of the battle, a service is held in the Visitor Centre to commemorate the fallen of both armies.

Just half a mile from the historic battlefield is **Leanach Farm B & B** which enjoys grand views overlooking the Nairn Valley and the Culloden viaduct carrying the main East Coast railway to Inverness. The farmhouse is an attractively-designed, white-painted modern building set at the heart of a working mixed stock and arable farm. Rosanne MacKay does all the cooking and her cuisine has received awards for healthy eating. She offers guests traditional farmhouse fare prepared with locally obtained fresh produce.

All the letting rooms are en suite, individually decorated, and well-equipped with TV and tea/coffee making facilities. A good indication of Leanach Farm's good food and superior amenities is its 4-star Commended

Leanach Farm B & B, Culloden Moor, Inverness IV1 2EJ
Tel/Fax: 01463 791027

rating from the Scottish Tourist Board. Rosanne's husband Ian trains Border collies and has had many successes in sheepdog trials. It is fascinating to see him at work with these super-intelligent dogs. As well as being close to Culloden battlefield, Leanach Farm is also near the Clava Cairns, an impressive group of prehistoric standing stones, and Cawdor Castle and Fort George are both about 8 miles distant.

DAVIOT

MAP 4 REF I6

4 miles SE of Inverness on the A9

Daviot is just a short drive from Inverness, and on the edge of the village **Torguish House** offers holiday-makers an excellent choice of accommodation. Bed and breakfast is available in the Old Manse which, interestingly, was the childhood home of the late Alistair MacLean, author of such action-packed novels as *The Guns of Navarone* and *Where Eagles Dare*. All the rooms are fully equipped to a high standard and most are en suite.

If you prefer self-catering, then you should go for the Old Steading in the grounds of Torguish House which has been converted into 4 compact, fully furnished cottages. Laundry facilities are available and in the garden there's a play area for children, complete with putting green, sand-pit, swings and tree house. Pets are welcome at no extra charge.

Owners Alister and Marjorie Allan ensure that visitors make the most of their holiday in this peaceful retreat which is also a perfect base for sight-seeing journeys to the north, east and west coasts. All of these can

Torguish House, Daviot, Inverness IV1 2XQ
Tel: 01463 772208

comfortably be reached on a day trip and en route you will pass through some of the most beautiful and spectacular scenery in Scotland. The Orkney Islands, too, are accessible as day excursions.

TOMATIN

MAP 4 REF I7

14 miles SE of Inverness off the A9

The name of this little village has become known around the world because of the products of the **Tomatin Distillery**. The distillery's 10-year-old Highland Malt, with its lightly-peated and delicate flavour, is well known to whisky connoisseurs, one of whom dubbed it "Simply a King among whiskies". Tomatin's whisky is also much in demand with major blenders for whom its distinctive flavour and quality is an essential part of their "recipes". That demand has made Tomatin the most productive distillery in Scotland. Visitors can join a 45-minute guided tour, sample the product, and browse in the Visitor Centre where there are informative displays and a full range of Tomatin whiskies on offer. The distillery is open weekdays throughout the year, and on Saturday mornings from May to October. Tel: 01808 511444

Set in the midst of the Monadliath mountains, in the valley of the River Findhorn, **Glenan Lodge** is an attractive stone house, built in the traditional style of a Scottish lodge. It's an ideal base for anglers, stalkers, birdwatchers, hillwalkers and tourists alike. Whatever your special inter-

Glenan Lodge, Tomatin, Inverness-shire, IV13 7YT
Tel: 01808 511217/Fax: 511356

ests, you can be assured of a very warm Scottish welcome from the owners, Mhorag and Tony Lucock. The Lodge has ten guest bedrooms, all centrally heated and all with tea and coffee-making facilities. Some are en suite, the others have wash-hand basins with hot and cold water. There's a large and comfortable TV lounge with an ample supply of books and magazines. A traditional home cooked breakfast is served in the dining-room where, if you wish, you can also have an evening meal, followed perhaps by a sampling of the fine selection of Highland single malt whiskies from the bar. You might want to follow this up with a visit to the Tomatin Distillery, Scotland's largest malt whisky distillery, which is within easy walking distance of Glenan Lodge.

BEAULY MAP 4 REF H6

12 miles W of Inverness on the A862

If you drive west from Inverness for about 4 miles along the A862, you will come to the **Ardfearn Plant Centre** at **Bunchrew**, established in 1987 by the well-known lecturer and TV personality, Jim Sutherland, and his son Alasdair. The nursery produces a fascinating range of shrubs, trees and herbaceous plants and the largest selection of alpines in Scotland. Plants from every continent in the world are raised here with new species continually being introduced. Ardfearn occupies a lovely position overlooking Beauly Firth with good views of its varied wild life, including seals and ospreys. More details on 01463 243250.

Another 4 miles to the west, stands **Moniack Castle**, which is actually a winery producing varieties such as elderflower and birch, as well as sloe gin and liqueurs. Tours are available, there's a shop and restaurant, and admission is free. The winery is open daily, except Sundays: for more details, telephone 01463 831283.

Four miles further west along the A862 is the peaceful little town of Beauly which, according to local legend, owes its name to Mary, Queen of Scots. On a visit in 1564 she apparently exclaimed "Ah, quel beau lieu!" (What a beautiful place!). An appealing story but in fact Beauly already had its name, derived from the Priory in which the Queen stayed during her visit. Founded in the 13th century, the Priory was recorded as the "monasterium de bello loco", - the monastery in a beautiful setting. Some beautiful fragments of the original building have survived and the north transept, restored in 1901, contains some interesting tombs and monuments of the Mackenzie family.

Beauly's town square is dominated by the Lovat Scouts Memorial, an impressive structure commemorating the raising by the 16th Lord Lovat of a Highland contingent to fight in the Boer War. Also worth a visit is the Kilmorack Gallery. It is housed in a beautiful 18th century church which retains most of its original features and provides an intriguing setting for a display of works by contemporary Scottish artists. To the south of the town, the Made in Scotland Shop is a showcase for a vast collection of Scottish made gifts, - knitwear, jewellery, pottery, furnishings, shortbreads and biscuits, jams and jellies, and much more. The shop is open every weekday all year, and on Sunday afternoons from April to September.

Five miles to the southwest of Beauly, on the A831, **Cluanie Park** offers visitors the chance to see some magnificent birds of prey at close quarters, amongst them golden eagles. There are regular talks and flying demonstrations, a gift shop, tea room and children's play area. The Park is open daily, except Saturdays, from June to September. More details on 01463 782534.

THE MORAY COAST

Stretching eastwards from Inverness, the coastal strip of the **Moray Firth** is a popular destination for those in search of a seaside holiday. Some 20 miles of sandy beaches run from Nairn to beyond Lossiemouth, and another major attraction is the colony of some 130 bottle-nosed dolphins which has taken up residence here. Known to scientists as *Tursiops truncatus,* this is the largest species of dolphin in the world, with a fully-grown adult attaining a length of 13ft and weighing between 400 and 660 pounds. Spectacular though they are to watch as they "bow-ride" in front of boats, the Moray Firth colony of dolphins has the uncharacteristic and unappealing habit of killing porpoises. Despite this unlovely trait, they are an irresistible sight and several companies run regular dolphin-spotting boat trips, although these are restricted during the dolphins' breeding season between late June and August.

The coastal area alongside the Moray Firth is one of the most fertile in the Highlands, and has always been comparatively well-populated, leading to the growth of attractive small towns such as Nairn, Forres, and Elgin with its magnificent ruined Cathedral. The region also boasts two major castles, Cawdor and Brodie, (both of which are still lived in by descendants of the original builders), and a huge 18th century military base, Fort George, which is generally considered to one of the finest fortifications in all Europe. Also well worth visiting is the century-old Dallas Dhu distillery near Forres where you can nurse a fine glass of malt whisky as you watch a film recording the history of this noble beverage.

ARDERSIER MAP 4 REF I6

11 miles NE of Inverness on the B9006 & B9039

If you take the B9039 about 5 miles out of Inverness, it will lead you past Inverness Airport and then along the shore of the Moray Firth before arriving at the little village of Ardersier. **The Gun Lodge Hotel** here is an outstanding establishment, a finalist in the 1996 Scottish Pub of the Year awards. Originally built to house the commander of Fort George, on the headland a mile away to the north, this traditional hotel, pub and eating place is personally run by the Mason family. The menu offers some of the finest Scottish cuisine in the area, including haggis, venison, salmon steaks

Gun Lodge Hotel, High Street, Ardersier, Inverness-shire IV1 2QB.
Tel: 01667 462734

and shellfish, as well as vegetarian dishes and a special choice for children. A good range of draught beers and over 20 malt whiskies are served in the bar, and for those looking for overnight accommodation, there are ten comfortable guest rooms equipped with washbasins and colour TVs; three also have en suite facilities. Karen, the youngest member of the family, takes great delight in welcoming young visitors and showing them her pet pigs and goats!

A mile or so beyond the village, on Ardersier Point, **Fort George** (Historic Scotland) is a remarkable example of 18th century military architecture and generally regarded as one of the most impressive fortifications in Europe. Its perimeter walls are almost a mile long and enclose an area of 42 acres, - Edinburgh Castle would comfortably fit onto its parade ground. Commanding the narrow entrance to the Moray Firth, the fort was designed by Robert Adam and building began in 1748, three years after the Jacobite rebellion, to house some 2000 soldiers garrisoned here to quell any attempt to rekindle the Stuart cause. The fort took 21 years to complete and cost nearly £1 billion in today's money, but it has never seen a shot fired in anger. Fort George is still a barracks, manned by the Queen's Own Highlanders whose glorious history is recorded in the Regimental Museum here. Bird-watchers will be delighted to find a colony of kittiwakes perched on the fort's roof-tops, and flocks of waders and seabirds on the sands and mud flats below. From the vantage position of the fort's lofty walls, you may even be lucky enough to catch sight of some of the bottle-nosed dolphins who have made the Moray Firth their home. Fort George is open daily, all year round. For more details, telephone 01667 462777.

Fort George, Nr Ardesier

CAWDOR

MAP 4 REF J6

5 miles SW of Nairn on the B9090

The lovely conservation village of Cawdor is best known for **Cawdor Castle**, home of the Thanes of Cawdor for more than 600 years. A fairy-tale building of turrets and towers, it must surely be the only castle built around a tree. A family tradition asserts that in a dream the 3rd Thane of Cawdor was told to load his donkey with gold and wherever the beast settled for the night, there to build his castle. The tree still stands, bare and limbless now, in the great vaulted room at the base of the central tower. It was a holly tree, one of the seven sacred trees of Celtic mythology, and has been carbon-dated to 1372. The presence of such a mystic tree was probably intended to ward off evil influences, but in the late Middle Ages it would have needed more than a tree to preserve the Cawdors from the rampant intrigue, murder and mayhem of the time. A typical (and true) story tells of Muriel, the 9th Thaness. She inherited the title at her birth in 1510, her father having died a few months before. As a rich heiress, the infant girl was promptly kidnapped by the most powerful man in Scotland, the Earl of Argyll, and "for future recognition, the babe was branded on the hip by her nurse with a key, and the top joint of her left little finger was bitten off". The rest of Muriel's long life, (she lived to be 77 years old), is strewn with similarly striking incidents.

Cawdor Castle

The castle is well worth visiting for its remarkable collections of tapestries, paintings (Reynolds, Lely, Lawrence, Romney, Stanley Spencer and John Piper amongst them), Chippendale furniture, and a wealth of family memorabilia. The grounds of Cawdor Castle are especially satisfying, with superb gardens (first laid out in the 1720s), a 9-hole mini-golf course, a topiary maze, picnic spots, and several Nature Trails.

Many visitors are still drawn to Cawdor because of its associations with Shakespeare's "Macbeth" although the present castle wasn't built until more than 300 years after Macbeth had died. Still worse, Macbeth never was Thane of Cawdor, - the title was retrospectively bestowed on him by the 16th century historian Hector Boethius to give the old story more dramatic spice. The Castle is open daily from May to early October: for more details, telephone 01667 404615.

Just outside the delightful village, and surrounded by open countryside, **Cantraydoune Cottages** provide a marvellously peaceful setting for a relaxing holiday. The building, a fine example of a traditional Scottish "long house", dates back to around 1745 when it was built as four linked cottages for farmworkers. It was totally refurbished in 1995 to an extremely high standard, with tiled floors, wood burning stoves and pine furniture. The guest rooms are individually and attractively decorated and all are en

Cantraydoune Cottages, Cawdor, Nairnshire IV12 5XY
Tel: 01667 493325

suite. There's a comfortable lounge, conservatory and dining room for guests' use. Christina Paul looks after her visitors well. She does all the cooking, - good quality home cooking using fresh local produce. Guests are welcome to bring their own wine and packed lunches are available on request if you are planning a day out. The area provides many interesting destinations: Cawdor and Brodie Castles, the historic battlefield of Culloden, the Moray coast and the urban attractions of Inverness and Elgin are all just a short drive away.

NAIRN MAP 4 REF J6

16 miles NE of Aberdeen on the A96

An attractive county town of mellow buildings and a popular holiday resort, Nairn has long been regarded as marking the boundary between the Lowlands and the Highlands. This divide was made abundantly clear to King James VI when he visited in the late 1590s. The fishermen, he found, spoke Gaelic; the farmers, English. He boasted sardonically that his kingdom was so extensive that people at one end of a town's main street could not understand those who lived at the other. Nairn marks the beginning of a seaside holiday coast: inviting sandy beaches stretch eastwards some 20 miles or so to Lossiemouth. To clinch the town's appeal as an inviting holiday resort, Nairn can truthfully claim to be one of the driest and sunniest places in all Scotland.

Nowadays, the few fishing boats sheltering in the harbour built by Thomas Telford are vastly outnumbered by pleasure craft, but for an insight into Nairn's maritime past, pay a visit to the tiny **Fishertown Museum** (free) which has an interesting collection of vintage photographs and artefacts connected with the herring fishing industry during the days of steam drifters. On the eastern edge of the town, the **Invernairn Mill Visitor Centre** offers a wide variety of attractions. There's a heritage museum, exhibition centre with working displays by local craftsmen, a working millwheel complete with all its gearing, a blacksmith's, craft and woollen shops selling high quality Scottish and locally crafted goods, an excellent delicatessen and a restaurant overlooking the Lethen hills. The centre is open all year round, but closed on Mondays from October to April. More information on 01667 455273.

AULDEARN MAP 4 REF J6

3 miles E of Nairn off the A96

Auldearn has a significant place in Scottish history for it was here, in May 1645, that Montrose raised his standard before achieving a brilliant victory over the forces of the Covenanters. The village had been founded as a royal burgh in the 12th century and a castle raised. Auldearn was intended to be the major administrative centre for the area but in time it was superseded by the better-sited settlement at Nairn. All that remains of 12th century **Eren Castle** is the motte, or mound, which it once crowned. In its place stands the 17th century Boath Doocot (NTS), or dovecote, and a board showing the plan of the critical battle that once raged here.

In the centre of this historic village is **The Lion Hotel**, originally built in the 17th century as an ale importing house and converted to a hotel some 20 years ago. It is now owned and personally run by Iain Reside who has been in the hotel trade all his working life and took over the Lion in

The Lion Hotel, High Street, Auldearn, IV12 5TH
Tel: 01667 456922

1996. He has quickly established an excellent reputation for good, wholesome, traditional cooking at very reasonable prices. The extensive menu, which changes daily, includes a good choice of fish, meat and vegetarian dishes, and half portions are available for children at half price. If you just want a snack, toasted sandwiches are also on the menu. The Lion also has a large function suite, with a separate bar, which is capable of catering for parties of up to 200 guests. And if you are planning to stay in this attractive corner of north-east Scotland, the hotel has several guest rooms, all well-equipped, pleasantly furnished, and all en suite.

BRODIE MAP 4 REF J6
4 miles W of Forres on the A96

Continuing westwards along the A96, follow the signs to **Brodie Castle**. The estate was granted to the Brodie family in 1160 by Malcolm IV and, although the house is now maintained by the National Trust for Scotland, the 25th Earl of Brodie still lives here. The present castle, built in a curious Z shape, replaced a medieval structure which was burnt down during the Civil War in 1645. Surrounded by lovely grounds, where each spring a sea of daffodils waves a golden haze, Brodie Castle houses an outstanding collection of porcelain, French furniture, and paintings, - amongst them works by Jacob Cuyp and Edwin Landseer. A wood-panelled dining-room, a grandiose Victorian kitchen and austere servants' quarters vividly evoke the disparities between life upstairs and downstairs in those days. Standing in the grounds, Rodney's Stone is a well-preserved stone slab sculpted

Brodie Castle

with Pictish symbols on one side and a cross on the other. The castle is open daily from April to September, and on weekends in October. Further details on 01309 641371.

FORRES Map 4 ref J6

12 miles W of Elgin on the A96

According to Shakespeare, it was on a blasted heath outside Forres that Macbeth first encountered the weird sisters who prophesied that he would be "king hereafter". Macbeth was on his way to King Duncan's castle at Forres, a building which has long since disappeared. This small town is most notable today for its attractive parks and for **Sueno's Stone**, one of the most remarkable Pictish stones in Scotland. Twenty feet high and elaborately carved, it most probably commemorates a medieval battle between the people of Moray and the Norse settlers on Orkney. The carvings are an early kind of war reporting. Reading from top to base, the story begins with the arrival of the leader and concludes with the decapitated bodies of the defeated at the bottom. The stone was found buried in 1726 and mistakenly named after Sweyn Forkbeard, King of Denmark. It stands just to the east of the town, enclosed in a glass booth to protect it from further ravages of the weather.

Housed in a splendid, porticoed building, **The Falconer Museum** contains a wealth of exhibits illustrating the heritage of Moray, from a

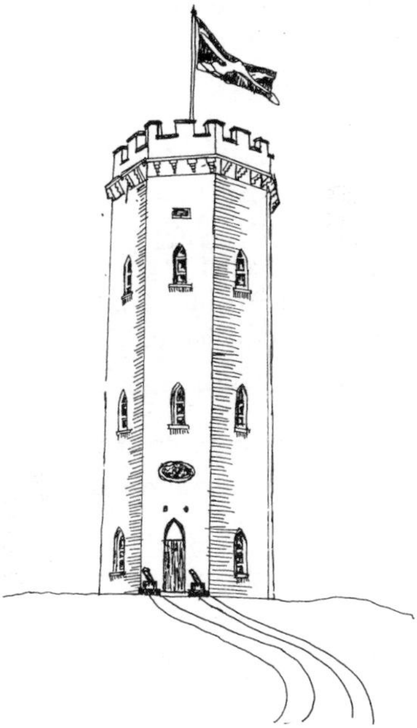

Nelson Tower

reconstructed Victorian shop window to the story of the "Corries" folk group. Another striking building is the **Nelson Tower** in Grant Park, a lofty octangular tower built by the Trafalgar Club in commemoration of Nelson's victory at Trafalgar. It was opened in 1812 and provides spectacular views over the Moray Firth, - once you have climbed its 96 steps.

If you are looking for bed and breakfast accommodation in this area, you should certainly try to stay at **"Morven"**. This Victorian House is situated in a quiet, town centre location and features a delightfully attractive and secluded large, mature garden which is stone-flagged with a patio area. There is also private car parking to the rear of the house.

The interior is beautifully decorated in a fresh, classic style all of its own, which gives the house the warm and friendly atmosphere that Barbara MacDonald has been able to maintain over the last 14 years. There are three letting rooms, all attractively furnished and well-equipped. Children are welcome at this Scottish Tour-

Morven, Caroline Street, Forres, IV36 0AN. Tel/Fax: 01309 673788

ist Board Commended Victorian house, which is conveniently located for exploring the golfing/fishing scene of the Speyside area, the Whisky Trail and Castle Trail as well as all the other many attractions of the Scottish Highlands.

A couple of miles south of Forres is the **Dallas Dhu Distillery**, the last distillery to be built in the 19th century. Visitors can wander freely through this perfectly preserved time capsule of the distiller's craft and then settle down with a free dram of whisky in the audio-visual theatre to watch a presentation of the story of Scotch whisky. There's also a gift shop and picnic area. The distillery is open daily from April to September, and most days from October to March, but opening hours vary. For more details, telephone 01309 676548.

FINDHORN

MAP 4 REF J5

12 miles W of Elgin via the A96 and B9011

This pleasant little fishing village, founded by the Abbot of Kinloss in 1532, is actually the third to bear the name of Findhorn. The first was destroyed by a sandstorm in 1694, the second was engulfed by a flood in 1701. Present day Findhorn boasts a superb beach, a picturesque harbour and a small Heritage Centre but its name is best known world-wide because of the **Findhorn Foundation**, a mile outside the village. The foundation was established in 1962 by Eileen and Peter Caddy, together with Dorothy Maclean as a community dedicated to spiritual values and ecological innovation. Dorothy espoused a theory that "devas", primal forces of light and energy, could be harnessed to grow healthy plants and vegetables on the unpromising sandy soil. She did indeed produce specimens far larger than had been grown in the area before. The Foundation has grown from an original nucleus of three adults and three children to a settlement of some 200 people, with around 8000 visitors a year. There are guided tours, residential workshops, and a well-stocked delicatessen on the site.

On the edge of Findhorn village, between the dunes and woodland, is **Heath House** offering spacious and comfortable bed & breakfast accommodation. Tony and Elizabeth Cowie have a talent for creating a relaxed and friendly atmosphere, and their modern house with its pleasant garden and outlook makes an excellent base for exploring this favoured corner of the country. Located just 200 yards from Findhorn Bay, Heath House offers visitors a choice of two double rooms (one en suite), and a twin-bedded room. Tony has many years experience of sailing and his yacht, a Jaguar 27, is available for chartered trips around the area. You might just want a few hours sailing in the Moray Firth, or a two day trip to Cromarty staying overnight on board the 3/4 berth vessel. Whether you go for one day or two, there's no better way of seeing the dolphins whose favoured

Heath House, Findhorn, Moray IV36 3WN
Tel: 01309 691082 e-mail: strandbo@aol.com

location is at the entrance to the Cromarty Firth. Being under sail means that minimum disturbance is caused to these fascinating creatures. Alternatively, Tony can usually arrange a real RIB-tickler, a high-speed trip on a Rigid Inflatable Boat along the Moray Coast. Water sports are Findhorn's forte but the area also offers excellent golf, fishing, and walking. As Tony says, this is where Findhorn excels, - search far and wide, nowhere else will you find such relaxation in being active!

Across the bay from Findhorn village, **Culbin Forest** (Forest Enterprise) was planted in the 1920s to control the extensive sand dunes which were frequently blown by North Sea storms onto neighbouring agricultural land. (A great tempest in 1694 drove so much sand onto the estate of the Laird of Culbin that "there was not a vestige to be seen of his manor house, yards, orchards and mains"). The forest has developed over the years and today it encompasses timber production, conservation projects, recreational uses such as walking, cycling and horse-riding, and is also an educational base for many schools, colleges and universities. Botanists especially will be in their element here, - a recent survey identified 550 flowering plants, many at their most northerly or southerly habitat, and more than 130 species of lichen. More information on 01343 820223.

ALVES

Map 5 ref K5

4 miles W of Elgin on the A96

In a peaceful location about a mile from Alves, **Carden Self-Catering** offers visitors a remarkable choice of holiday accommodation. The Old Steading, or farmhouse buildings, are some two centuries old and have been inventively converted into six houses. Each one has been individually designed to take advantage of the setting, giving views into the south-facing courtyard and over open farmland to the northern hills. "The Barn" sleeps six, "The Cart House" and "The Mill House" accommodate four each, while the other three houses are designed for two each. (Don't hesitate about booking "The Bothy" - it's far more luxurious than the name would have you believe!) The fitted kitchens are all extremely well-equipped, (even a dishwasher, washing machine and tumble dryer are included), and the comfortably furnished living rooms have a colour TV with text and video. Each house has its own enclosed private patio garden with furniture, and barbecues are available.

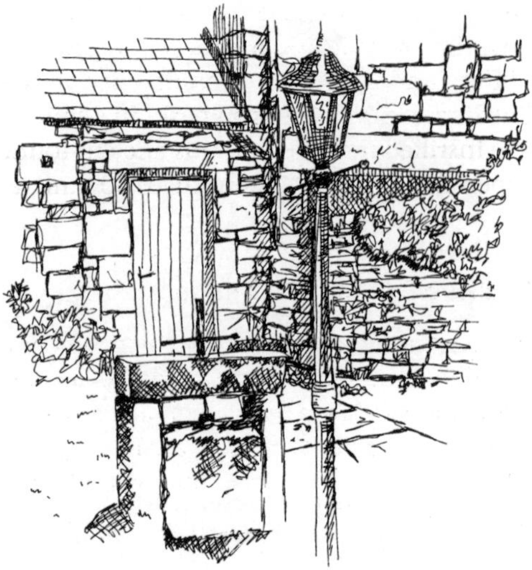

Carden Self-Catering, The Old Steading Garden, Alves, Moray IV30 3UP
Tel: 01343 850222 Fax: 01343 850626
e mail: carden @ enterprise. net

Outdoor facilities include an all weather tennis court, children's play area, and farm walk, while the indoor Games Room is equipped with table tennis, a pool table and a video games machine. Carden Self-Catering also has two farm cottages, Grieves and Claydales, both equipped and furnished to the same high standards. All the recreational facilities on offer at the Old Steading are also available to guests staying in these cottages. Dog lovers will be pleased to know that a maximum of two dogs is permitted in Grieves Cottage. Open all year round, Carden Self-Catering also offers weekend and short breaks. If you would like to know more, there's a detailed brochure available which even includes ground plans of each property.

About 4 miles south of Alves as the crow flies, and roughly twice as far by road, stands **Pluscarden Abbey**, one of the very few monastic establishments in Scotland still functioning. Surrounded by attractive countryside, the Abbey was built on a very grand scale around 1230, knocked around quite badly by the English Edward III in 1303, and even more seriously damaged by the Scottish Earl of Buchan in 1390 during his feud with the local bishop. Pluscarden's monks struggled valiantly to restore the Abbey, only to have it completely suppressed in 1560. More than three centuries of neglect and slow decay followed, halted only in 1897 when the 3rd Marquis of Bute, a Catholic antiquarian, bought the ruinous building and began to restore it. His son later donated the Abbey to the Benedictine monks of Prinknash, in Gloucestershire, and since 1948 they have instilled new life into this ancient foundation. This striking building is open daily from 5 a.m. until 10.30 p.m.; admission is free.

ELGIN

Map 5 ref K5

38 miles NE of Inverness on the A96

This handsome market town, which developed around the River Lossie in the 1200s, still retains most of its medieval street plan. The bustling High Street gradually widens to a cobbled Market Place where the architectural focus is an elegant neo-classical building, the **Church of St Giles**, erected in 1828. Eight years later, at the top of the High Street, the townspeople of Elgin subscribed funds to build one of the first municipal museums in Britain. The **Elgin Museum** offers a good display of local artefacts, some fine Pictish stones, pre-Columbian pottery, and also houses an eclectic anthropological collection which includes a shrunken head from Ecuador and a gruesomely grinning mummy from Peru. When the museum first opened, Johnstons of Elgin Mill was already well-established. For almost two centuries, Johnstons has been noted for its fine fabrics and finished garments. Modern day visitors can watch the whole process by which raw cashmere from China and Mongolia is transformed into finished garments. Following the disastrous floods of July, 1997, when the Lossie burst its banks and swamped the mill with 4ft of water, Johnstons undertook massive rebuilding and refurbishment of their Shop and Visitor Centre. These smart new facilities are situated in original mill buildings of 1865 and contain a wide range of stylish products. Mill tours are available, there's an audio-visual presentation, and a new Coffee Shop serving home-made Scottish baking, freshly ground coffee, speciality teas, and light meals. For more details, telephone 01343 554099.

Elgin has a particular resonance in Scottish history for it was here that Bonnie Prince Charlie spent eleven days in 1746 just before taking to the field of Culloden where the hopes of the Stewart cause were finally and brutally annihilated. During his stay, the Prince visited the ruins of **Elgin Cathedral** which is possibly the most accident-prone ecclesiastical building in the country. Founded in 1224, barely fifty years later it was severely damaged by fire. Rebuilt, the Cathedral was described as *"the ornament of the district, the glory of the kingdom, and the admiration of foreigners"*. Then in 1390 the *"Wolf of Badenoch"*, (the epithet applied to the lawless Earl of Buchan), with his *"wyld, wykked Helendmen"*, set fire to the building along with the rest of the town. It was the Earl's way of expressing his displeasure towards the Bishop of Moray who had excommunicated him for leaving his wife. Rebuilt once again, the Cathedral flourished for a century and a half until the Reformation. Then it was stripped of all its priceless treasures, the lead was salvaged from its roof in 1667, and on Easter Sunday 1711, the central tower collapsed. The ruins were cannibalised as a "common quarry" until 1807 when steps were taken to preserve what remained. And what remains is still remarkably beautiful.

A short distance from the Cathedral, in a small paved piazza off the High Street, is Sandra Stewart's delightful coffee-shop and restaurant, **The Rowan Tree**. One satisfied regular customer has described The Rowan Tree as the "only real coffee shop around" and he's almost certainly right. Customers can either sit outside overlooking the quiet piazza, or inside where the decor has an appealing Victorian flavour. The aura of times past is enhanced by the crisp white blouses and mob caps worn by the staff. Sandra opened The Rowan Tree in 1997 but has been in catering all her life. (She also offers an outside catering service: anything from a finger buffet to a banquet). Her wide experience is reflected in the sumptuous home-baked cakes on offer and in the meals listed on the extensive menu. This friendly and relaxed coffee-shop also stocks an exclusive range of coffees and teas from around the world. The Rowan Tree is open every day from 9am until 5pm, and during the summer months stays open later.

The Rowan Tree, 55 High Street, Elgin, Moray IV30 1EE Tel: 01343 551273

SHERIFFSTON MAP 5 REF K6

2 miles E of Elgin off the B9103

Chalet holidays are fast growing in popularity and those offered by **North East Farm Chalets** at Sheriffston provide particularly good value. Scattered around three different owner-occupied farms, each of the three properties is a well-appointed modern A-frame chalet with 2 bedrooms sleeping up to 6 people. These purpose-built holiday lodges, all with comfortable furnishings by Habitat, combine up-to-date amenities with the

North East Farm Chalets, Sheriffston, Elgin, Moray IV30 8LA
Tel: 01343 842695

good old-fashioned pleasure of a warm farmhouse welcome and the personal attention of the farm family who will do everything possible to help you enjoy your favourite activities, - or if you prefer it, inactivity! Located in peaceful rural surroundings, the chalets make an ideal holiday destination for families with children and pets.

The safe, sandy beaches of the Moray Firth are uncrowded and easily accessible, and facilities for almost every kind of sport are within easy reach. In each chalet you'll find full information about local events and attractions: everything from the historic castles of Mar, Cawdor and Brodie, to the local agricultural shows; from hang-gliding or fishing, to rough shooting or water-sports. Walkers are spoilt for choice in this area, with the Speyside Way and many other waymarked paths waiting to be explored. Accommodation is available to rent all year round, but to get the very most from this lovely countryside you should perhaps consider high summer when the sun hardly sinks below the horizon.

To the north and west of Elgin, three historic buildings definitely merit a short diversion. **St Peter's Kirk** near Duffus dates back to 1226, and although only mournful fragments of that original structure remain, the church is worth visiting to see its fine 14th century cross, the exquisite calligraphy on many of the tombstones, and the watch-house built in 1830 to protect the newly-interred from the depredations of grave-robbers. Duffus is also home to **Gordonstoun School**, founded in 1933 by Kurt Hahn, a refugee from Nazi Germany who by manic force of character successfully established a dire educational establishment. Gordonstoun managed to incorporate the worst elements of the English public school ethos Hahn so greatly admired, along with a glorification of physical prowess borrowed from the Nazi regime he so much detested. Prince Philip was happy as a pupil here: his son, Prince Charles, rather less so.

Duffus Castle, about a mile and a half to the southeast of Duffus village, owes its present dramatic appearance to some Norman builders who didn't get their calculations exactly right. The great earthen mound on which they erected their huge castle eventually gave way under the massive weight of so much stone, undermining the impressive 14th century tower which has sunk, split open, and now leans at an ominous angle. Admission to Duffus Castle is free, but take care which side of the tower you inspect it from.

The third of this group of historic buildings close to Elgin is **Spynie Palace** (Historic Scotland). Tacked on to a much older building, the palace was built in the 1460s as a residence for the Bishop of Moray, David Stewart. Taking into account the less-than-respectful attitude of the locals at that time to the established church, the bishop decided that a well-fortified building might be appropriate. The colossal, four-square David's Tower, named after him, is the largest tower house in Scotland, - a clear indication from His Grace to his flock that in this part of Moray, at least, the meek would not be inheriting the earth for a while.

LOSSIEMOUTH

MAP 5 REF K5

6 miles N of Elgin on the A941

Four miles north of Spynie Palace is Elgin's nearest seaside resort, Lossiemouth, with two sandy beaches swept by invigorating breezes. Once important for its herring fishing, the town is generally known as Lossie, and its residents as "Lossie loons". The town's most famous loon was Ramsay MacDonald, the first Labour prime minister, and the house in which he was born in 1866 stands at 1, Gregory Place, identified by a plaque. The interior is not open to the public but, curiously, there is a reconstruction of MacDonald's study in the **Lossiemouth Fisheries & Community Museum** which is otherwise devoted to the town's fishing industry and includes some interesting small scale models of fishing boats.

2 Strathspey

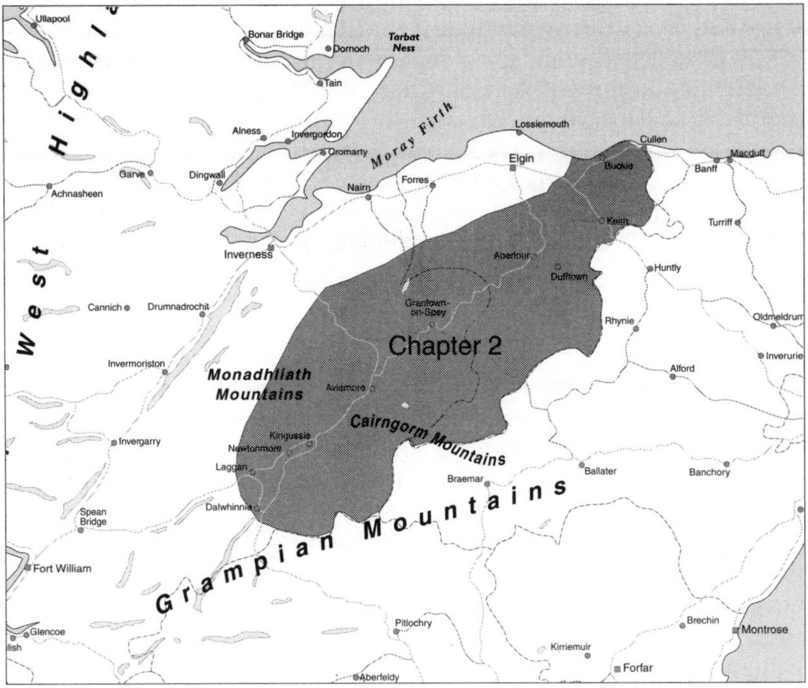

"Strath" is a word that many visitors to Scotland may not be familiar with. In northern England, it would be called a dale; in southern England, a valley; in Wales a cwm; and in Devon, a combe. Five different names within mainland Britain for five distinctive kinds of landscape surrounding the same topographical feature, a river.

A remarkable river in this case. The Spey is Scotland's second longest river (110 miles), and its fastest flowing. It is famous for salmon, sea trout and brown trout fishing of the highest quality, and from the start of the season in early February, the Spey salmon fishing intensifies throughout the summer.

The Spey's unpolluted waters are also much appreciated by the producers of malt whisky, - half of all Scotland's malt whisky distilleries are located in the surrounding glens. The **Malt Whisky Trail** is a 70-mile route which links up seven of them and a cooperage. They all offer visitors a guided tour, a free dram, and, if they charge an entrance fee, usually part of it can be redeemed against a bottle of whisky from the distillery shop. In addition to these distilleries, there are many others which also welcome visitors. Parts of the Malt Whisky Trail overlap with the **Speyside Way**, a 45-mile long path which follows disused railway tracks for much of its length. For most of its route, the path stays close to roads and small villages, and so is ideal for shorter walks or cycle rides. A leaflet is available which gives details of the route and also lists conveniently located bed & breakfast establishments and camping sites. The path begins at Spey Bay on the Moray Firth and runs southwards to Tomintoul on the edge of the Cairngorm mountains. We begin our tour of Strathspey at the point where the River Spey flows into the Moray Firth and then follow the river, (with occasional short diversions), upstream and southwards, for almost one hundred miles, to its source in the Monadhliath Mountains.

SPEY BAY — MAP 5 REF K5

14 miles NE of Elgin on the B9104

This small village at the mouth of the Spey is nowadays best known for the **Tugnet Ice House** (free), the largest industrial ice house in Scotland. Built in 1890, it's an odd-looking building, rather like three grassed-over Nissen huts. The Ice House is now a museum, telling the story of shipbuilding and salmon fishing on the Spey through models and displays, while a video programme takes the visitor on a journey down the river from its source to the mouth. The museum is open from May to September.

FOCHABERS — MAP 5 REF K6

9 miles SE of Elgin on the A96

Fochabers is one of many Scottish villages which were re-sited from their original location when an 18th century Laird, embarking on a programme of improving his property, decided to remove his tenants' unsightly hovels from view. Normally, this could be achieved with a few strokes of a lawyer's pen, but at Fochabers the ancient contract of "feu tenancy" involved the Duke of Gordon in a quarter of a century of expensive litigation before he finally removed the last blot on his landscape in 1802. The Duke's gracious Georgian residence, Gordon Castle, overlooking the now-sanitised view, is not open to the public.

A century or so after the building of Gordon Castle in 1776, one of the 50 gardeners who tended its extensive grounds made a momentous decision. George Baxter resigned his job, borrowed £100, and together with his wife Margaret, an inspired cook, opened a small grocery store in Spey Street, Fochabers. In the back of the shop, Margaret magicked the fruits of local hedgerows into unbelievably tasty jams and jellies. George's former employer, the Duke of Gordon, was captivated by them. They graced his breakfast and tea tables, and so introduced his many rich and aristocratic friends to these very Scottish specialities. As a result of the Duke's patronage George and Margaret Baxter's business thrived. But it was their daughter-in-law, Ethel, who in 1929 created the firm's most famous product, Baxter's Royal Game Soup, still savoured by gastronomes around the world. Today, the **Baxters Visitor Centre** at Fochabers welcomes almost a quarter of a million visitors each year, drawn here by its historic appeal, its Old Shop Museum, (a re-creation of George Baxter's original establishment in Fochabers), and its constellation of other attractive specialty shops. Apart from Christmas, New Year, and factory holidays, the Centre is open all year: for further details, telephone 01343 820666. In Fochabers itself, the **Fochabers Folk Museum** (free) in the High Street has more than 4,000 exhibits, amongst them collections of horse-drawn vehicles, costumes, and items illustrating local history. Housed in a converted church, the museum is open daily all year. Tel: 01343 820362

KEITH — MAP 5 REF L6

17 miles SE of Elgin on the A96

From Fochabers, we make a short diversion to Keith, a small town which nevertheless has three distinct areas: the medieval town set around the **Auld Brig**, built in 1609 by Thomas Murray and Janet Lindsay whose names are carved on its south side; New Keith, laid out by the 2nd Earl of Seafield in 1750; and Fife Keith on the opposite bank of the River Isla, founded by the Earl of Fife in 1817. The town's oldest building is **Milton Tower**, in Station Road, the only surviving part of a much larger castle built in 1480.

Keith stands at the northeastern tip of the popular **Whisky Trail**, a 70-mile wander around the area which will guide you to 7 major distilleries and a working cooperage. One of the best known is the **Strathisla Distill-**

Strathisla Distillery

ery at Keith, famous for its Chivas Regal blended scotch which is exported all over the world. Founded in 1786, Strathisla is the oldest working distillery in the Highlands and, with its curious twin pagodas serving as vents, one of the most architecturally interesting. Visitors are welcomed with complimentary coffee and shortbread, then given a free guide book for a self-guided tour during which they will be tutored in the art of whisky "nosing" before returning to the Isla Room for a dram of the "real cratur". Half the entrance fee is redeemable against the purchase of a bottle of the house product. Strathisla is open daily from mid-March to the end of November; weekdays only from February to mid-March. Tel: 01542 783044

ROTHES — Map 5 ref K6

9 miles SE of Elgin on the A941

We return to Speyside at Rothes where, just outside this little town, the **Glen Grant Distillery & Garden** stands in a sheltered glen surrounded by a beautifully landscaped Victorian garden. The distillery was found in 1840 by two Grant brothers and produces a light, floral malt whisky which is quite distinctive. Visitors can enjoy a tour and discover the secrets of the distillery, wander through the delightful garden, and sample a dram from "Major Grant's whisky safe". Most of the entrance fee is refunded when

Craigellachie Iron Bridge

you buy a bottle from the Distillery Shop which also stocks a wide range of high quality gifts. Glen Grant is open daily from mid-March to October, but times vary. For more details, telephone 01542 783318.

CRAIGELLACHIE

MAP 5 REF K6

13 miles SE of Elgin on the A941/A95

Four miles south of Rothes, the village of Craigellachie sits on the hillside looking down on the meeting of the bright waters of the Rivers Fiddich and Spey, the latter spanned by the elegant **Iron Bridge** built by Thomas Telford in 1815. The village lies on the Whisky Trail, not because of a distillery, but because of **Speyside Cooperage** where visitors can see highly skilled coopers practising their ancient craft. Each year, they prepare some 100,000 oak casks which will be used to mature many different whiskies. It's like watching an industrial ballet as the coopers circle the casks, rhythmically hammering the iron bands into place. This award-winning attraction also has a Visitor Centre, viewing gallery, gift shop and picnic area. Tel: 01340 871108.

Housed in the former Gospel Hall at Craigellachie, **The Green Hall Gallery** stands on the edge of this beautiful Speyside village, The timber-clad building is, naturally, painted green, set off by colourful shrubs and hanging baskets. The Gallery is a showcase for the work of two gifted artists: Maggie Riegler, who specialised in tapestries, and Stewart Johnson in ceramics, now devoting their time to painting. The Gallery also displays a wide range of attractive handmade cards on handmade petal flower paper, as well as prints on parchment and handmade paper. There's also a strik-

The Green Hall Gallery, 2, Victoria Street, Craigellachie Banffshire AB38 9SR Tel: 01340 871010

ing selection of original oils and watercolours featuring local scenes, animals, flowers, fish and birds. All the artwork is their own and they also do the printing themselves to ensure the highest quality. Maggie and Stewart, who live right next door to the Gallery, also run a small and friendly bed & breakfast facility in their family home. Visitors are assured of a warm welcome and there's an additional incentive for keen walkers who will find that private steps from the house lead to the Speyside Way, just 20 metres away.

A popular stopping-off place for walkers along the Speyside Way and the Malt Whisky Trail is the **Highlander Inn** in Craigellachie. You don't have to be a walker though to appreciate the charms of this attractive, white-painted hostelry. Built in the late 19th century, it used to be the village bank so it is sturdily constructed with traditional "doubled-up" windows and appealing touches of grandeur in the decor.

**The Highlander Inn, 10, Victoria Street, Craigellachie
Banffshire AB38 9SR Tel: 01340 881446**

Jock and Alison Anderson have owned the Highlander Inn since 1995 and they have brought a relaxed and comfortable atmosphere to this well-appointed inn. They have 4 letting rooms, all of them en suite, and each room is individually decorated with a fresh, classic decor. The food served at the inn is quite outstanding. The menu concentrates on the "Taste of Scotland", - the natural cooking of such local specialities as salmon, trout, venison and beef. Fittingly for a hotel in the heart of distillery country, the bar stocks more than 50 single malt whiskies and Jock, as an expert taster, will happily help you appreciate the subtle differences between the various brands of Scotland's national drink. After that, you may not feel like immediately tackling the rest of the Speyside Way but it's well worth a short stroll to see Thomas Telford's graceful bridge over the Spey, built in 1814 and part of the main road until 1974 when a new bridge was built.

About 3 miles southeast of Craigellachie, stands another famous distillery, **Glenfiddich** which is still owned and managed by the Grant family who built it more than a century ago. They take great pride in the fact that Glenfiddich is the only *"château-bottled"* malt whisky made in the Highlands. Bottling at the distillery, using a single source of water, gives Glenfiddich, they believe, its unique purity of taste and enables visitors to observe the whole process from *"barley to bottle"*. In the early years of the 20th century, when successive British governments imposed increasingly savage duties on whisky, Glenfiddich cannily advertised the medicinal properties of their malt, *"manufactured under the Careful and Personal Supervision of a Fully Qualified Doctor"*. The attractions at Glenfiddich include an audio-visual presentation (available in 6 languages), an exhibition, gift shop and picnic. The distillery is open daily, Easter to mid-October; weekdays only at other times, and is closed for 2 weeks from mid-December. Admission is free. Tel: 01340 820805.

Standing beside the distillery, overlooking great piles of whisky barrels, are the substantial and picturesque ruins of **Balvenie Castle** (Historic Scotland), a moated stronghold originally built by the "Black" Comyn Earls of Buchan in the late 1200s and extended during the 15th and 16th century by the Earls of Atholl who added the great round tower which still looks formidable. It was here that Mary, Queen of Scots, stayed during a brief visit in 1562. The castle was stormed by Royalists in 1649, and occupied during both Jacobite rebellions, after which it was abandoned. The grand old fortress steadily decayed until 1929 when its last owner, the 6th Earl and 1st Duke of Fife entrusted its still imposing ruins to the care of the state. The castle is open daily from April to September: there's a modest entrance charge.

DUFFTOWN — MAP 5 REF K6

17 miles SE of Elgin on the A941

A local saying claims that "While Rome was built on seven hills, Dufftown stood on seven stills". Today, this agreeable market town asserts its title to being *"Malt Whisky Capital of the World"* with some legitimacy since it is surrounded by no fewer than 7 distilleries and exports more of the amber liquid than anywhere else in Britain. Originally named Balvenie, after the nearby castle, Dufftown is elegantly laid out with spacious streets, a legacy of its creation as a new town in 1817 by James Duff, 4th Earl of Fife, with the aim of creating employment following the Napoleonic wars. Its four main streets converge on an attractive **Clocktower** of 1839 which now houses the town's **Museum** (free) and Tourist Information Centre.

Decorated with colourful baskets of flowers hanging outside, **The Mason Arms** stands out in this town of beautiful open bright and wide streets, and clean and crisp stone buildings. Graeme Edmonstone has owned this attractively furnished and decorated pub/restaurant for more than ten years and is well-known for his friendly and welcoming approach to customers. Open from 11am to 11pm, The Mason Arms welcomes families and offers visitors an extensive choice of wholesome, well-prepared food served all day. Specialities include local game and steaks but there's always a vegetarian dish available. Graeme also serves a good selection of fine ales and, as you might expect in this distillery town, a large choice of malt whiskies. The famous Glenfiddich distillery is just a mile or so away, and Glen Grant, Strathisla, Glenfarclas and Glenlivet distilleries all lie within a few miles radius of Dufftown. Lovers of the amber nectar could scarcely find a more appropriate place in which to settle down with a wee dram!

The Mason Arms, 22, Conval Street, Dufftown
Banffshire AB55 4AE Tel: 01340 820302

Dufftown Clocktower

Over to the west from Dufftown, are two distilleries featured on the Whisky Trail. At the tiny village of **Knockando, Cardhu Distillery** has the distinction of being the only malt distillery pioneered by a woman. In the early days, she would raise a red flag to warn local crofters with their unlicensed stills that the Excise authorities were in the area. Cardhu stands in Speyside, close to the source of its success, - the ice-cold fresh mountain spring water. To this day, the art of distilling here is unhurried and unchanging, with the resulting malt maturing for at least twelve years in old oak casks. Cardhu has a gift shop and a picnic area, and is open weekdays all year and also on Sundays from Easter to September. Tel: 01340 872555. A few miles away, to the south, is **Glenfarclas Distillery** where, since 1836, five generations of the Grant family have been distilling the spirit of Speyside into a premium malt whisky of outstanding character. A professional whisky taster recently declared that a dram of Glenfarclas *"goes down singing hymns"*. (Hymns? Shouldn't that be drinking songs?). The distillery has a cask-filling gallery, gift shop, and picnic area, and your admission fee includes a voucher redeemable in the distillery shop. Apart from the last two weeks of December, Glenfarclas is open weekdays all year round, and daily from June to September. Tel: 01807 500245

About 4 miles southwest of Glenfarclas stands an ancient house which is not just one of the most beguiling in Strathspey, but in the whole of Scotland: **Ballindalloch Castle**. The charm, as always, derives from the fact that the same family has lived here for generations: the Macpherson-Grants who have managed to both preserve their heritage intact while also imaginatively adapting to 20th century economic imperatives. According to family legend, its original builder back in the 16th century, the Laird of Ballindalloch, intended his new castle to crown a nearby hill. But each morning, when his masons returned to their work, they found their previous day's construction strewn across the ground. So, one stormy night, the Laird, accompanied by his masons, kept vigil on the hill site. Great gusts of wind swept across them, each blast somehow conveying the repeated message, *"Build it in the coo haugh,* (cow pasture)". Deeply impressed by this wind-borne supernatural advice, The Laird complied and so his new castle was built on a level plain beside the River Spey, a location which also happened to provide one of the most picturesque settings for all inland Scottish castles. A vigorous stream of supernatural events continues to flow through the castle's history.

General James Grant inherited Ballindalloch in 1770, died here in 1806, and was buried in his favourite spot overlooking the River Spey. From his grave, the General, who was a noted *bon viveur,* rises each evening, and "walks to the dungeon passage to refresh himself from his beloved wine cellar". Inside the castle itself, a vaporously beautiful lady, dressed in a pink crinoline gown and wearing a large straw hat, is said to regularly visit the Pink Bedroom. These spectral appearances cannot be guaranteed, but you can certainly see an extraordinary collection of 16th and 17th century Spanish paintings acquired by Sir John Macpherson during his tenure as Secretary of the British Legation in Lisbon. Painted on a small scale, these fine and delicate paintings provide an interesting cultural contrast with the grandiose portraits by Allan Ramsay of George III and Queen Charlotte displayed in the Great Hall of the castle.

In the grounds outside roam the famous herd of Ballindalloch Aberdeen Angus cattle, the oldest registered herd of its kind in existence. Other attractions include extensive gardens and grounds; river walks; craft workshops; gift shop, and tea room. The castle is open daily from Good Friday to September 30th. Tel: 01807 500206.

GLENLIVET — MAP 5 REF K7

13 miles SW of Dufftown on the B9008

"The celebrated **Glenlivet Distillery**" Queen Victoria called it in her diary after passing its lonely hillside setting one windy autumn day in 1867. Established some 40 years earlier by George Smith, The Glenlivet's much appreciated fragrant single malt whisky swiftly acquired a dedicated following of connoisseurs. Modern-day visitors are welcomed to a guided tour of the production process, given the opportunity to see inside the vast bonded warehouses where the spirit matures for 12 years, and to browse through the multimedia exhibition devoted to The Glenlivet's history. A free leaflet, "Discover Glenlivet", provides further details of walks and trails, and historic places of interest close by. The distillery is open daily during July and August; weekdays only on other dates between mid-March to the end of October. Most of the admission fee is redeemable in the distillery shop against the purchase of a bottle of Glenlivet. Tel: 01542 783220.

TOMINTOUL

MAP 5 REF K7

19 miles SW of Dufftown on the A939/B9008

Surrounded by bleak moorland, Tomintoul, pronounced *Tom*-in-towel, sits 1160ft above sea level, the highest village in the Highlands although, strangely, not the highest in Scotland. (That distinction belongs to Wanlockhead in "lowland" Dumfries & Galloway). The village was plonked down in this raw countryside by the Duke of Gordon in 1779. Fifteen years later a visitor noted that 37 families lived here, *"with not a single manufacture to employ them, but all of them sell whisky and all of them drink it"*. A century later Queen Victoria, passing through, described it as *"the most tumble-down, poor looking place I ever saw"*. She was told that it was the *"dirtiest, poorest village in the whole of the Highlands"*. Things have changed greatly since those days, particularly in recent years when Tomintoul has become a base for ski-ers on the area nearby known as **the Lecht**. The Lecht provides dry ski-slope-skiing all year and snow-making equipment helps to extend the snow season in winter. In the village itself, the **Tomintoul Museum** (free) features a re-created crofter's kitchen and smiddy, with other displays on the local wildlife, the story of Tomintoul, and the Cairngorms. The museum, which also houses a Tourist Information Centre, is open from May to October. Tomintoul is also the southern terminus of the Speyside Way, the long-distance footpath which is described at the beginning of this chapter.

Just outside the village is **Auchriachan Farmhouse** where bed and breakfast guests find a warm Highland greeting, along with tea, scones and pancakes awaiting them on arrival. The lovely old stone farmhouse was built more than 250 years ago, after its predecessor had been razed to the ground by English troops returning south after the Battle of Culloden. It

Auchriachan Farmhouse, Mains of Auchriachan, Tomintoul Ballindalloch AB37 9EQ Tel: 01807 580416

stands on the banks of Conglass Water, which eventually courses into the River Spey, and anglers will be delighted to know that free fishing is available. Irene Duffus runs this attractive B & B establishment which offers visitors a choice of four guest rooms, all en suite and all comfortably appointed with a welcoming warm decor. Auchriachan enjoys a wonderfully peaceful setting, surrounded by open fields and woods. It stands at the southern end of the Speyside Way Country Walk, is also close to the famous "Whisky Trail", and the great bulk of the Cairngorm Mountains rises just a few miles to the south. It is spectacular countryside, and Auchriachan Farmhouse makes a wonderful base from which to explore it.

BRIDGE OF BROWN MAP 5 REF K7

9 miles SE of Grantown on Spey on the A939

Set on the hillside overlooking the bridge is Graham and Sue Larrington's **Bridge of Brown Tea Room & Craft Shop**, offering visitors an outstanding collection of home baked cakes, tarts, puddings and pies, along with a well-stocked Craft Shop packed with a wide range of pictures, jewellery, pottery, speciality jams, and many other eye-catching items. Dating from about 1800, the Tea Room has served various functions in its time, from a threshing barn to a coffin maker's workshop. Enjoying fine views across the countryside and with a welcoming open fire for days when there's a nip in the air, the Tea Room serves everything from a simple cup of coffee, through light snacks to a full and satisfying meal. Amongst the desserts, Sue's hot bread pudding with cream deserves a very special mention.

Bridge of Brown Tea Room & Craft Shop, Tomintoul, Ballindalloch Banffshire AB37 9HR Tel: 01807 580335

Graham has a special interest in model engineering, building fi models for private and commercial collectors. Ready-built models located and supplied. Graham will also build model aircraft and can t you how to fly them using his trainer fitted with dual controls - the easy way to learn!. Advice and help with models is always available, and with somethinginteresting being built or restored in the workshop, the Bridge of Brown Tea Room, set in the wild and beautiful countryside in the foothills of the Cairngorm Mountains, makes a very pleasant stop.

GRANTOWN-ON-SPEY — MAP 4 REF J7

23 miles SE of Nairn on the A939

One of Queen Victoria's favourite little towns, Grantown-on-Spey was originally laid out in 1776 with wide, tree-lined streets leading to a central square. This traditional Highland resort grew in stature when doctors began recommending its dry, bracing climate for those *"requiring rest and quiet on account of nervous overstrain and debility"*. The town stands close to several busy tourist routes and is a popular centre all year round: many winter visitors for the skiing at Aviemore preferring Grantown's elegant Georgian and Victorian appeal to the decidedly charmless surroundings at Aviemore itself.

To the south of Grantown, on the B970, is a rather unusual tourist attraction, **Revack Estate**, where the estate's owner, Lady Pauline Ogilvie Grant, invites visitors to explore its 15,000 acres of splendid Highland countryside. You can wander along trails through wet ground habitats which provide nesting sites for oystercatchers, lapwings, skylarks and curlews, and also attract colourful colonies of butterflies. There's an exotic collection of orchids on display and for sale; a generously equipped Adventure Playground; gift shop; licensed restaurant and cafeteria. The Revack Estate is open all year round, daily from 10am to 6pm: for more details telephone 01479 872234.

About 6 miles southwest of Grantown, at Skye of Curr, you can acquire a living memento of your visit to Scotland at the **Speyside Heather Garden & Visitor Centre** which has more than 300 varieties of heather growing in its landscaped show garden. Its Heather Heritage Centre houses an exhibition on the varied historical uses of the plant in thatching, ropemaking, for doormats and baskets, as well as in medicine, cooking, drinks, and dyeing wool. In the heather craft shop you can buy the plants themselves and gifts associated with them, (including heather wine). There's also a restaurant, garden & produce shop, art gallery, and antiques shop. The Centre is open weekdays all year, and also on Sundays during the summer season. Tel: 01479 851359.

DUTHIL

Map 4 ref J7

9 miles NE of Aviemore on the A938

Standing in two acres of its own grounds and surrounded by towering pine trees, **The Pines Country House** is a well-appointed, comfortable country house offering its guests excellent bed and breakfast, or half-board accommodation. Lynn and Dave Benge have been welcoming visitors to their home for more than 16 years now, throughout that time providing the best of Highland hospitality and a personal service in a warm and friendly, relaxed atmosphere. Their success as hosts is indicated by their Scottish Tourist Board rating of 3 Crowns, Commended. The centrally-heated house offers a choice of family, double or twin rooms, all en suite

**The Pines Country House, Duthil, Carrbridge
Inverness-shire PH23 3ND Tel: 01479 841220**

and all well-equipped with tea/coffee facilities plus radio and colour television. Children and pets are welcomed and a baby sitting service is available. Everything on the breakfast and dinner menus is home cooked, and your hosts will be pleased to cater for any special diets. The Pines enjoys a wonderfully peaceful, south-facing location with splendid uninterrupted views of the Spey Valley, and it's so rural Lynn and Dave often find red squirrels and wild birds on their doorstep. Open all year, The Pines makes an admirable base for exploring this dramatically beautiful part of the country.

CARRBRIDGE

Map 4 ref J7

7 miles N of Aviemore off the A9

The stone bridge that gives Carrbridge its name still survives, an elegant, single high-arched span. It was built in 1717 following the deaths of two men who had drowned here while attempting to cross the treacherous ford over the River Spey. Today, Carrbridge's other prime attraction is its imaginative Landmark Forest Heritage Park which has as its focus a striking modern building surrounded by pine trees. Inside, you can watch a dramatic, triple-screen, audio-visual history of the Highlands. Outdoors, you can wander through a sculpture park; trace your way through its woodland maze or nature trail; climb a 65ft high observation tower; and even, securely raised on timber stilts, strut your stuff along a tree-top-level trail. A great place for children. The Park is open daily throughout the year: for more details, telephone 0800 731 3446.

AVIEMORE

MAP 4 REF J7

29 miles SE of Inverness on the A9

Scotland's premier skiing resort was built almost from scratch during the 1960s, - Europe's first purpose-built leisure, sports and conference centre. The developers threw in everything they could think of: high-rise hotels, a cinema, a theatre, ice rink, swimming pool, go-karting track, and a dry-ski slope. And since this was the 1960s, everything was built, of course, in concrete. A more recent addition is a children's amusement park, **Santa Claus Land**, set in the heart of a mature pine forest and offering a range of attractions, - amongst them go-karts, a Lego play area, a pets' farm, dinosaur safari ride, craft village, and Techno Land where kids can don a virtual reality helmet and step into an interactive video game. Santa Claus Land is open daily all year: telephone 01479 810624.

For adults, Aviemore's most attractive feature, apart from the glorious mountain scenery all around, is the **Speyside Railway** whose steam trains run for some five miles from here to Boat of Garten, along the track of the old Highland Railway which opened in 1863 and closed in 1965. The railway's vintage rolling-stock includes a functioning restaurant car that was once part of the Flying Scotsman and, depending on the time of year, there are from five to eight return trips each day. The Aviemore station is worth visiting just to see its engine shed full of burnished locomotives. The shed itself is original, but the other station buildings were imported from Dalnaspidal, and the turntable from Kyle of Lochalsh. Services run from April to October: for more details, telephone 01479 810725.

One of Speyside Railway's special offers should not be resisted, - an inclusive tour which combines train travel from Aviemore to Boat of Garten with a 4-mile bus journey to the **RSPB reserve** on the shores of **Loch Garten**. For bird-watchers, Loch Garten is a holy place, the nesting place of one of Britain's rarest birds, the osprey. In the mid-20th century, it was assumed that this fearsome grey-and-white eagle had disappeared for ever from the British Isles. Then, in 1954, a single pair arrived mysteriously and set up home in a tree about half a mile from the loch. Ever since then, a steadily increasing number of ospreys have flown from Africa each spring to nest here. Between late April and August, the RSPB opens a special observation hide where with the aid of powerful binoculars and live television monitoring visitors can watch these magnificent birds in their nests.

COYLUMBRIDGE

MAP 4 REF J7

2 miles SE of Aviemore on the B970

Set amongst towering Caledonian pine trees, the award-winning **Rothiemurchus Camp & Caravan Park** offers sheltered camping in a unique wilderness setting. Open every day of the year, the park has a wide range of Thistle Award cabins for hire and provides a full range of facilities including toilets, hot showers and a launderette. The Park lies within the vast Rothiemurchus Estate which stretches from the River Spey at Aviemore to the granite peaks of the Cairngorm Mountains. In recognition of the quality of its landscape, wildlife and natural beauty, the area has been part of the Cairngorm National Nature Reserve since 1954. Within its boundaries there is an enormous range of recreational activities on offer: bankside or boat fishing, clay pigeon shooting, 4x4 off-road driving, cycling and mountain biking, birdwatching, guided walks with a Rothiemurchus Ranger, or tours of the estate by Landrover. There's far too much going on to give

Rothiemurchus Camp & Caravan Park, Coylumbridge, Aviemore Inverness PH22 1QU Tel: 01479 812800

a complete list here, but the Rothiemurchus Visitor Centre will happily provide full information. The Centre is also worth visiting for its Card Shop which stocks a wide selection of books, maps, cards and much more, and its Old School Shop displaying an excellent range of Scottish craftwork, designer knitwear, quality stone and glass ware, and exclusive jewellery.

Also within the Rothiemurchus estate is **Loch an Eilean**, "Loch of the Island", an island on which stands a picturesque ruined castle. There's a gentle one-hour walk which wanders around the loch: details of this walk and of the many other woodland trails in the area can be obtained from the Rothiemurchus Visitor Centre.

To the west of Rothiemurchus, the **Glen More Forest Park** covers some 4000 acres of the northwest slopes of the Cairngorms. At its heart is Loch Morlich, around which Scotland's only free-ranging herd of reindeer have found a congenial habitat, and in winter the Siberian Husky Club hold their races in the surrounding area. Beyond the loch, the road bends south towards the Cairngorm Ski Area, and climbs steadily above the forest to the high-level car parks which in winter and early spring service the ski-lifts. The whole year round, a chair-lift operates to the Ptarmigan Restaurant which, at 3,600ft, is the highest building in Britain.

KINGUSSIE — MAP 4 REF I8

12 miles SW of Aviemore on the A9/A86

Southwest of Aviemore, the A9, the B9152, and the railway run alongside each other towards the little resort village of Kingussie, (pronounced King-*yoo*-see). The B9152 will give you better views of Loch Alvie, and of Loch Insh, where there's a watersports centre, and also bring you to the excellent **Highland Wildlife Park** near **Kincraig**.

The Park is owned and run by the Royal Zoological Society of Scotland, a registered charity which also owns Edinburgh Zoo. Its declared mission is to promote the conservation of animal species and wild places by captive breeding, environmental education and scientific research. Visitors drive around the huge reserve where herds of red deer, secretive roe deer, enormous bison, ancient breeds of sheep, and wild Przewalski horses, one of the world's rarest mammals, all roam freely. The rest of the Park can be explored on foot, wandering through themed habitats such as the Wolf Territory where a raised walkway takes visitors right into the heart of the enclosure. An informative free guidebook is provided and there's a Children's Trail, play area, gift shop, visitor centre, and coffee shop. The Park is open daily all year from 10am but may close in bad weather: for more details, telephone 01540 651270.

Kingussie, small though it is, can also boast a major visitor attraction, the **Highland Folk Museum**. Across an 80-acre site, this outstanding museum displays a fascinating collection of buildings, amongst them a reconstructed Lewis "black house", an old smokehouse, a water-powered sawmill, a 19th century school, a clock maker's workshop, and a traditional herb and flower garden. Indoors, the farming museum has a stable, barn, dairy, and a large range of old carts, ploughs and other farming implements. On most days during the summer there are also demonstrations of various traditional crafts. For further information, telephone 01540 661307

A mile or so away, on the south side of the Spey, stand the substantial remains of **Ruthven Barracks**. Built in 1719 to keep Highlanders in check following the 1715 Rising, the barracks were extended by General Wade in 1734. After the tragedy of Culloden, Jacobite survivors rallied here hoping that Bonnie Prince Charlie might once again take to the field. When they received a brusque message advising that every man should seek his safety in the best way he could, they blew up the barracks and fled. The stark ruins of the once-mighty military outpost they left behind look their best at night when they are floodlit.

A mile or so from Ruthven Barracks is the **RSPB reserve at Insh Marshes**, one of the most important wetlands in Britain. In spring, lapwings, redshanks, and curlews all nest here, and in the winter, when the marshes flood, they attract flocks of whooper swans and greylag geese. The best months for visiting are from November until June. The reserve is always open and admission is free.

NEWTONMORE — MAP 4 REF I8

16 miles SW of Aviemore on the A86

This small village is home to the **Clan Macpherson Museum**, one of whose prize exhibits is a black chanter allegedly presented to the Macphersons by the "little people", and to the Newtonmore Highland Games, held on the first Saturday in August, when clan members from around the world rally here.

A few miles south of Newtonmore, at Laggan, a minor road strikes off westwards alongside the Spey but fizzles out some 10 miles short of the source of this famous river and so puts a full stop to this tour of Strathspey.

Although it's not in Strathspey, you may want to make a short detour to **Dalwhinnie Distillery**, about 7 miles south of Laggan on the A889. The highest distillery in Scotland, Dalwhinnie produces a single malt whisky with a light heather fragrance. Guided tours are available and the admission charge includes a voucher redeemable in the distillery shop against the purchase of a bottle of malt whisky. The distillery is open weekdays from March to December, weekends during the season.Tel: 01528 522208.

3 The Great Glen

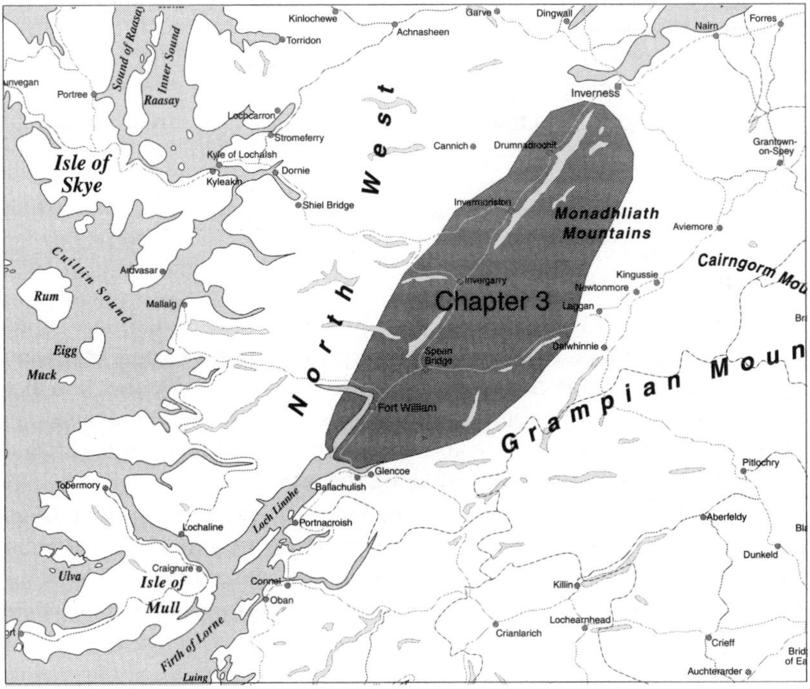

© MAPS IN MINUTES ™ (1998)

The single most impressive feature of the Highlands is the Great Glen, a vast geological fault that stretches some 60 miles in a diagonal line from Inverness to Fort William. Two thirds of its length is filled by the waters of Lochs Lochy, Oich and Ness, and the construction of the Caledonian Canal in the early 1800s linked them together, creating a navigable waterway running all the way from Fort William to the Moray Firth at Inverness.

The most famous of the three lochs in the Great Glen is, of course, **Loch Ness**, and whether or not a fabulous creature lurks in its depths, the loch is remarkable in itself. Twenty-four miles long, it is fed by eight rivers, its bed lies deeper than anywhere in the North Sea and even much of the Atlantic, and it has never been known to freeze. Because of its great depth and length, the loch is one of Europe's largest freshwater systems, holding more water than all the reservoirs and lakes in the whole of England and Wales.

A monstrous creature swimming in its waters was first reported in AD 565 by no less a witness than St Columba, but the "Leviathan of the Loch" was then not spotted again until the 1930s, a sighting which sparked off huge enthusiasm for tracking down the beast. Echo-sounders, a submarine and devices to obtain a piece of Nessie's skin or flesh have all been employed in the massive search, so far without the slightest success. Various photographs of the monster, including the familiar "Surgeon's" photograph taken in 1934, have all subsequently proved to be fakes. On the other hand, there have been numerous credible witnesses who claim to have seen Nessie, and many respected scientists are convinced that an as yet unknown species of aquatic life, a "bio-mass", does indeed inhabit the loch.

DOCHGARROCH

MAP 2 REF I6

3 miles SW of Inverness, on the A82

It was at this small village on the River Ness that Queen Victoria stepped ashore in September 1872 after travelling the length of the Great Glen from Banavie. She was charmed when "two little girls put down bunches of flax for me to walk upon, which it seems is an old Highland custom". Like so many travellers before and since, the Queen had been enthralled by the superb views she had seen along the way.

There's surely no better way to experience this stunning Scottish scenery than by navigating your own boat through the magnificent Caledonian Canal and the Great Glen. **Loch Ness Charters** make this possible by offering their superb range of sailing and cruiser boats for charter. In business

Loch Ness Charters, Dochgarroch, Inverness IV3 6JY
Tel: 01463 861303

for more than twenty years, the company offers a great choice of boats, from 23ft to 27ft sailing crafts, (Voyager, Leisure, Mirage and Westerly), as well as two motor cruisers. Each offers different levels of comfort and space. Some have showers and hot water; all have toilets and gas cookers with ovens as standard. The boats can accommodate from 3 to 5 people in comfort and there's space for a further crew member if required. If you can't sail, or are a little bit rusty, Loch Ness Charters offer lessons to start you off or get you back into the frame. All yachts are also equipped with a motor to help you out of any sticky situations that may arise.

DRUMNADROCHIT — MAP 2 REF H7

15 miles SW of Inverness on the A82

Before beginning our tour down the eastern side of the loch, we make a diversion to Drumnadrochit, in effect the headquarters of the "Nessie" industry. This little town has two exhibitions devoted to the elusive monster: the Original Loch Ness Monster Exhibition which is little more than a souvenir shop with a half-hearted audio-visual show as an afterthought seemingly, and the **Official Loch Ness Monster Exhibition** which takes its subject rather more seriously with photographs, sonar scans, eye-witness accounts from across the ages, and reconstructions of the various research projects carried out in the loch. Outside, emerging from its own lochan, rears a "life-size" model of a rather mean-looking Nessie. Cruises around Loch Ness can also be booked here.

If you fancy the idea of seeing the monster yourself, the most likely viewpoint apparently is at **Castle Urquhart**, to the east of the town. More sightings of the monster have been reported from this point than from

Castle Urquhart, Nr Drumnadrochit

anywhere else on or around the loch. Perhaps significantly, the water here is the deepest in the whole of the loch, reaching some 750ft in depth. The castle, reached by a steepish climb up a hundred steps, was built in the 14th century to guard this strategic point in the Great Glen. It is dramatically sited on a bluff and looks particularly splendid at night when it is floodlit. The castle was deliberately blown up in 1692 to prevent it falling into the hands of the Jacobites, but the keep and four square turrets are still very imposing.

A couple of miles to the south of Castle Urquhart stands the **John Cobb Memorial**, honouring the land-speed record holder who, in 1952, had just established a new water-speed record in his jet-engined craft, *Crusader*, when his boat disintegrated on the loch near this point. Still alive, Cobb was recovered from the wreckage and carried up this hillside. He died a few metres from where the monument now stands.

It was along this road that Dr Johnson and James Boswell made their way in August 1773, the first occasion on which Boswell had seen the bulky doctor on horseback and, he observed, riding well. As they continued southwards to Fort Augustus, they noticed an elderly woman at the door of a wretched hovel, and asked if they might see inside. The house was made of earth "and for a window had only a small hole, which was stopped by a piece of turf that was taken out occasionally to let in light". Johnson was curious to know where the woman slept. A guide translated the question into Erse. "She answered with a tone of emotion, saying, as he told us, she was afraid we wanted to go to bed with her". The exchange gave the good doctor and his biographer much cause for merriment as they resumed their journey. Boswell maintained that it was Johnson who had alarmed the poor woman's virtue. "No, sir" said he. "She'll say, There came a wicked young fellow, a wild dog, who I believe would have ravished me, had there not been with him a grave old gentleman who repressed him". "No, sir" replied Boswell, "She'll say, There was terrible ruffian who would have forced me had it not been for a civil, decent young man who, I take it, was an angel sent from heaven to protect me".

AULT-NA-GOIRE

Map 2 ref I7

18 miles SW of Inverness on minor road off the B852

From Inverness, two roads strike southwest through the Great Glen. Most visitors take the A82 which follows the western shore of Loch Ness to Fort Augustus, but on the eastern bank the B862/B852 is usually much quieter and offers equally grand views. About 15 miles along this road is Farigaig Forest and if the idea of holidaying in a secluded forest setting appeals to you, then **Loch Ness Hideaways** have the very thing. Silver Birch Chalet and Rowan Cottage both enjoy superb locations, about a quarter of a mile apart, at the head of the Pass of Inverfarigaig. Each has views over the

Loch Ness Hideaways, Ault-na-Goire, Errogie IV1 2UH
Tel: 01456 486641

Farigaig forest, and fabulous Loch Ness is little more than a mile away. Deer, red squirrels, buzzards and pine martens are all abundant here, and patience may be rewarded with the sighting of even more elusive wildlife. Silver Birch Chalet was designed and constructed by Finnish craftsmen. It is extremely well insulated and fully double-glazed, making it comfortable in all seasons. The chalet sleeps four people, as does Rowan Cottage which is also of timber construction and is set in 1½ acres of fenced natural garden. Styled on the bungalows in Kashmir, it has a lovely tranquil atmosphere and combines old-world charm with modern comforts. Both these properties are very much Hidden Places, - and eminently well worth seeking out.

FOYERS

MAP 2 REF H7

20 miles SW of Inverness on the B852

From Whitebridge, the road descends steeply to Foyers, on the banks of Loch Ness. Just before entering the village, hidden away in woods to the left, are the **Falls of Foyers**. The two waterfalls, one 40ft high, the other 90ft, were admired by no less a personage than Robert Burns. In 1896, though, the waters were diverted to provide power for Britain's first aluminium plant which, with extraordinary insensitivity, was sited beside Loch Ness. The plant closed in 1967 but the building is now used as a Hydro-electric pumping station. Despite the loss of volume, the Falls still remain impressive, especially after a good storm. The generation of electricity here is something of an engineering marvel, although it's mostly out of sight. Underground tunnels and piping link Loch Ness to Loch

Mhor, high on the hills to the east. During the day, water is released from Loch Mhor and rushes downhill, generating power as it goes. Then at night, when demand is at its minimum, excess power on the grid is used to pump the water back up again. According to its operators, the power produced is outstandingly "green", - the entire facility causing less pollution than a single cottage chimney.

In Foyers village itself and occupying a superb position close to Loch Ness, **Foyers House** had an unusual history before it became a guest house. It was originally built just before World War II as a Cottage Hospital. At that time, the authorities feared that there would be air raid casualties from attacks on the aluminium plant beside the loch. Happily, the raids never happened and after the war the building was used as a social club for

Foyers House, Foyers, Inverness-shire IV1 2XU
Tel: 01456 486405

the village before being converted to a guest house in 1991. Most of the bedrooms here have a grand view over the famous loch and there's an attractive visitors' lounge with a stone fireplace and wood-burning stove. Neil and Brenda Ellis take good care of their guests, serving traditional home cooking, using only the finest local ingredients, and offer an extensive range of local draught beers and bottled ales. Trout fishing is available "on the doorstep" and Neil is happy to supply local guide-books, maps and advice. For anyone on a tight budget, Neil and Brenda have additional, economically priced accommodation available, including a walkers' hostel with self-catering facilities.

WHITEBRIDGE

MAP 2 REF H7

24 miles SW of Inverness on the B862

From Inverness the B862 follows the course of one of General Wade's military roads along the eastern side of Loch Ness. The route passes Loch Tarff and then climbs up to the Whitebridge View Point which, at 1162ft, gives some glorious views eastwards to the Monadhliath Mountains. The tiny village of Whitebridge, a mile or so south of magnificent Loch Ness, takes its name from the bridge erected by General Wade across the River Fechlin, the last remaining high-arched bridge and the best example of his work.

Hidden along the river bank adjacent to the bridge are **Wildside Highland Lodges**. Beautifully situated, they appeal to anyone who appreciates a haven of peace and tranquillity, set amidst granite mountains and steep wooded glens. This is a small private complex of 12 Lodges, each of which

Wildside Highland Lodges, Whitebridge, Inverness-shire IV2 6UN
Tel: 01456 486373 e mail; wildside@enterprise.net
Web address: www.assc.co.uk/wildside

can accommodate from one to six people. The Lodges are sturdily constructed from Fyfestone and cedar, well-insulated and warm with full central heating. The generous open-plan living area has pine furniture and soft furnishings designed with relaxation in mind. Each lodge looks out to open country, picturesquely framed by large double-glazed picture windows, and the complex has a small central shop as well as a laundry with payphone. The surrounding countryside of Stratherrick is superb. Sheltered by the wild Monadhliath mountains, it enjoys a drier climate than the west Highlands but shares the same rugged scenery, studded with lochs.

FORT AUGUSTUS

MAP 2 REF H8

38 miles S of Inverness on the A82

The modest village of Fort Augustus takes its imposing name from the military base established here in the wake of the 1715 Jacobite rising. The fortress was built by General Wade and named after George II's younger son, Augustus. At that time, Augustus was a plump lad just 8 years old but he would later be reviled as the Duke of Cumberland, the "Butcher of Culloden". Following that battle, it was at Fort Augustus that the Duke expressed his gratification at receiving the head of Roderick Mackenzie, a young Edinburgh lawyer who had maintained the pretence of being Bonnie Prince Charlie in order to help the real prince escape.

After Culloden, the fort no longer had any useful purpose and in 1876 it was demolished, giving way to a **Benedictine Abbey**. The Abbey is still a monastery but also houses a particularly lively **Heritage Centre** where, with the aid of a walkman and a sound-and-light show, visitors are provided with an interesting insight into the history and culture of the area with exhibits on Loch Ness and the Great Glen, the Jacobite uprisings,

Ben Nevis from the Caledonian Canal

and the story of the old fort. The Abbey has been acclaimed as "one of the finest heritage centres in Britain" and the attractions also include a living museum of 17th century Highland life, staged at the Clansman Centre; peaceful grounds; a gift shop; the Abbot's Table restaurant, and 50-minute cruises around Loch Ness aboard the cruiser *Old Catriona* which featured in the film, *"Loch Ness"*. You can even take a helicopter ride over the loch and stay overnight in budget accommodation in the Abbey's guest rooms. During the season there are special Highland Gatherings featuring events such as tossing the caber, piping competitions, and Scottish dancing. The Centre is open every day except Christmas Day, but times vary: for more details, telephone 01320 366233.

Running through the centre of Fort Augustus is the **Caledonian Canal**, linking Loch Ness to Loch Oich with the help of six locks. Designed by the celebrated engineer Thomas Telford, the canal completed a waterway along the Great Glen that provided a 60-mile through route from the Atlantic Ocean to the North Sea, and spared shipping the perilous, perennially storm-tossed route around Cape Wrath.

Just to the north of the village is **The Brae Hotel**, a former Victorian Church Manse although there's nothing austere about its comfortable appointments or the welcome you'll receive from the owner, Andrew Reive. The hotel stands in its own attractive grounds overlooking Fort Augustus, in the very heart of the Great Glen at the southern end of Loch Ness. The village's central location, with the North and Western Highlands within

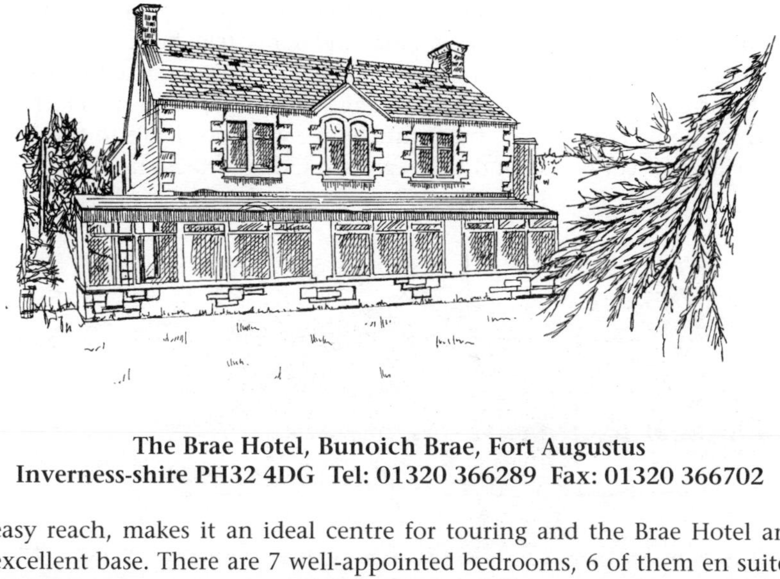

The Brae Hotel, Bunoich Brae, Fort Augustus
Inverness-shire PH32 4DG Tel: 01320 366289 Fax: 01320 366702

easy reach, makes it an ideal centre for touring and the Brae Hotel an excellent base. There are 7 well-appointed bedrooms, 6 of them en suite and one with a private bath/shower room. All rooms have colour TV and tea/coffee making facilities. Most of the bedrooms, and the dining room, are non-smoking. Downstairs, there's a cosy Lounge Bar where you can enjoy a drink in comfort, made even more pleasant with a welcoming fire in the chillier months. For the more active, the hotel has a pair of mountain bikes for hire; golf, pony trekking and fishing are all available locally, and if you enjoy walking you will be well-satisfied with the numerous forestry roads and paths which strike off in all directions.

INVERGARRY MAP 2 REF H8

40 miles SW of Inverness on the A82/A87

South of Fort Augustus, the A82 runs alongside Loch Oich to Invergarry. In medieval times this little town was important as the base for the MacDonnells of Glengarry, staunch Jacobites whose **Invergarry Castle** was destroyed by the Duke of Cumberland after Culloden but not before the fugitive Bonnie Prince Charlie had stayed there the night after the battle. The ruins still stand in the grounds of Glengarry Castle Hotel.

With its abundance of wildlife, Invergarry is a perfect base for touring, walking or fishing holidays and, just outside the village, **Faichemard Farm Chalets** provide the ideal accommodation. Joan and Duncan Grant, whose family has lived on this working hill farm since 1868, have four attractive chalets to let, all situated out of sight of each other, and all enjoying grand views along the glen to Loch Garry. Peaceful and private, the chalets are nevertheless within walking distance of the local shop, restaurant and bar. Each chalet can sleep a maximum of five people, is fully equipped, has its own parking area, and there's a laundry and public telephone at the reception area. There are three golf courses within 25 miles, and also three pony trekking centres within easy reach. There are countless rivers and lochs to fish in, (some requiring permits), and ample walks available to suit both the experienced walker and the beginner. Other attractions just a short

Faichemard Farm Chalets, Invergarry, Inverness-shire PH35 4HG
Tel: 01809 501314

drive away include Loch Ness and the Monster!, Inverness, the Isle of Skye, Culloden Battlefield, Glencoe, the Sands of Morar, Glen Affric and Aviemore, the Caledonian Canal and the Great Glen cycle route, and of course Ben Nevis! The chalets are open from April to October, and prices start from £150 per week per chalet.

SPEAN BRIDGE MAP 2 REF G8

8 miles NE of Fort William on the A82/A86

There are in fact two bridges at Spean Bridge: Thomas Telford's elegant bridge of 1819, and a couple of miles downstream, the older High Bridge built by General Wade in 1736. One hundred feet high it spans the deep gorge here. In 1913, one of its arches collapsed and has never been repaired. Spean Bridge offers some excellent views of the Ben Nevis range, especially from the Commando Memorial atop a hill just outside the village. This much-admired bronze sculpture, designed by Scott Sutherland, shows three soldiers looking west to the Cameron country of Lochiel where they trained during World War II. Spean Bridge has another notable military connection for it was nearby, on August 16th, 1745, that a mere dozen of MacDonald of Keppoch's Highlanders "armed with little more formidable than bagpipes and blood-curdling cries" managed to rout two companies of government troops. The incident is regarded as the first skirmish of the '45 rebellion, formally declared two days later by Bonnie Prince Charlie.

Completely restored and refurbished in 1995, **Smiddy House** is a family-run establishment offering an excellent base for touring and sightseeing

Smiddy House, Spean Bridge, Inverness-shire PH34 4EU
Tel: 01397 712335 Fax: 01397 712043

in this spectacular corner of the Western Highlands. Amanda and Kirk McLuskey provide a warm welcome at this inviting guest house which also incorporates a first class, licensed café bistro. Smiddy House has four large letting rooms, all with en suite facilities, and all the bedrooms have been refurbished to the highest standard with solid pine beds and furnishings. Each room has a colour television and coffee-making facilities, a guest-only laundry room is also available, and there is a spacious residents' lounge where you can relax after indulging perhaps in the highland hospitality of the bistro. Children and pets are welcome, there's ample parking space, and if you are thinking of travelling by rail, the little village has its own station on the wonderfully scenic West Coast line from Glasgow to Mallaig. Whether you come for the skiing, climbing, or are just looking for a relaxed informal atmosphere with a personal touch, Smiddy House makes an ideal choice.

If you would like a souvenir of the Highlands which will last and last, pay a visit to **The Heather Centre** about 200yds from Telford's bridge on the Inverness road. As well as the traditional purple variety, the Centre also has lucky white heathers, and a whole range of golden, orange, or bronze modern hybrids. There's an Exhibition of Scottish plants, many of which, along with imported species, are for sale. The Centre is open daily from April to October: more details on 01397 712619.

About halfway between Spean Bridge and Fort William, at Nevis Range, Britain's only **mountain gondola system** offers an exhilarating ride up Aonach Mor (4006ft). The gondolas rise up through the forest at the base station to an altitude of 2150ft in just 15 minutes. The views, needless to say, are staggering. At the top station, there's a restaurant and bar with a full range of self service meals and snacks, and two gift shops. Walkers will find a good choice of paths, both here and through the forest at the base station. During July and August, additional facilities include dry slope skiing, mountain bike hire, and slide shows. Nevis Range is open daily from Christmas to early November, with extended opening hours in July and August. More details on 01397 705825.

FORT WILLIAM

With its excellent road, rail and waterway links, Fort William has become the business and tourism "capital" of the Western Highlands. It occupies a glorious position overlooking Loch Linnhe, (although an ill-conceived dual carriageway has blocked off access to the shore). The town is the main shopping centre for a huge area and the High Street, with inviting little squares set back from it, gets very busy during the season. The major attraction for tourists is, of course, **Ben Nevis**, at 4406ft Britain's loftiest mountain and with a base which is said to be 24 miles in circumference.

Despite its height, there are several undemanding and well-worn routes to the top. The record time achieved during the annual race to the summit is one and a half hours, but for those walking at a more realistic pace between four and five hours should be allowed. The views from the top are incredible, extending halfway across Scotland to the distant Hebrides.

In the town itself, the **West Highland Museum** has collections covering almost every aspect of Highland life, an extensive and well-presented display. The museum's most famous exhibit is the "secret portrait" of Bonnie Prince Charlie, - a meaningless smudge of colour until viewed against a curved mirror when a charming miniature of the Prince, wearing a brown wig and an elaborate satin coat comes into focus. The portrait dates from the time when the penalty for anyone possessing an image of the Prince was death. Another intriguing exhibit is the long Spanish rifle used in the assassination of a local factor in 1752, the notorious "Appin Murder" that inspired Robert Louis Stevenson's *Kidnapped.* The museum also traces the town's history from 1655 when General Monk first built an earthwork fort here and called it Inverlochy. During the reign of William III the fort was rebuilt in stone and re-named Maryburgh. Subsequently, it was known as Duncansburgh and Gordonsburgh before finally settling down as Fort William. The Fort itself was demolished the 1890s to make way for the West Highland Railway station which in turn was dismantled to make room for a car park.

One experience not to be missed while you are in Fort William is a **seal cruise** along **Loch Linnhe**, followed by lunch or dinner in the award-winning **Crannog Scottish Seafoods restaurant**. During the season, the excursions leave daily from Fort William pier, travelling in the comfortable cruiser, the *Souter's Lass*. The route along this lovely loch takes in Seal Island, home to many common and grey seals, passes modern fish farms

Crannog Scottish Seafood Restaurant & Cruises, Fort William Town Pier Tel: 01397 705589 Crannog Scottish Seafoods, Smokehouse, Blar Mhor, Fort William PH33 7NG Tel: 01397 700072

along the way and offers a good chance of seeing the many species of wildlife resident in and around the loch. Some of the finest views of Ben Nevis are to be had from the water and the cruiser has a comfortable all-weather lounge with snacks and refreshments available. Back at the pier, it's just a few steps to the restaurant which in 1995 won the Booker Prize for Excellence as the Best UK Caterer for its integrated Crannog concept. The name Crannog was chosen by West Highland fisherman, Finlay Finlayson, to symbolise his concept of catching, curing and cooking the finest West Coast seafood in one integrated operation. Fish caught in his own boats is prepared in the Smokehouse and then made available to customers throughout the country and, of course, in his own restaurant on the pier. Finlay adopted the name Crannog because in Celtic times a Crannog was a fortified, self-sufficient island where fishing played a vital rôle in the community. The idea has been brilliantly successful and visitors to the restaurant can enjoy a superb lunch or dinner, fully assured of the quality and freshness of the beautifully cooked fish dishes on offer. The restaurant also offers a choice of fine wines and, as an extra bonus, you can admire the stunning views across Loch Linnhe as you relax and enjoy the authentic taste of Scotland.

Another highly recommended excursion from Fort William is a day trip on the **Jacobite Steam Train** to Mallaig. The 45-mile journey passes alongside Loch Eil and on to the west coast through some of the most spectacular scenery in the country. En route, it crosses the massive **Glenfinnan Viaduct** and makes an extended stop at Glenfinnan Station, allowing time to visit the **Station Museum**. Drinks, snacks, souvenirs and

Jacobite Steam Train

audio line-guides are available from the on-train shop. Trains run weekdays from mid-June to the end of September, and also on Sunday during the high season. Tel: 01524 732100.

Whisky lovers will undoubtedly want to make their way to the **Ben Nevis Distillery & Visitor Centre** on the A82 just north of Fort William. The major product here is The Dew of Ben Nevis, a distinctive blend of choice whiskies from all over Scotland. Visitors can follow the whole process of whisky making, find out about the "mighty Ben" itself, and discover the part that a legendary hero, big Hector MacDram, played in its creation. The distillery is open daily except Sundays from Easter to October: for more details, telephone 01397 700200.

Just off the A82 are the ruins of **Inverlochy Castle**, a stronghold of the Comyns. Historians say the castle was built in the late 1200s, but a durable legend claims that this was the site of a Pictish city whose king signed a treaty with Charlemagne in AD 790. The castle's original walled square with four corner towers still stands but there is little else of interest to be seen. A mile or so to the northwest of the castle, at **Banavie**, is **Neptune's Staircase**. Designed by Thomas Telford in 1822, this is a remarkable feat of engineering - a series of 8 locks which in the course of just 500 yards raise the level of the Caledonian Canal by 72 feet.

Finally, to the west of Fort William, on the A830 "Road to the Isles", **Treasures of the Earth** features one of Europe's finest collections of priceless gemstones and beautiful crystals, displayed in intriguing simulations of cave, cavern and mining scenes. The gift shop offers a wide selection of gemstone giftware, jewellery, geological specimens, healing crystals and much more. Treasures of the Earth is open daily, all year: telephone 01397 772283.

BALLACHULISH — MAP 2 REF G9

15 miles S of Fort William on the A82

On her way to visit Glencoe, Queen Victoria noted the village of Ballachulish, *"where the slate quarries are"*. The miners had *"decorated every house with flowers and bunches or wreathes of heather and red cloth"*. The slate quarries at Ballachulish had provided a living for the villagers since 1693 and at the time of Victoria's brief visit were at the height of their productive life with some 26 million slates being shaped and shipped in 1875. The quarries finally closed in 1955 but their legacy lives on in the slate gravestones in the churchyard, many of them elegantly engraved, and in the unique loch-side boat sheds constructed almost entirely of slate, their survival guaranteed by preservation orders.

Standing at the gates of the former slate quarry, and opposite the Tourist Information Centre, **The Arches Craft Shop** was originally the village

The Arches Craft Shop, East Laroch, Ballachulish, Argyll PA39 4JB
Tel: 01855 811866

Post Office. It now stocks much more interesting items, most notably its fascinating Wood Exhibition of Ancient Scots Pine Root sculptures by a local craftsman, Brian Dickie. These weird and wonderful creations justify a special trip by themselves, but Margaret Dickie's shop has a great deal more on offer. There are hand-crafted bowls, large and small, carved by Hamish Small of Kinlochleven from Scottish woods, and locally-made jewellery - hand-painted, copper and brass, semi-precious stone and silver. You'll also find unusual Celtic crafts; clothing (with a difference); toys for the tots; exquisite glass; and beautiful cards and gift wrap, - in fact, a comprehensive showcase for local crafts from Scotland and around the world. As Margaret says, "There's an awful lot in such a wee shop!", which, incidentally, is open all year round.

"The best hospitality I ever had on my travels was at Ballachulish House" wrote the 5th Duke of Argyll in 1760. More than two centuries later, John and Liz Grey ensure that visitors to their handsome hotel go away echoing His Grace's sentiments. Set between the mountains and loch, with superb views of Loch Linnhe and the Morven Hills, **Ballachulish House** was fairly new when the Duke visited. It had been rebuilt after the previous house was burnt down in 1746 by Hanoverian troops in the wake of the Jacobite Rebellion. The house already had a certain notoriety because of the Appin Murder of 1752 when Colin Campbell, the King's Factor, was assassinated about a mile away. Robert Louis Stevenson immortalised the event in his novel, *Kidnapped*, but the real killer has never been identified. In these quieter times, Ballachulish House offers guests great peace and tranquillity

Ballachulish House, Ballachulish, Argyll PA39 4JX
Tel: 01855 811266

in hospitable and friendly surroundings. The rooms are furnished with antiques, and even on summer evenings a log fire adds to the atmosphere of warmth and comfort. All bedrooms have en suite bathrooms and telephone, there's a billiard room, and in the drawing-room guests may help themselves to a drink before dinner from the "trust" bar. The food served at Ballachulish is in keeping with the style of the house and is complemented by an excellent wine list. The best local ingredients are used, with fish straight from the sea port of Mallaig, shellfish, venison, lamb and beef from local sources, - and with no concessions to nouvelle cuisine!

On the edge of the town, **Highland Mysteryworld** promises to take you back in time to a world of bogles, kelpies, fachans, and the Blue Man of the Minch, with the help of energetic actors in costume, special effects and lots of models. Children garbed in Viking helmets and cloaks can have great fun in the adventure playground, and there's a lochside trail, a gift shop specialising in herbal mixtures and books of legends, and a restaurant. Mysteryworld is open daily from Easter to October: more details on 01855 811660.

To the east of Ballachulish opens up one of the starkest and most sombre glens in Scotland, **Glen Coe**. Translated from Gaelic, the name means "Valley of Weeping". Here, in the early hours of February 13th, 1692, during a howling blizzard, some forty men of the Clan MacDonald were slaughtered by soldiers under the command of Campbell of Glenlyon. It was a heinous crime, "murder under trust", since for the previous ten days Campbell's soldiers had been entertained with traditional Highland hospitality by the MacDonalds. The legal pretext for the government-ordered massacre was that the MacDonalds had failed to meet the deadline of New Year's Day, 1692, for signing an oath of loyalty to William III. In fact, the necessary papers had been signed but, because of bad weather, arrived a few days late at Edinburgh. Secretary of State Sir James Dalrymple seized on the opportunity of making an example of the MacDonalds who, besides being notorious for their thievery, were also known Jacobite sympathisers. The MacDonalds may have been unpopular but the treachery of their slaughter outraged the whole country. Three years later, an official enquiry confirmed that the killings were indeed murder. Dalrymple was forced to resign, but no-one else was ever brought to account. The massacre at Glencoe poisoned the history of western Scotland for generations and even now a sign on the door of an inn in the village still proclaims: "Nae Campbells".

Today, most of this gloomy, melancholy glen is owned by the National Trust for Scotland which maintains a small **Visitor Centre** where, along with a gift shop and the usual amenities, you can also watch a video retelling the dreadful events of February, 1692.

KENTALLEN OF APPIN

MAP 2 REF G9

17 miles S of Fort William off the A828

This tiny village was the setting for the real-life "Appin Murder" which captured the imagination of Robert Louis Stevenson and inspired his novel *Kidnapped*. The murdered man was Colin Campbell of Glenure, known as the Red Fox. In the aftermath of the 1745 Jacobite rising, the Appin lands of the Stewart clan had been forfeited to the Crown. As government factor, the Red Fox had been charged with evicting the Stewarts and replacing them with men of Campbell blood. In May, 1752, Campbell was riding through Kentallen when two rifle shots rang out from a holly tree on the hillside. The Red Fox was killed immediately. A certain Alan Breac Stewart was suspected of the crime but as he could not be found, James Stewart of the Glens was arrested instead. After a travesty of a trial, with a blatantly prejudiced jury, eleven of whose members were Campbells, James was hanged at Ballachulish. Even this outrageous injustice failed to satisfy the Campbells. James' body was hung in chains for two months, and when only the bones remained, the skeleton was wired together and hung up again. The name of the true murderer of the Red Fox was known to leading Stewarts of the time, but for reasons of clan loyalty it has never been disclosed and remains to this day a family secret.

The charming village of Kentallen seems far too pretty for such a gruesome story, enjoying as it does breathtaking views across Loch Linnhe to the mountains of Morven. Sharing this spectacular view is **Ardsheal House**, a magnificent 18th century granite and stone manor set in scenery that is exceptionally beautiful, even for the West Highlands. An earlier 16th century mansion on this promontory of pink marble was destroyed by fire as a result of the 1745 uprising, and the present house was built around 1760.

Ardsheal House, Kentallen of Appin, Argyll PA38 4BX
Tel: 01631 740227 Fax: 01631 740342
e-mail: ardsheal97@aol.com Website:www.ardsheal.co.uk

Ardsheal has an inviting country house ambience with spacious public rooms panelled in warm oak, and the six delightful bedrooms are furnished with family antiques and pictures. The feeling that you are visiting a welcoming private house is re-inforced by the owners of Ardsheal House, Neil and Philippa Sutherland. As one noble guest, Lord Wilson of Tillyorn, remarked, it was "memorable and wonderful to find such accomplished hosts, delicious food and courteous attention". The food, wine, and malt whiskies are indeed memorable. Philippa serves 4 course dinners, with set menus changing daily, in the attractive dining room or the garden fronted conservatory. The innovative cooking makes full use of the abundant local produce, together with vegetables, herbs and fruit from the house garden, all served with home-baked bread. With Ben Nevis, Glencoe and Loch Ness all within easy reach, this outstanding hotel makes a perfect base for exploring the scenic glories of the West Highlands.

4 Oban and the Isle of Mull

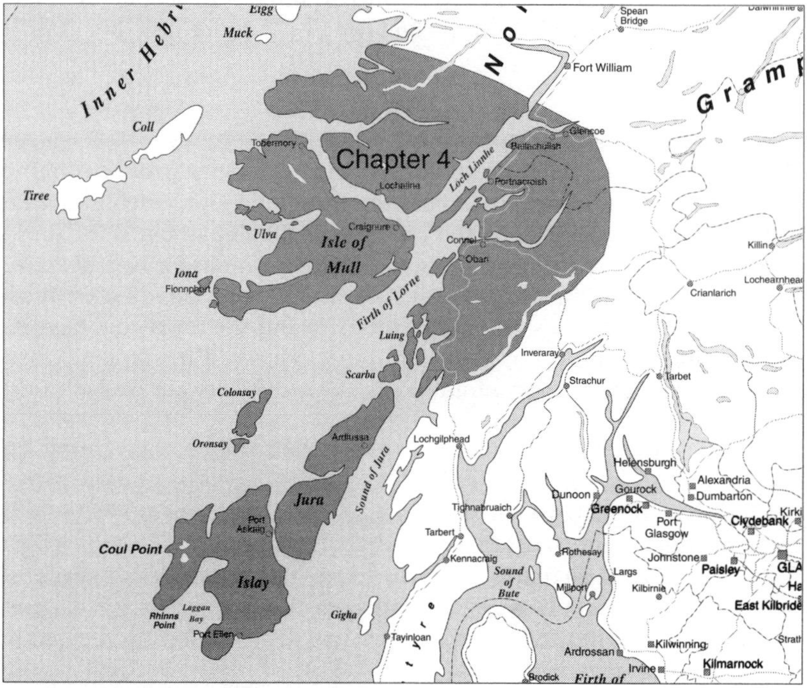

The undisputed holiday centre of the West Highlands, Oban has excellent road and rail communications and a generous choice of regular car and passenger ferries serving the main islands of the Inner Hebrides, and seasonal day trips to many of the smaller islands. The town stands at the heart of what was the 5th century Kingdom of Lorn, supposedly founded by the legendary Irish Celt of that name. Lorn later formed part of the great early Kingdom of Dalriada, whose kings were inducted at Dunstaffnage Castle, just north of Oban, on the hallowed "Stone of Destiny", or Stone of Scone. The stone was also known as "Jacob's Pillow", the stone on which he was sleeping when he dreamed of the ladder of angels rising from earth to heaven. It was taken from there to the Abbey of Scone, near Perth, in 838, and for the next 500 years was used in the coronation ceremonies of every king of Scotland. Then Edward I made off with it and installed the Stone in Westminster Abbey where, apart from a few months in 1950 when it was spirited away by Scottish nationalists, it remained for another 700 years. It was finally returned to Scotland in 1996 and now stands in Edinburgh Castle.

The area's main attraction, of course, is its magnificent coastal and mountain scenery, but the formidable Duart Castle on the Isle of Mull should be on every visitor's itinerary, the holy island of Iona has a very special mystical charm, and anyone with an interest in Scotland's industrial heritage will want to visit the Bonawe Iron Furnace near Taynuilt.

OBAN

This handsome and lively Victorian port is always busy with boat traffic criss-crossing between the islands of the Inner and Outer Hebrides. Protected by the length of the island of Kerrera, Oban's harbour is the finest on the west coast, with three piers and plenty of room for its still-active fishing fleet, a multitude of holiday craft, and the ever-busy ferries. Tourism is by far Oban's most important industry, but the town does have its own **distillery**, founded in 1794, and the producer of the famous Oban West Highland Malt. Forty-minute tours of the distillery are available during the season. The tours conclude with a free dram and your admission fee is refunded if you buy a bottle of their product. (Tel: 01631 64262). Another local industry is glass, and **Oban Glass**, part of the Caithness Glass group, also welcomes visitors to watch the process of glass-making from the selection of the raw materials to finished articles such as elegant paperweights. Samples of their products are on sale in the factory shop. On the North Pier, **World in Miniature** displays some 50 minuscule "dolls' house" rooms in a variety of historical styles, including two furnished in the manner of Charles Rennie Mackintosh and, like the others, built to a scale of one-twelfth.

McCaig's Tower, Oban

The most striking feature of Oban however is a completely useless building. High on the hillside overlooking the town stands one of Britain's most unforgettable follies, **McCaig's Tower**, erected by John McCaig between 1897 and 1900. On the foundation stone McCaig describes himself as "Art Critic, Philosophical Essayist, and Banker". He was motivated by a wish to provide work for unemployed masons in the area and, while a less romantic man might have built a Town Hall or a school, McCaig decided to build a replica of the Colosseum of Rome which he had admired on a visit there. His enormously costly project was designed from memory and its similarities to the original building are general rather than precise. McCaig had intended that a museum and art gallery would also form part of the complex and that large statues of his family would be stationed around the rim. None of this came to pass. He died in 1902 and his sister Catherine, who inherited his fortune, didn't share her brother's taste for such a grandiose monument. John McCaig's Colosseum remained a dramatically empty granite shell, a wonderful sight when floodlit and adding an oddly Mediterranean aspect to this picturesque town.

Just two miles from the bustling centre of Oban, **The Anchorage Guest House** is an inviting white-painted house, standing by itself beside a rocky hill and just yards from the shore. Here David Doak offers top quality bed and breakfast accommodation from April to September. The location is so attractive it was featured during the filming of *Ring of Bright Water,* starring Virginia McKenna and Bill Travers. The Anchorage is also ideally located for walking and fishing, the Sub-Aqua Centre is nearby and there's a boat hire centre just along the road. The guest house is also close to the Old

The Anchorage Guest House, Gallanach Road, Oban PA34 4QH
Tel: 01631 562088

Harbour and the ferry to the Isle of Kerrera, the low-lying island that protects Oban from the most ferocious of the westerly winds. Kerrera measures just five miles by two so it's easy to explore on foot and there are some grand panoramic views over to Mull, Jura, Lismore and beyond.

Just to the north of Oban stand the ruins of **Dunollie Castle**, much admired by both Sir Walter Scott and William Wordsworth. It was once the seat of the MacDougalls, Lords of Lorne, who still live nearby at Dunollie House (private), but little remains of the castle now apart from an impressive ivy-covered Keep rising majestically from a crag. **Dunstaffnage Castle** (Historic Scotland), a couple of miles further north, also sits atop a crag, and offers some superb views across the Lynn of Lorne to the island of Lismore. Substantial parts of the castle's 13th century fabric have survived, including walls 66ft high and 10ft thick in places, a curtain wall with 3 round towers, a large well surrounded by four small turrets, and a ruined chapel. As mentioned earlier, the castle was the original home of the Stone of Scone.

About 2 miles east of Oban, the **Rare Breeds Farm Park** has been a winner of the Scottish Tourist Boards "Tourism Oscar" and is very popular as a family day out. In its 30 acres of attractive countryside, visitors can meet a large number of rare, but mostly indigenous, species of deer, goats, cattle and sheep. There's a children' corner where kids can meet the baby animals at close quarters, a woodland walk, conservation centre, and tea room.

LERAGS — MAP 1 REF F11

2 miles S of Oban off the A816

Lerags is a glen steeped in clan history with the burial ground of the chiefs of the clan MacDougall, the ruins of Kilbride church, and the 16th century **Campbell of Lerags Cross** all within a one mile radius. The Cross, carved in 1526 with a depiction of the Crucifixion, was discovered centuries later lying in three pieces beside the ruined church. The figure of Christ escaped almost undamaged and is still a striking image.

What a pleasure to find a pub which positively welcomes children. Karen and Seoras Lindsey's friendly family pub and restaurant, **The Barn**, is located in beautiful, tranquil countryside on the outskirts of Oban, secluded yet only minutes from the bustle of the town centre. Accompanied children under the age of 14 are welcome here until 8pm.; there are pets to say hello to, children's portions available, and regular special offers for families. The food is all home-made, with some irresistible puddings and vegetarian choices included in the tempting menu. During the season, every Friday evening is "fantastic fish" night, with the very best of the day's catch of offer; on Thursday evenings there's a Scottish Ceilidh featur-

The Barn, Lerags, Oban, Argyll Tel: 01631 564618

ing a mix of traditional Scottish music and popular tunes; and on Sundays there's an informal evening of live music. In good weather, you can relax in the beer garden and enjoy a game of draughts on the outdoor board. This exceptionally inviting pub is open from 11 a.m. (weekdays), 12 noon (Sundays), from April to October. Winter opening hours vary.

George and Joan Waugh, the resident proprietors of the **Foxholes Country Hotel** have a straightforward philosophy: they are there to spoil you. They certainly spoil you with the food served in the hotel's smart dining-room with its panoramic views over the glen. The 6-course table d'hôte menu offers a choice of 3 starters, soup of the day, 3 main courses and 3 desserts, (all changed daily). At a reasonable extra cost, you can choose from the à la carte menu, offering excellent, top-quality local fish, steaks

Foxholes Country Hotel, Cologin, Lerags, Oban, Argyll PA34 4QA
Tel: 01631 564982

and game. There's a large selection of sensibly priced wines to complement your meal, and an equally wide choice of spirits, beers and soft drinks available in the bar servery. The accommodation at Foxholes is rather special too: all bedrooms are tastefully furnished with the added convenience of en suite bathroom or shower, colour television, tea, coffee and hot chocolate-making facilities, and radio alarm clock. A spacious and peaceful residents' lounge, a sunny patio with splendid views, miles of open countryside all around, - no wonder the Waughs feel confident that their outstanding hotel provides all the ingredients for an enjoyable and memorable holiday.

Dotted throughout 7 acres of wooded hillside in the peace and calm of Lerags Glen, **Lagnakeil Highland Lodges** provide a haven of tranquillity guaranteed to revitalise the most world-weary guest. There are 17 lodges in total, of four different types, each designed to offer modern comforts while blending harmoniously into the surrounding countryside. Each Lodge is completely self contained with fitted kitchen, complete with microwave and all the other necessary amenities, en suite bedroom decorated to a high standard, and a spacious dining/living room with colour TV. If you don't feel like cooking for yourself, a short walk up the glen will bring you to a country pub serving fine food and ales. At Lagnakeil you'll find a warm Highland welcome from resident owners Colin and Jo Mossman

Lagnakeil, Lerags, nr Oban, Argyll PA34 4SE. Tel: 01631 562746

who will do everything they can to ensure you have a memorable holiday. And there's certainly no shortage of activities to keep you occupied: Lagnakeil is a great base for exploring the superb countryside on foot; Oban's many attractions are just a few minutes drive away; some thirty spectacular gardens are within easy reach; and horse-riding or golf at Oban's 18-hole golf course are just some of the many other options available.

TAYNUILT

Map 1 ref G10

13 miles E of Oban on the A85

During the 1300s, someone built a house beside a stream that runs into Loch Etive. At that time everyone hereabouts spoke Gaelic so the "House by the Stream" was known as "Tigh-an-Uillt", and from this original single dwelling present-day Taynuilt takes its name. **The Taynuilt Hotel** stands on the site of that medieval house and, although not quite so ancient, is a grand old building enjoying wonderful views across the Argyll country-

The Taynuilt Hotel, Taynuilt, by Oban, Argyll PA35 1JN
Tel: 01866 822437

side. Visitors enter the hotel by way of a four-columned classical-style porch and then find themselves instantly at home in a traditionally decorated and furnished hostelry where they will meet a warm welcome from the owners, Gregor and Heather MacKinnon. Open log fires add to the warmth and, should the weather also be warm, there's a beer garden outside in which to enjoy it. Best of all is the home-cooked food: prime Scottish produce, carefully prepared and attractively presented.

Located in the heart of this lovely village, **The Robin's Nest Tearoom** offers the very best of home baking. The bright and airy room is exquisitely decorated, with pine floor and furniture, open fire, flowers on the tables and stylish pictures and decorations. The home made bread, freshly baked cakes and scones are all prepared daily by Maireadh Sim and her friendly staff, and so too are the excellent pancakes, soups and snack lunches. This is a tea room definitely not to be missed. The Robin's Nest is

The Robin's Nest Tearoom, Main Street, Taynuilt, Argyll PA35 1JE
Tel: 01866 822429

open daily from spring to the end of October (10am - 5pm), and from Thursday to Sunday (10am - 4.30pm) throughout the winter. To make a really good day of it, you might want to combine a visit to The Robin's Nest with a cruise on nearby Loch Etive, generally regarded as one of the loveliest lochs in Scotland and inaccessible except by boat. The boat cruises the 20 miles of sheltered water from Connel Bridge to the mountains of Glencoe and an on-board commentary guides you through this glorious mountain country, rich in history and legend.

Located in a quiet leafy corner of this attractive village, away from the public road, the **Kirkton Cottage and Chalet** have been carefully designed to integrate with their rural environment. The spectacular mountain scenery all around is a haven for hill walkers, nature lovers, and indeed for anyone who enjoys peace and tranquillity. Both the chalet and the cottage have been furnished and equipped to a high standard, with total-control electric heating, colour television, microwave, and bed linen (including duvets). Just about everything in fact to make your stay comfortable. "Kirkton Cottage" is a cosy dwelling which sleeps up to four people, (one double, one twin room). It has an open plan sitting-room with dining and kitchen area, and a shower room with w.c., washhand basin and shower. The chalet "Mountain View", across the lane, is ideal for two people and contains a double bedroom with en suite shower, and w.c., and an

Mrs L Beaton, Kirkton Cottage & Chalet, Dalry, Kirkton Taynuilt PA35 1HW Tel: 01866 822657

open plan kitchen/dining/living area. Both properties have their own parking areas and garden furniture is also provided. With the glorious scenery of Loch Etive and majestic Ben Cruachan just a few miles away, Kirkton Cottage and Mountain View are definitely Hidden Places to seek out.

Most of beautiful Loch Etive is not accessible by road, and by far the best way to explore its 20-mile length is by boat. During the season, **Loch Etive Cruises** runs daily 3-hour trips to the head of the loch on its modern cruiser *Anne of Etive* which has seating for 125, a licensed bar, serves teas

Loch Etive Cruises, Etive View, Taynuilt, Argyll PA35 1JQ Tel: 01866 822430 Fax: 01866 822555

and snacks, and provides an on-board commentary identifying points of interest along the route. The grand scenery includes the peaks of Ben Cruachan (3,695ft) and Ben Starav (3,538); the silvery walls of rock known as the "Etive Slabs"; waterfalls, and golden sands. *Anne of Etive* pauses close to a seal colony to enable photographs to be taken and, towards the head of the loch, golden eagles can be seen on most days. History and legend add extra colour to the commentary: the story of Deirdre of the Sorrows, for example, and of how the Clan McIntyre tricked their landlord, the Earl of Breadalbane, into accepting a flask of wine encased in a ball of snow as their annual rent. Free transport from Taynuilt to the pier is available, and during June and July there are special evening cruises by arrangement.

To the north of Taynuilt, near the shore of Loch Etive, stands **Bonawe Iron Furnace** (Historic Scotland), the well-preserved remains of a charcoal furnace, or "bloomery", for iron smelting. Built in 1753, it was in operation until 1876, - "the longest-lived blast-furnace in the Scottish Highlands".

Bonawe Iron Furnace, Taynuilt

At its peak, the furnace gave employment to some 600 men in an isolated and self-contained community in the middle of the countryside. Its major products were lengths of pig iron, cannonballs and shot. During the Napoleonic wars, the workers took great pride in their contribution of ammunition for the British forces and when they learnt of Nelson's death, they set up a monument to him in the churchyard, - the very first of the many to be set up in memory of the hero of Trafalgar.

For a really satisfying day out, combine a look at Bonawe Furnace with a visit to **Inverawe Fisheries, Smokery & Country Park** nearby where you'll find a huge choice of activities. You could try to spot all 75 species of birds in the Bird Sanctuary, or fish in one of the 3 lochs which provide full scope for all fly fishermen from the novice to the expert. A full-time

Inverawe Fisheries, Taynuilt, Argyll PA35 1HU
Tel: 01866 822446 Fax: 822274 e-mail: info@inverawe.co.uk

fishing instructor is on hand who will give anything from a half hour basic lesson for beginners to full day lessons and weekend courses. Or you could simply roam through the lovely, unspoilt countryside, follow the Nature Trail, or walk along the riverbank to Loch Etive. An informative tour of The Smokery demonstrates the true old fashioned highland way of preparing the salmon and you can find out how they slice the salmon so thinly! Then there's The Smokery Tearoom which enjoys panoramic views of the river and parkland and offers a variety of salads, open rolls, sandwiches and home baking. And in the shop you'll find a magnificent display of over 50 products from the smoke-house along with a selection of other Scottish gourmet delicacies. You may well want to linger in the idyllically peaceful surroundings of the Country Park: if so, there are three cottages on the estate available for holiday bookings.

DALAVICH Map 1 ref F11

28 miles SE of Oban on minor road off the A816

From Taynuilt, the B485 leads to Loch Awe and then a minor road follows the lochside southwards. It's a pleasant drive but an even better way to enjoy the 23 mile length of Loch Awe, with its islands and crannogs and 13th century castle on Innischonnel, is to hire a motor or rowing boat. Dalavich, on the west side of the loch, midway between Ford and Kilchrenan, is an ideal place from which to begin your exploration of this most beautiful loch, and here you will find **Lochaweside Marine** where Norman Clark has a fleet of boats (including canoes) available for hire by

Lochaweside Marine, 11 Dalavich, by Taynuilt, Argyll PA35 1HN
Tel: 01866 844209

the hour, half day, or full day. His modern fleet includes boats of various sizes, all available with or without engines, and the largest can accommodate parties of up to 8 people. Norman can also issue you with fishing permits for trout or pike, in season, supply you with all the necessary fishing tackle, and is also very knowledgeable about all aspects of the loch. He also has boats for hire at Loch Avich, a few miles to the northwest, another marvellously scenic stretch of water, reached by a minor road that passes through the wooded hills of Inverinan Forest.

ISLE OF MULL & ARDNAMURCHAN PENINSULA

For ten months of the year, from September until June, the 3000 residents of Mull virtually have its 370 square miles to themselves, - a spectacular landscape of moorland dominated by the massive bulk of Ben More (3170ft), with a west coast gouged by two deep sea-lochs, and an east coast unusually well-wooded for the Hebrides. During July and August, it's quite a different story as visitors flock to this unspoilt island. Its charming "capital", the little port of Tobermory, becomes crowded and the narrow roads congested. But as always in the Highlands, one only has to travel a mile or so from the popular venues to find perfect peace and quiet. Getting away from the pestilent swarms of summer midges may not be quite so easy.

Some 200 years ago, there were more than three times as many permanent residents on the island, but the infamous Highland Clearances of the early 19th century saw a constant stream of the destitute and dispossessed pass through Tobermory, boarding ships which would take them to an uncertain future in the slums of Glasgow or on the distant shores of America, Canada, and Australia. The island is still littered with the ruins of the crofts from which these refugees were driven or, quite often, even smoked out. Today, Mull is well-served by vehicle and passenger ferries from Oban, either by the 40-minute crossing to Craignure on the south-eastern tip of the island, or to Tobermory in the northeast. In this survey of Mull, we begin at Craignure and then travel more or less anti-clockwise around the island, with an excursion from Tobermory to the Ardnamurchan peninsula, finally ending up at the pilgrim destination of Iona.

CRAIGNURE — MAP 1 REF E10

East Coast of the Isle of Mull on the A849

As one approaches Craignure on the ferry from Oban, the great fortress on *dubh ard,* the "black height", becomes ever more imposing. **Duart Castle**, with its huge curtain wall 30ft high and 10ft thick, was built in the 13th century by the Macleans of Duart to protect them from their inveterate enemies, the Campbells. A century later, around 1360, they added the massive Keep that still stands today. Like most of the clans at that time, the Macleans were a pretty blood-thirsty bunch, but the behaviour of one of their early-16th century Chiefs appalled even his contemporaries. Lachlan Maclean had taken as his second wife, Catherine, sister of the powerful Earl of Argyll. When Catherine failed to produce an heir, Lachlan decided to dispose of her. One night, he bound her, took her to a rock in the Sound of Mull that becomes submerged at high water, and abandoned her there. The next day, he informed her brother of Catherine's death by drowning. In fact, she had been rescued by fishermen and taken to the Earl's castle at Inverary. A few days later the grieving Lachlan arrived at the castle with his "late" wife's coffin and was ushered into the Great Hall to find Catherine sitting at the head of the table. Throughout the meal that followed no-one made mention of her amazing resurrection, but later that year, 1523, Catherine's family had their revenge. Lachlan was visiting Edinburgh when he was surprised by her uncle, the Thane of Cawdor, and stabbed to death in his bed.

At low water, the skerry on which Catherine was marooned, now known as The Lady Rock, can be clearly seen from the Sea Room at Duart Castle. The splendid vista takes in Lismore lighthouse, the town of Oban and, on a clear day, the lumpy profile of Ben Nevis, some thirty miles distant.

In the Macleans' long connection with the castle there is a huge gap of more than 200 years. In 1691, Duart was sacked by their relentless enemies, the Campbells; after the Battle of Culloden, the Maclean estates were confiscated by the Crown and the castle was allowed to become increasingly dilapidated. Then in 1911, Sir Fitzroy Maclean, 10th Baronet and 26th Chief of the Clan Maclean, was able to buy Duart and begin the daunting work of restoration. To his eternal credit, Sir Fitzroy disdained any fake medieval additions, - none of the extraneous castellations and pepper-pot turrets favoured by most Victorian and Edwardian restorers. When he died here at the age of 101 in 1936, he left behind a castle that was faithful in essentials to the uncompromising spirit of his forefathers who had laid its foundations some 700 years earlier.

Duart Castle is open daily, from May to mid-October, there are sea- and loch-side walks, a shop and tea room, and, weather permitting, a motor launch from Oban esplanade will bring you direct to the castle slipway. For more details, telephone 01680 812309.

Craignure village itself offers a number of guest-houses, an inn, and a part-time Tourist Information Centre, but perhaps its most popular attraction is the **Mull and West Highland Railway**, a miniature-gauge line which runs southwards for a couple of miles to Duart Bay and Torosay Castle. The ancestral home of the Guthrie family, **Torosay Castle** is an extravagant 19th century mansion, a full-blooded example of the Scottish Baronial style of architecture. The opulent Edwardian interior contains an interesting collection of family portraits by artists such as Sargent and de Laszlo, and wildlife paintings by Landseer, Thorburn and Peter Scott. Even more impressive are the magnificent terraced gardens which include a Japanese garden area and an avenue lined with 19 elegant life-size statues by the 18th century Venetian sculptor, Antonio Bonazza. Torosay Castle is open daily, from mid-April to mid-October: more details on 01680 812421.

TOBERMORY — Map 1 ref E9

21 miles NW of Craignure on the A848

This picture-postcard little town, (population 700), is set around an amphitheatre of hills which cradle one of the safest anchorages on Scotland's west coast. Oddly, Tobermory's potential as a port was not recognised until 1786 when the British Society for the Encouragement of Fisheries decided to develop the harbour and build a quay. Despite the Society's encouragement, the fishing industry never really prospered. (Lacking modern aids, the fishermen were baffled by the arbitrary movements of the herring shoals). By the early 19th century, the port's main traffic was the sad stream of near-destitute refugees from the Highland Clearances who came here to board ship for destinations in the "New World", destinations that few of them had ever heard of before. That tragic episode of Scotland's history has been re-told many times, but it never loses its power to excite both anger and compassion.

The British Society's development of Tobermory port did, however, leave behind a charming legacy of (now) brightly-painted, elegant Georgian houses ranged along the quayside. Combined with the multi-coloured pleasure craft thronging the harbour, they help to create an atmosphere that is almost Continental: bright, cheerful and relaxed. The town's other attractions include its recently-opened arts centre, An Tobar, which stages exhibitions and live events; the tiny **Tobermory Distillery** where visitors are offered a guided tour and a complimentary dram of its famed single malt whisky; and the **Mull Museum** on Main Street where one of the exhibits is devoted to the most dramatic incident ever recorded on the island. It occurred in 1588 when a galleon of the routed Spanish Armada sought shelter in Tobermory harbour. The Spaniards were received with Highland courtesy; their requests for fresh water and victuals amply fulfilled. At some point, though, the people of Tobermory suspected that their guests intended to sail away without paying the bill for these provisions. Donald Maclean of Duart was deputed to go on board the Spanish ship and demand immediate payment. The Spaniards promptly locked him up and set sail towards their homeland. The ingenious Donald somehow managed to release himself, find his way to the ship's magazine, blow it up, and consign himself, the crew and the ship's rumoured cargo of fabulous amounts of gold bullion to the deep. Ever since then, strenuous efforts have been made to locate this watery Eldorado of Spanish gold. So far, all the divers have been rewarded with is a few salt-pocked cannon and a handful of coins.

Just a few minutes walk from the busy harbour, **Highland Cottage Hotel** is a charming small hotel of quality located in the quiet elegance of Upper Tobermory's Conservation Area. In the hotel's restaurant, excellent food is served in an attractively informal ambience, - top-quality fresh, local ingredients, imaginatively cooked and impeccably presented. After your meal, you can relax with a post-prandial liqueur or a dram of the famed Tobermory single malt whisky, and perhaps settle down with a good book from one of the hundreds on display throughout the hotel. And so to bed. The extremely well-appointed bedrooms all have an "Island" theme and thoughtful extra little touches which should help to ensure a good night's sleep. David and Josephine Currie are the owner/managers of this friendly and welcoming hostelry and will do everything they can to make

Highland Cottage Hotel, Breadalbane Street, Tobermory, Isle of Mull Argyll PA75 6PD Tel: 01688 302030 Fax: 01688 302727

sure that you return home with very pleasant memories of your stay in Tobermory.

During the summer months, a vehicle ferry plies the 35-minute crossing from Tobermory to Kilchoan on the wild Ardnamurchan peninsula, famed for its abundance of birds, animals and wildflowers. (The area can also be reached by road from Fort William). From Kilchoan, with its ruined 13th century Mingary Castle dramatically sited on the cliff top, a five mile drive will bring you to **Ardnamurchan Point**, the most westerly point in mainland Britain, offering some grand views across to the islands of Coll, Mull and Tiree. The unmanned lighthouse here is not normally open to the public but there's a café, gift shop, children's play area and a Visitor Centre dedicated to the theme of lighthouses and lighthouse people. Two of the keepers' cottages have also been converted into self-catering accommodation.

GLENBORRODALE MAP 1 REF E9

30 miles SW of Fort William via the A830, A861 & B8007

Travelling eastwards from Kilchoan, the B8007 loops inland around the bulk of Beinn nan Losgann (1026ft), then rejoins the coastline near Glenborrodale where banks of rhododendrons line the roadside for almost a mile. (This is Gulf Stream country with an almost sub-tropical warmth). The many islands in the loch are used as breeding stations by numerous different birds, among them goosander and merganser, whilst on the lochside many colonies of sandpipers nest between the road and shore. At the **Glenmore Natural History Centre**, an attractive timber building with turf roof, you can watch live television pictures of the surrounding wildlife, including views from an underwater camera in the nearby river. The centre was established by the gifted local photographer Michael MacGregor and his outstanding images, accompanied by specially composed music, are featured in a fascinating audio-visual show. For watching coastal wildlife, there are boat trips from Glenborrodale available through Ardnamurchan Charters who also run trips to Fingal's Cave and Tobermory on the Isle of Mull.

Enjoying panoramic views across Loch Sunart, and with the lofty Ardnamurchan Hills as an imposing backdrop, **The Clan Morrison Hotel** occupies an exceptionally beautiful situation. The hotel owners, the Morrison family, have committed themselves to providing guests with a free-and-easy holiday away from the hustle and bustle of modern city life, yet with all the modern conveniences to which they are accustomed. All the hotel facilities, (which include a games room with a full-size pool table), are on the one floor level, with a separate ramp access for disabled guests. Meals are served in the smartly-appointed dining-room where picture windows frame the lovely views, and the menus offer a choice and price to meet all tastes and pockets. Children are welcome, and separate

The Clan Morrison Hotel, Glenborrodale, Acharacle
Argyll PH36 4JP Tel: 01972 500232

meal-times, menus, and a large play area are provided for their enjoyment. And, as the area is a remote one, the Morrisons are quite happy for you to also bring your pets. The well-designed bedrooms are all en suite, and the excellent facilities include a baby-listening service. For those who prefer a self-catering holiday, the Clan Morrison Hotel also offers a modern 3-bedroom bungalow equipped with just about every imaginable amenity. A mere fifty yards from its front door, you have access to the loch for boating and diving, and this glorious corner of the West Highlands is ideal for hill-walking, bird-watching, stalking, sea-angling and much more. Unleaded petrol and diesel are also available at the hotel.

From Glenborrodale, the B8007 follows the shoreline of Loch Sunart before joining the A861 at Salen. If you turn left here, the road will take you across the peninsula to the village of Acharacle, 4 miles to the north.

ACHARACLE — MAP 1 REF E9

30 miles SW of Fort William via the A830, A861 & B8007

Undoubtedly the most attractive way of arriving at Acharacle is to take the passenger boat from Glenfinnan which travels the whole 17 mile length of Loch Shiel to deliver you at this pleasing village surrounded by gentle hills at the southern tip of the loch. Small though it is, Acharacle is the main stronghold for Gaelic speakers on the peninsula, and a lively little community where ceilidhs are often held in the village hall.

About 3 miles north of Acharacle is **Dalilea**, a unique farmhouse built in the traditional style of a Scottish country house. Parts of the house date

Dalilea House, Acharacle, Argyll PH36 4JX Tel: 01967 431253

back to the 15th century. The striking white-painted building with its twin turrets and corbie gables stands in its own grounds on the banks of Loch Shiel, a very popular loch for salmon and sea trout fishing. The surrounding area is ideal for those looking for an active country holiday, or who simply wish to get away for a quiet, relaxing break. There is brown trout fishing in hill lochs nearby, pony trekking with Kirsty, beautiful beaches, many tracks and hill walks for all abilities, and several local sights of historical significance. Dalilea's proprietor, Mairi Macaulay, is committed to providing her guests with a warm and comfortable base in this remote yet wonderful corner of the West Highlands. She provides traditional and inventive home cooking for breakfast and dinner, and is happy to cater for any dietary requirements. A selection of wines and spirits is available to accompany your meal, and in the lounge you can relax by the cosy fire with a plentiful supply of games, jigsaws and books to hand.

From Dalilea House it's just a few miles to **Castle Tioram**, (pronounced "Cheerum"), which is romantically sited on a lonely islet in Loch Moidart and can be reached at low tide by a sandy causeway. The medieval masons who built the castle adroitly adapted its design to fit the rock on which it stands, so the building is pentagular in shape. Tiorum was deliberately burnt down by its Jacobite owner, MacDonald of Clanranald, in 1715 to prevent it falling to his Hanoverian enemies.

We return now to Tobermory and continue our tour of the Isle of Mull.

DERVAIG

Map 1 ref D10

6 miles SW of Tobermory on the B8073

From Tobermory, the B8073 to Dervaig follows a tortuously twisting route through dramatic scenery, - one of the more demanding stretches of the annual round-the-island Mull Rally held in October. Nestling at the head of Loch a'Chumhainn, Dervaig itself is a pretty village of white-washed houses set in pairs along the main road. It's best known perhaps for being the home of the **Mull Little Theatre**. Housed in a former cow byre, this is the smallest professional theatre in Britain with just 43 seats for the audience. Each season, nevertheless, it stages a varied programme of plays, some of which are adapted for the small number of resident actors.

An attractive white-painted building, the **Bellachroy Hotel** dates back to 1608 and is believed to be the oldest continuously inhabited dwelling on the island. It was originally a drovers' inn but nowadays it's an inviting hotel, set in its own grounds, where visitors receive a warm welcome from the owners David and Karen Gervers who have been here since 1992. The hotel offers a menu that changes daily, served either in the welcoming bar (an excellent place to retreat if the weather is unkind), or in the Dining Room. Bellachroy has 7 comfortable guest rooms, 4 of them en suite and

Bellachroy Hotel, Dervaig, Isle of Mull, Argyll PA75 6QW
Tel: 01688 400314

all pleasantly furnished. The residents' lounge has lovely views of the River Bellart, Ben More and Dervaig village. Dog lovers will be pleased to know that David and Karen have a dog of their own and visitors' dogs are made more than welcome! Located in the centre of the village, the Bellachroy is within easy reach of Dervaig's famous Mull Little Theatre and just a little further away is the well-known Old Byre Heritage Centre.

About a mile south of Dervaig, **The Old Byre Heritage Centre**, housed in a lovely old building of variously-coloured stone, has become an essential stop on any visitor's tour of the island. The Centre explores the history of the island's inhabitants and dwellings, from the first settlers to the present day, with the help of over 25 specially created models. These striking models also feature in a 30-minute film presentation, "The Story of Mull and Iona", with a commentary accompanied by specially composed music played on the Clarsach, or Celtic harp. A video of the film is available in the large Gift Shop which also has a wide range of gifts, souvenirs crafts, and items to suit all pockets and ages. In 1998, The Old Byre's licensed tea room received an award from "The Taste of Scotland" for excellence in food preparation and presentation: scrumptious home baking is the speciality, with light meals served throughout the day. The Centre is open daily from Palm Sunday to the end of October, with programmes (including the film) starting hourly from 10.30am to 5.30pm.

The Old Byre Heritage Centre, Dervaig, Isle of Mull
Argyll PA75 6QR Tel: 01688 400229

Five miles west of Dervaig, still on the B8073, the tiny village of **Calgary** has one of the best sandy beaches on the island and enjoys enchanting views across to Coll and Tiree. Calgary has been known as an ideal holiday spot for generations, and one of its earliest visitors was a certain J.F. McLeod. Later, as a Colonel in Canada's North West Mounted Police, he founded what later became the capital of the province of Alberta and christened the new settlement with the name of this remote Scottish village.

Twenty miles further along this road, just after it joins the B8035 at **Gruline**, another famous founder is commemorated at the **Macquarie Mausoleum** (NTS). This is the burial place of Lachlan Macquarie, the "Father of Australia", served as Governor of New South Wales for 12 years from 1809 when he was appointed to succeed the highly unpopular William Bligh, former captain of *HMS Bounty.* Macquarie's simple tomb looks across Loch na Keal to the island of Ulva where he was born in 1761.

Travelling southwestwards from the Mausoleum, along the B8035, there is a spectacularly scenic drive as the road runs between the edge of the loch on one side, and mighty Ben More (3170ft), an extinct volcano, rises in terraced slopes on the other. Then, as the road swings south, it passes beneath the formidable, overhanging Gribun Rocks. Some years ago, one of them tumbled down the hillside and smashed through the hamlet of Gribun, demolishing one of the houses. The boulder is still there.

After another 8 miles or so, the B8035 joins the A849. Turn right here, and you now enter the Ross of Mull, a 20-mile narrow, rocky promontory bounded by Loch Scridain to the north and the Firth of Lorne on the south.

PENNYGHAEL MAP 1 REF E11

20 miles SW of Craignure on the A849

Situated on the shores of Loch Scridain, a deep inlet on Mull's western coast, **Pennyghael Hotel** commands magnificent views ranging from Ben More to Iona. On summer evenings, the pleasure of your evening meal in the dining room overlooking the loch may well be made even more memorable by a breathtaking sunset. The food here is all home-cooked, using local produce wherever possible, such as wild salmon, scallops, Mull cheese and venison. The hotel has 5 bedrooms, (3 double, and 2 twins on the ground floor), all with private bathrooms, colour TV, direct-dial telephones, and tea/coffee making facilities. Tony Read, who owns and runs this attractive, white-painted hostelry, also has 3 self-contained holiday cottages to let. Oak Cottage, a detached stone building, has the unusual history of having served first as a barn, then as the village cinema, until being converted to its present use in the 1980s. Clansman Cottage and Pine Cottage are semi-detached stone cottages which have been converted to provide spacious self-catering accommodation for up to 4 people. The Scottish Tourist Board's rating for Pine Cottage is currently awaited: the other two cottages enjoy an STB 4 Crowns Commended award. The hotel and the cottages are open from Easter to the end of October.

The Pennyghael Hotel, Pennyghael, Isle of Mull, Argyll PA70 6HB
Tel: 01681 704288 Fax: 01681 704205

A short drive from Pennyghael across the peninsula will bring you to **Carsaig**, a small village noted for its scenic setting, picturesque old stone pier, and the Carsaig Arches, dramatic columns of basalt some 750ft high which have been sculpted by the sea into fantastic caves and arches. Returning to the A849 and continuing southwestwards, we pass the Angora Rabbit Farm (seasonal) where children can stroke these appealing floppy-eared creatures, and watch their fur being clipped and then spun. About 7 miles further, the A849 ends at the village of Fionnphort.

FIONNPHORT

MAP 1 REF D11

37 miles SW of Craignure on the A848

Pronounced Finnyfort, Fionnphort is busy during the summer with ferries plying the one-mile crossing to the pilgrim island of Iona, or the 20-mile round trip to the Isle of Staffa to see the celebrated **Fingal's Cave**. In the village itself, the **St Columba Centre** has a small museum telling the story of the saint's life with the help of audio-visual effects and original artefacts. Opened in 1997 to celebrate the 1400th anniversary of his death, the centre is open daily throughout the year. A mile or so south of Fionnphort, there is a superb beach at Fidden, looking across to the Isle of Erraid where Robert Louis Stevenson stayed when he was writing *Kidnapped*. (He even had the hero of the book, David Balfour, shipwrecked here).

Back in Fionnphort, and a mere one minute's walk from the Iona and Staffa ferries, **Seaview Bed & Breakfast** is a traditional Hebridean home, sturdily built with thick walls of local pink granite. After recent refurbishment by its owners, John and Tania Noddings, Seaview has been elevated

Seaview Bed & Breakfast, Fionnphort, Isle of Mull, Argyll PA66 6BL
Tel: 01681 700235 Fax: 700669 e-mail: tania.noddings@ukonline.co.uk

to a 3-Star B&B rating by the Scottish Tourist Board and its new dining room enjoys splendid views across to Iona and its historic Abbey. Evening meals are available, and since John is a fisherman it is his daily catch of fresh sea food which provides the wholesome basis for Tania's cooking. John is also happy to take guests out into the Sound of Iona on his 20ft Orkney Fastliner, "Wanderer", to see crab and lobster fishing under way. Back at Seaview, you can relax in the comfortable sitting room where you'll find a good selection of books, guides and magazines. The five individually furnished and decorated bedrooms provide all the comforts you would expect, including bathrooms and colour TV. In the morning, prepare yourself for Tania's celebrated "Fingal's Breakfast", a meal worthy of the legendary giant himself! Seaview is open all year, there is parking for residents and pets are welcome. During the spring and autumn, short breaks are available with special rates for a stay of three or more nights.

IONA

Each year, hundreds of thousands of visitors make the 5-minute crossing from Fionnphort to Baile Mór, the only village on this historic island. (No visitor cars are permitted incidentally). They are continuing a tradition of pilgrimage which began shortly after St Columba's death in 597 at the then-venerable age of 75. Born in Donegal, Columba arrived on the island in 563 with 12 companions and founded a monastery of which nothing now remains. From Iona he travelled widely, even as far as the Shetlands and Iceland, pursuing his eventually successful mission of converting the whole of Scotland to Christianity. After his death, Columba was buried on Iona, but 200 years later, following a raid by Norsemen in which 68 monks were slaughtered, his bones were returned to Ireland and all trace of them lost.

Columba's monastery was replaced around 1200 by the **Cathedral Church of St Mary**, (usually referred to as the Abbey), but most of the present building dates back to the early 1500s and was heavily restored earlier this century. Opposite the Abbey's west façade stands the superb 8th century St Martin's Cross, 14ft high and lavishly decorated with Christian figures on one side, Pictish symbols on the other. South of the Abbey is the island's oldest surviving building, St Oran's Chapel, said to have been built by Queen Margaret in 1080. In the surrounding burial ground, Reilig Odhràin, are interred no fewer than 62 kings: of Scotland (48), Norway (8), Ireland (4), and France (2). One of the last Scottish kings to be buried here was Duncan (1040), followed in 1057 by his murderer, Macbeth. Soon afterwards, Dunfermline superseded Iona as the royal burial ground. The leading Highland chiefs, however, continued to be buried on Iona, and in 1994, John Smith, the former leader of the Labour party and a frequent visitor to the island, was interred here in the face of much local protest. Many of the cemetery's medieval grave slabs are now preserved in the **Infirmary Museum** at the back of the Abbey, along with an interesting collection of Celtic crosses.

Most visitors to Iona do not stray far from the Abbey complex so the rest of this small island, just 3 miles long and barely a mile wide, is ideal for walking and for the quiet contemplation that this holy island inspires but which is difficult to achieve within the busy environs of the Abbey.

Just a few yards from the Abbey and close to the parish church and Bishop's House, the **St Columba Hotel** offers a high degree of personal attention from its dedicated and enthusiastic staff. One of the hotel's most appealing features is its central sun lounge which provides glorious views, in ever-changing colours, over the Sound of Iona to the Ross of Mull and the mountains beyond. Anyone in search of a truly peaceful refuge from

St Columba Hotel, Isle of Iona, Argyll PA76 6SL
Tel: 01681 700304 Fax: 01681 700688

modern life will be delighted to know that there is not a single television set within the hotel and, because visitors' cars are not allowed on the island, children do not have to be so closely guarded. Since the arrival of the new chef the hotel is becoming renowned for its excellent cuisine. Th hotel offers visitors a choice of 19 twin-bedded rooms and 8 single rooms, all with private facilities and well-appointed. When you arrive on the island, your luggage will be picked up and transported to the hotel, about half a mile from the jetty. One further recommendation: the St Columba Hotel has produced a model brochure which is not only fully informative about its own facilities but also includes a detailed map of the island marking Iona's many historic sites. Send for it!

5 South Argyll and the Isle of Arran

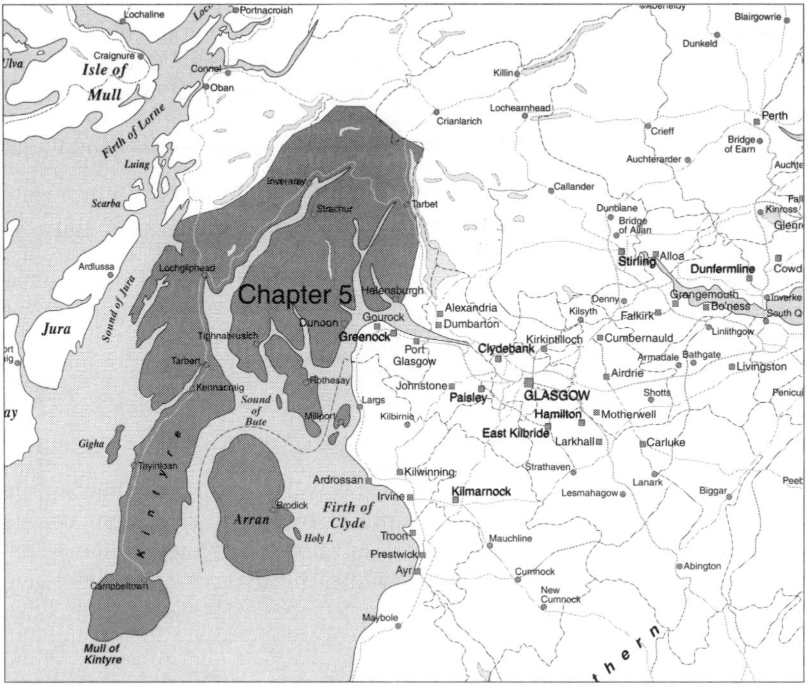

This exploration of southern Argyll begins to the south of Oban at Carnasserie Castle, a 16th century fortified house whose great age dwindles into insignificance compared with the extraordinary collection of prehistoric cairns, stone circles and inscribed stones a few miles away, near Kilmartin. This is by far the most striking of the prehistoric sites on mainland Scotland, rivalled only by those on Orkney. The route continues down the 40-mile length of the Kintyre Peninsula which only a mile-long isthmus near the pleasant little port of Tarbert prevents from being an island. We then travel eastwards to the Cowal Peninsula with its deeply-fretted coastline and with vast tracts of the Argyll Forest Park covering some 125,000 acres of the north-east corner. The most heavily-populated area of the peninsula is around Dunoon, a legacy from Victorian times when steam ferries from Gourock, a few miles across the Firth of Clyde, made the coastline here easily accessible to affluent Glasgow citizens in search of healthy weekend and holiday retreats. A mere half-mile of water, the Kyles of Bute, separates the northern tip of the Isle of Bute from the Cowal Peninsula, although most visitors arrive at the handsome Victorian resort of Rothesay, "capital" of the island. The eastern side of this small island has long been a popular destination for Clydesiders, but you only have to travel a few miles to the west coast for splendidly open spaces with only a handful of villages scattered along its length. Finally, we visit the Isle of Arran, "a great arrogant lion of an island" with massive mountains dominating its northern half. With tourism as its major industry, Arran offers good sandy beaches, walking, fishing and a wide range of sporting facilities, including no fewer than seven golf courses, (3 of them 18-holers).

Our survey of the area begins about 27 miles south of Oban, on the A816, at Carnasserie Castle (Historic Scotland), an outstanding example of a 16th century fortified house. Although the castle was sacked during the Monmouth rebellion of 1685, enough remains to give a good idea of what the house was like with features such as the huge open fireplace in the kitchen, large enough to roast a whole ox.

KILMARTIN

MAP 1 REF F12

29 miles S of Oban on the A816

Two miles south of the castle, Kilmartin is well-known to archaeologists for the astonishing number of prehistoric chambered cairns, stone circles, burial cists, and rocks inscribed with ritual cup-and-ring signs, all concentrated to the west and south of the village. The most ancient and impressive is the **Nether Lairg South Cairn**, some 5000 years old, where visitors can enter the large chambered tomb with its stone-slabbed roof. A little further south, the two Stone Circles at Templewood, excavated as recently as the 1970s, appear to have been the main centre for burials from Neolithic times to the Bronze Age. The various sites are well-signposted, have useful information boards, and are normally open throughout the daylight hours. The village of Kilmartin is itself notable for the early Christian crosses in the church, some medieval graveslabs in the churchyard, and a ruined 16th century tower which was once the home of the rectors.

Nestling in the hills outside Kilmartin, **Tibertich** is a working farm with a flock of Blackface sheep and a small herd of Luing suckler cows. Here, well off the beaten track, with guaranteed fresh air and beautiful scenery, Barbara Caulton offers guests a choice of either Bed and Breakfast, or self-catering accommodation. B & B is available in the main house where on arrival you will be offered a welcoming cup of tea and coffee, served in the sitting room with its view of rolling hills, grazing sheep and subtle colours. There are 3 cosy bedrooms (a single, double and twin), all with views of the hills. Evening meals are available by arrangement. If you prefer self-catering, Barbara has two cottages to let, both of them sleeping up

Tibertich, Kilmartin, Argyll PA31 8RQ Tel/Fax: 01546 810281

to 4 people, and both full of character. Calltuinn, (Gaelic for Hazel), is a traditional stone cottage, tucked away on its own with marvellous panoramic views. The spacious grassed area outside is completely fenced off, making it safe for both children and pets. Ròs-Mhuire, (Gaelic for Rosemary), is a renovated stone cottage with a high ceiling and galleried loft area. Well-furnished, comfortable, and centrally heated, Ròs-Mhuire makes an ideal retreat whatever the season. Please note that pets are allowed only at Calltuinn Cottage, and that all the accommodation at Tibertich is non-smoking.

KILMICHAEL GLASSARY

MAP 1 REF F12

32 miles S of Oban on minor road off the A816

About 5 miles south of Kilmartin, there are yet more prehistoric remains, some of the most important in the country. The rocky outcrop of **Dunadd Fort** was the seat of power in western Scotland from around AD 500, - the capital of the Pictish Kingdom of Dalriada. Here, generations of Scottish kings were crowned, one of them, Aidan, by St Columba, and the ceremonies are recorded in some remarkable stone carvings along with an inscription in the ancient Irish language of Ogham. Dunadd thrived for nearly 4 centuries, until 873, when Kenneth McAlpin conquered the Picts and moved his capital to Scone, near Perth.

Kilmichael Glassary takes its name from yet another prehistoric survival, a rock inscribed with the typical cup and ring markings of that period. In this tiny village, the gleaming white walls of **The Horseshoe Inn** beckon an invitation that should not be resisted. Your hosts at this welcoming, family-run inn are Mary Dodds, Chris Finch and Lucy Atter and they take pains to provide both good food and good accommodation. Bar meals to suit every taste are available from 12 noon until 9.00 p.m., seven days a week, with a limited menu on offer until 10.30 p.m., Sunday to Thursday, and until half past midnight on Friday and Saturday. That really does count

The Horseshoe Inn, Bridgend, Kilmichael Glassary, Lochgilphead Argyll PA31 8QA Tel: 01546 606369 Fax: 01546 602305

as dedicated customer service. Vegetarian options and special meals for children are also available. Accommodation at the Inn consists of double or twin rooms, all with en suite facilities, tea & coffee-making equipment, and colour television. (Children and pets are very welcome, but please note that smoking is not permitted in the bedrooms). The Inn is located in the heart of mid-Argyll, an area steeped in history, with many archaeological and historic sites nearby, such as the Kilmichael Cup and Ring Marks, Kilmartin Glen, Carnasserie Castle, and Dunadd Hill, the site of an Iron Age Fort where the ancient Kings of Dalriada were crowned.

MINARD

MAP 1 REF F12

26 miles NE of Tarbert on the A83

Standing in its own grounds in beautiful countryside on the northwestern shore of Loch Fyne, **Minard Castle** provides visitors with an exceptional choice of either Bed and Breakfast, or self-catering accommodation. This grand old house was built in the 18th century and was known then as Knockbuie House. In the mid-19th century an impressive castellated front was added and the building re-named Minard Castle. The present owners, Reinold and Marion Gayre, offer a warm welcome to visitors to their family home where there are 3 comfortable bedrooms (1 double, 2 twins), all

Minard Castle, Minard, Argyll PA32 8YB Tel/Fax: 01546 886272

well-equipped with colour television, facilities for making tea and coffee, and en suite bathrooms. Breakfast in the Morning Room, relax in the Drawing Room, stroll through the extensive grounds (some 70 acres), or use the castle as your base for touring this scenic area. Please note that smoking is not allowed in the house. In the castle courtyard, there are two first-floor flats sleeping 4/5 people, both comprehensively equipped. Another option is The Lodge which sleeps up to 6 people, has a view through the trees to Loch Fyne and its own small private garden with tables and chairs. Self-catering guests are also welcome to use the castle grounds. An additional attraction for guests at Minard Castle is that they may take advantage of its salmon fishing rights which extend along the shore in both directions from the house, and include Brainport Bay, Minard Bay and Union Bay.

TARBERT

Map 1 ref F13

32 miles N of Campbeltown on the A83

At Tarbert, an isthmus, or "tairbeart", just one mile long links the Kintyre Peninsula to the mainland. A venerable, but true, story recounts that in 1093 the wily Viking King Magnus Barefoot made a surprise attack on the west coast while the Scottish king, Malcolm Canmore, was away fighting the English. Malcolm was forced to cede the Hebrides, but seeking to keep Magnus off the mainland, he stipulated that the 20-year-old invader might only retain any island he could navigate his ship around. Magnus coveted Kintyre, at that time much more fertile than the Hebridean islands, so he mounted his galley on wooden rollers and "sailed" his ship across the isthmus near Tarbert thus claiming the whole of the peninsula. More than three centuries later, Robert the Bruce performed an identical manoeuvre while establishing his supremacy over the region. The Bruce was also responsible for building a Castle at this strategic point, but today only the ivy-covered ruins of the Keep remain, standing atop a 100ft mound. This appealing little town, backed by low green hills, was once a busy fishing port but nowadays it is pleasure craft which throng the harbour, particularly during the last week in May when the yacht races in the Rover series take place. They are followed the next week by the powerboat Grand Prix.

A mile or so south of the town stands an attractive family-run 18th century coaching inn full of character, the **West Loch Hotel**, occupying a lovely position on the shore of West Loch Tarbert. With its open fires and

West Loch Hotel, by Tarbert, Loch Fyne, Argyll PA29 6YF
Tel: 01820 820283 Fax: 01820 820930

friendly, cosy atmosphere, the West Loch is as inviting an hotel as you could find anywhere, and it enjoys a well-earned reputation for its good food, providing excellent dinners as well as bar lunches and suppers, - all of them complemented by a wide choice of affordable wines, beers and spirits. Surrounded by some of Scotland's most breathtaking scenery, this impeccably maintained hotel has 7 bedrooms, all with private facilities, with a choice of doubles, twins, singles, or a family room for three. The attractive little port of Tarbert is just a couple of miles away, offering pleasant day excursions to the islands of Islay and Jura, or, in the other direction, you can take a ferry across to the "high island" of Arran with its dramatic, rugged mountains. You don't have to take to the water to find great scenery: south of the West Loch Hotel, a drive through the huge open spaces of Kintyre should surely soothe the most troubled soul.

GLENBARR

Map 1 ref E14

24 miles S of Tarbert on the A83

From Tarbert, the A83 skirts the rugged coastline, providing some excellent views of the islands of Jura and Islay, and if you are lucky, sightings of Atlantic grey seals, Britain's largest wild animals, draped across the offshore rocks. There are no settlements of any size along this route until you come to Glenbarr which has been described as *"the most pleasing village of south Kintyre"*.

Visitors to Scotland are understandably fascinated by the clan system, and at **Glenbarr Abbey** they can enjoy a privileged insight into this unique element of Scottish society, as notable for its ferocious loyalties as for its sometimes barbarous feuds. The family seat of the Macalisters of Glenbarr, Glenbarr Abbey was built in the late 18th-century and then greatly enlarged around 1815 with the addition of a striking west wing in the Gothic Revival style. This beautiful house is the home of Angus, 5th Laird of Glenbarr and Representer of Macalister of Glenbarr, and his wife, Jeanne, who personally conduct visitors around its many treasures. Guided by the people who know and love them best, you will be introduced to a veritable wealth of exhibits: antique toys, a Spode dinner service, a collection of

Glenbarr Abbey, Glenbarr, by Tarbert, Argyll PA29 6UT
Tel: 01583 421247

Sevres and Derby china, family jewellery, 19th century fashions, wonderful patchworks, a unique thimble collection, and even a pair of gloves worn by Mary, Queen of Scots. You can also learn about the Macalister Clan's long history, with its origins dating back to the 13th century and to Alasdair Mor, brother of Angus Mor of the Isles. There are still many Macalisters living in this area of Kintyre, but the 5th Laird is the only major landowner. In 1984, he gifted Glenbarr Abbey and its contents to a charitable trust to create this Macalister Clan Visitor Centre, where in addition to exploring the grand old house itself, visitors can also wander through the lovely grounds with its riverside and woodlands walks, browse in the Gift Shop, and enjoy refreshments in its tearoom.

CAMPBELTOWN

MAP 1 REF E14

38 miles S of Tarbert on the A83

Campbeltown enjoys a very scenic position at the head of a deep bay sheltered by Davaar Island and surrounded by hills. In its 19th century heyday, when Campbeltown boasted a large fishing fleet and a thriving shipbuilding industry, it was said that there were 34 distilleries and almost as many churches in the town. A glance at the skyline here shows that most of the churches seem to have survived, although not necessarily for religious purposes. The former Longrow Church for example is now the **Campbeltown Heritage Centre** and where the altar once stood there's now a beautifully crafted wooden skiff constructed in 1906. There are displays on the area's whisky industry, and exhibits relating to the 6th century St Kieran, the "Apostle of Kintyre". Kieran lived in a nearby cave which can still be visited at low tide. The saint believed in self-abnegation of an extreme kind. His food consisted of three equal parts of bread, herbs and sand; he heaped his body with heavy chains, and slept in the open air with a flat stone for his pillow. One is not surprised to learn that, after sleeping outside during a snowfall, St Kieran died of jaundice at the age of 33.

Of Campbeltown's numerous distilleries which, it was claimed, produced such a powerful aroma that boats could find their way through thick fog to the harbour by following its bouquet, only two remain: Glen Scotia and Springback. They produce a malt which is quite distinctive from those made at nearby Islay or at any other of the Highland and Lowland distilleries. The family-owned **Springback Distillery** has tours by appointment.

The most striking feature of the town is the **Campbeltown Cross** overlooking the harbour.The 15th century cross is carved with highly intricate ornamentation of Biblical figures and Celtic designs.

A popular outing from Campbeltown is to **Davaar Island** which at low tide is linked to the mainland by a mile long causeway. The uninhabited island is used for grazing, (so no dogs are allowed), and its main attraction is a cave in which a wall-painting of the Crucifixion mysteriously appeared in 1887. Years later, in 1934, a local artist, Archibald MacKinnon, admitted that the painting was his work, and in the following year, at the age of 85, he returned to renovate it.

Ten miles south of Campbeltown, Keil, just to the west of Southend, is best known as the spot where St Columba first landed in Scotland, in AD 563. It's claimed that two footprints carved into a rock mark his first steps ashore, and that the ruined medieval chapel stands on the site of the one he founded here.

Beyond Keil, a minor road leads to the most southwesterly point of the peninsula, the Mull of Kintyre. The road ends a mile short of the lighthouse of 1788 which stands 300ft above sea level, exposed to the full force of Atlantic gales. It's a bleak, wild spot, but on a clear day worth the trek for the views across to Ireland, just 12 miles away.

THE COWAL PENINSULA

Bounded by Loch Long and Loch Fyne, the Cowal Peninsula is like a three-taloned claw with the Isle of Bute clutched in its grip. (The name Cowal is believed to come from an old Norse word meaning a forked piece of land). In this comparatively small area there's a wide variety of scenery, from the extensive forests smothering the Highland peaks of the north, to the low-lying coastline of the southwest. Apart from the area around Dunoon, where two-third's of the peninsula's 16,500 population live, Cowal is sparsely-populated with an abundance of wildlife untroubled by too much human disturbance. The area is particularly popular with bird-watchers. In addition to the prolific variety of indigenous species, including hawks, buzzards and eagles, there are even more exotic birds to be seen at the Cowal Bird Garden, near Dunoon.

CAIRNDOW — Map 1 ref G11

39 miles N of Tarbet on the A83

Cairndow stands at the head of Loch Fyne, a small village with a curiously shaped white-washed church. Built in 1816, the **church** is hexagonal in shape with Gothic style windows in pairs and a tower crowned by an elaborately carved parapet and four turrets.

Cairndow Stagecoach Inn has entertained some distinguished guests during its long history. Dorothy Wordsworth visited in 1803 and "at our landlord's earnest recommendation" enjoyed a herring fresh from the loch; in 1875, Queen Victoria stopped here to change horses. Delightfully situated just off the A83, on the upper reaches of Loch Fyne, Cairndow is one

Cairndow Stagecoach Inn, Cairndow, Argyll PA26 8BN
Tel: 01499 600286 Fax: 01499 600220

of the oldest coaching inns in the Highlands. The stables from those days of the stage coach have been converted into the Stables Restaurant, brimming with old-world charm and with grand views over the loch. Both table d'hôte and à la carte menus are offered and include superbly prepared dishes such as sauté haunch of venison in red wine sauce, and Loch Fyne salmon steaks. At dinner time, the candlelit setting adds to the appeal. If you are looking for something less substantial, "Pub Grub" is served in the bar all day. The inn is under the personal supervision of Douglas and Catherine Fraser who also offer excellent accommodation in 14 well-equipped, centrally heated, bedrooms. If you really want to indulge yourself, book into one of the two de-luxe rooms with two-person spa baths, king-size beds, and 20" television.

Just behind Cairndow village, **Ardkinglas Woodland Garden** can boast the tallest trees in Britain, - conifers more than 200ft high, and hundreds of other attractive trees and shrubs, including many exotic rhododendrons. The garden is open daily from dawn to dusk.

Standing on a promontory overlooking Loch Fyne, Castle Lachlan was first mentioned in a charter of 1314 and was the ancient home of the Maclachlan of MacLachlan. Today the clan Chief, Madam Maclachlan of Maclachlan, lives in a nearby 18th century castle/mansion and if you are a member of the MacLachlan clan you are welcome to visit by appointment.

INVERARAY

MAP 1 REF G11

11 miles SW of Cairndow on the A83

Although not strictly speaking within the Cowal Peninsula, the charming little port of Inverary is just a few miles from Cairndow and should on no account be missed. A striking example of a planned "new town", Inverary was built in the mid-1700s by the 3rd Duke of Argyll, chief of the powerful Clan Campbell. He demolished the old settlement to build his grand new Castle and re-housed the villagers in the attractive Georgian houses lining Main Street. The Duke also provided them with an elegant neo-classical church, All Saints, which was originally divided into two parts: one for services in English, the other for Gaelic speakers. A later addition, erected as a memorial to Campbells who fell in World War I, is the free-standing Bell Tower, equipped with ten bells which are reputedly the second heaviest in the world. During the summer season, the tower is open to visitors and there are splendid panoramic views from the top.

One of the most popular attractions in the area is **Inverary Jail**, yet another of the 3rd Duke's benefactions to the town. The stately Georgian courthouse and the bleak prison cells were last used in the 1930s and have since been converted into an award-winning and imaginative museum where costumed actors re-create the horrors of prison life in the past. Visitors can also seat themselves in the semi-circular courtroom and listen to excerpts from real-life trials that took place here. The Jail is open daily throughout the year, with restricted hours from November to March. For more details, telephone 01499 302381. A few minutes walk from the Jail stands the grand neo-Gothic **Inveraray Castle**, still the family home of the Duke of Argyll whose ancestor, the 3rd Duke, began building it in 1746. Despite two major fires, in 1877 and 1975, the most important treasures survived and include portraits by Gainsborough, Ramsay and Raeburn, superb furniture, and a mind-boggling array of weaponry which includes the dirk, or traditional Highland dagger, used by Rob Roy. Outside, the grounds are extensive with many pretty walks, some by waterfalls on the River Aray, and the old stables now house the Combined Operations Museum which recalls the period leading up to the D-Day landings when some quarter of a million Allied soldiers were trained in amphibious warfare on Loch Fyne. The Castle is open daily from April to October, except on Fridays outside the main season; the Museum is open for the same months, but always closed on Fridays. Tel: 01499 302203.

REST AND BE THANKFUL

MAP 2 REF G11

6 miles SE of Cairndow on the A83

The modern A83 makes easy work of the pass through Glen Croe along which William and Dorothy Wordsworth struggled "doubling and doubling with laborious walk" in 1803. As they reached the summit, 860ft above sea level, the Wordsworths noted with approval the plaque inscribed "Rest-and-be-thankful", placed here by the army troops who repaired the old stone road in 1743. The viewpoint provides superb vistas of Beinn an Lochain (2,992ft) to the west, and Ben Ime (3,318ft) to the east.

LOCHGOILHEAD — MAP 2 REF G11

10 miles S of Cairndow on the B839

From Rest-and-be-Thankful, the B828 climbs to almost 1,000ft, drops sharply down into Glen Mor and then passes through the Argyll Forest Park before reaching this little town set in a lovely position at the head of Loch Goil. The town is mostly a resort centre offering a wide range of watersport activities, but if you follow the lochside road southwards it will bring you to the ruins of **Carrick Castle**. A classic tower house castle, built around 1400, it was used as a hunting lodge by James IV. A stronghold of the Argylls, the castle was burned by their enemies, the Atholls, in 1685, but the lofty rectangular great hall is still imposing in its solitary setting beside the loch.

From Lochgoilhead, return along the B839 to the A815 near Cairndow. The last four miles of this route traverses the narrow Hell's Pass, a lonely, rockstrewn landscape ideal for the footpads and highwaymen who earned the pass its name. At the junction with the A815, look out for the Wedding Ring, a group of inset white stones in the shape of a heart marking the spot where the gypsies of Argyll once solemnised their marriages. South-westwards from this point, the A815 runs alongside Loch Fyne, where seals are a common sight, to Strachur, a straggling village where the road forks. The A886 runs down the western side of the peninsula, the A815 leads to the area's major town, Dunoon, on the east coast. We begin by following the latter which passes through more than 20 miles of the **Argyll Forest Park** before reaching the village of Kilmun. En route it passes the celebrated **Younger Botanic Gardens** at **Benmore**. They were established in the late 1800s by the Younger family who bequeathed them to the Royal Botanic Gardens, Edinburgh, in 1928. The 120 acres of gardens contain a staggering collection of shrubs and trees, most notably some 250 species of rhododendron, azaleas, giant Californian redwoods, and more than 200 varieties of conifers, about one third of all those in existence. One of them, a fir tree, now stands at more than 180ft high, (although there's an even loftier one near Cairndow which exceeds 200ft.).

KILMUN — MAP 2 REF G12

5 miles N of Dunoon on the A880

Kilmun stands on the shore of Holy Loch which, according to tradition, was given its name when a ship carrying earth from the Holy Land, destined for the foundations of Glasgow Cathedral, was wrecked here. It was taken for granted that the exotic soil had sanctified the loch, hence its name. The village itself was an important early Christian site, with a chapel founded here around AD 620 by St Mun, a contemporary of St Columba. The present church was built in 1816, but looming behind it is the domed mausoleum of 1794 which contains the earthly remains of all the Earls and Dukes of Argyll since 1442. Amongst them are the Earl Archibald who died at the Battle of Flodden, and the 8th Earl who was beheaded in 1661. In the church's graveyard running up the hillside is the grave of Dr Elizabeth Blackwell (1821-1910), who struck an early blow for Women's Lib by becoming the first woman doctor registered in Britain. Just to the west of the village, the **Forestry Commission's Arboretum** will appeal to anyone who loves trees, and its Information Centre can provide copious details of the many forest walks throughout the Argyll Forest Park.

Occupying a splendid position close to the shore of Holy Loch, **The Cot House Hotel** is an attractive white-painted building with traditional crow-stepped gables. It was originally built as a ferryman's home and toll house, "cot" being the local word for the small boat used to cross the river. The hotel is a favourite with fishermen angling on the nearby River Eckaig, famous for its trout and salmon, and also with anyone who appreciates good Scottish food, expertly and imaginatively prepared. The hotel has received many plaudits for its excellent cuisine which is based on the "Natu-

The Cot House Hotel, by Sandbank, Kilmun, Dunoon Argyll PA23 8QS Tel: 01369 840260

ral Cooking of Scotland" theme, featuring seasonally available local produce from the sea, rivers and glens of Argyll. The extensive choice includes meat, fish, and vegetarian options, as well as a children's menu, and vegans can also be catered for. The restaurant has a welcoming log fire, as does the bar where you'll find a great range of malt whiskys and drinks to suit all tastes. For fairweather days, there's a patio, and a Beer Garden overlooking the children's play area set in an idyllic rural environment. The Cot House Hotel is ideally located for exploring the Cowal Peninsula and offers guests a good choice of rooms, all tastefully decorated, well-equipped, and en suite. The hotel has won the Licensed Trade News Awards for the Family Welcome of the Year, and was runner-up in the Independent Hotel Caterer of the Year Award.

DUNOON

Map 2 ref G12

29 miles S of Cairndow on the A818

A popular resort in the 19th century for Glaswegians, (it was, and still is, linked to Clydeside by a regular ferry), Dunoon is by far the largest town in Argyll, with some 13,000 inhabitants. In the years following World War II, the town benefited greatly from the establishment of a US nuclear submarine base on nearby Holy Loch, and later suffered badly from the economic effects of the base's closure in 1992. But Dunoon is once again a lively resort, well-known for the **Cowal Highland Games**, Scotland's largest, which take place on the last Friday and Saturday of August and completely take over the town. Upwards of 150 bands, more than 2000 pipers and drummers, take part in the centrepiece march past, and some 40,000 visitors come to watch the spectacle.

On Castle Hill are some sparse remains of the 12th century **Dunoon Castle**, notorious as the setting for a grisly massacre in 1646 when the Marquis of Argyll had scores of his Lamont prisoners hanged from "a lively, fresh-growing ash tree" and their bodies tossed into a shallow communal grave. The grave was rediscovered in the 19th century during construction of a new road and a memorial now marks the site. Forty years after that massacre, the castle was burnt down and remained derelict until 1822 when James Ewing, Provost of Glasgow, cannibalised its stone to build Castle House, a castellated "marine villa" which is currently used as council offices.

At the foot of Castle Hill is an appealing **Statue of Mary Campbell**, the Dunoon-born lass who became one of Robert Burns' many lovers. It was an intense affair and, despite being already married, Burns became engaged to Mary. At that time he was obsessed with the idea of emigrating to the West Indies and poems such as *Will you go to the Indies, my Mary?* make it clear that the poet's then-pregnant wife was not his preferred partner in the enterprise. Mary died at the age of 22, officially of a fever, but there has been persistent speculation that she died giving birth to a still-born baby. Dunoon Grammar School merits a special mention since it is second only to Eton in the number of its former pupils who have become Members of Parliament, amongst them Ken Livingstone, Virginia Bottomley, Brian Wilson and the late leader of the Labour Party, John Smith.

Dunoon's popularity as a resort in Victorian times is evident at the **Abbot's Brae Hotel** which was built originally, in 1843, as a holiday retreat for an affluent Glasgow glass merchant and still maintains many of the house's original features. This splendid Victorian country house enjoys an idyllic setting, standing peacefully in its own 2-acre secluded woodland garden with breathtaking panoramic views of the sea and surrounding hills. The owners, Gavin and Helen Dick, pride themselves on creating a hospitable home-from-home atmosphere, with the emphasis placed on relaxation and comfort. All of the hotel's seven spacious bedrooms have en suite facilities and are well-equipped with central heating, colour television, radio, hospitality tray, direct-dial telephones, and other thoughtful extras. Two of the bedrooms are large family rooms which can accommodate 4 people comfortably, one double bedroom is situated on the ground floor, and one has a four-poster bed, ideal for a special celebra-

Abbot's Brae Hotel, West Bay, Dunoon, Argyll PA23 7QJ
Tel: 01369 705021 Fax: 701191 web-site:www.abbotsbrae.ndirect.co.uk
email: enquiry@abbotsbrae.ndirect.co.uk

tion or romantic break. The hotel's Dining Room, which enjoys impressive open views over the garden and the Firth of Clyde, offers the best of Scottish ingredients prepared in traditional ways. A fully stocked bar and an imaginative wine list are available to complement your meal. Astonishingly, despite its peaceful setting, the Abbot's Brae Hotel is only 7 miles from the motorway network of Great Britain, by way of the Gourock - Dunoon ferry.

Less than a mile to the north of the town, on the A885, the **Cowal Bird Garden** makes an ideal venue for a family outing. Set in some 10 acres of oak and birch woods, this award-winning attraction is home to a fascinating variety of exotic birds, amongst them macaws and parrots who, if they're feeling like it, may well croak back a "Hello!" in response to yours; brightly-hued budgerigars; kakarikis from Australia, and many other species. There's a wild bird hide from which you may catch sight of a great spotted woodpecker, and a nature trail through the ancient woodlands where, if you are quiet, there's a chance of seeing roe deer, red squirrels, tawny owl and those woodpeckers again. Children love playing amongst the farmyard pets. There's Millie, Smoky and Felix, pygmy goats; Jock and Dumpling, Vietnamese pot-bellied pigs; Jack and Coco, the donkeys; Blacksox, a breeding billy goat, "lovable but smelly", and many more. Refreshments are available at the garden's gift shop, but you are also wel-

Cowal Bird Garden, Lochan Wood, Sandbank Road, Dunoon Argyll PA23 8QR Tel: 01369 707999

come to bring your own picnic. Hopefully, you'll be visiting the Cowal Bird Garden in good weather, but if it does rain the friendly staff will even provide you with a brolly!

TIGHNABRUAICH

Map 2 ref F13

34 miles S of Cairndow on the A886/A8003

Moving across to the western side of the peninsula, the picturesque village of Tighnabruaich, set on the lochside looking across to the Isle of Bute, manages to stay wonderfully peaceful despite being a popular sailing resort. The benign influence of the Gulf Stream creates a lovely climate in which tropical plants flourish in colourful domestic gardens. Do visit the Pier, which is still fully functioning, and walk up the hillside to the viewpoint where you can enjoy a magical view across the Kyles of Bute

Situated on the water's edge of the Kyles of Bute, one of the most scenic and unspoilt areas of the West Coast, the **Royal Hotel** has been a landmark to visiting yachtsmen for more than 150 years, and offers far-travelled visitors traditional Scottish hospitality along with a warm welcome. This family-owned and family-run establishment has comfortable bars with open fires, and a restaurant where lovers of good food and

Royal Hotel, Tighnabruaich, Argyll PA21 2BE
Tel: 01700 811239 Fax:811300 E-mail: royalhotel@btinternet.com

wine will appreciate jumbo prawms, clams, lobsters, mussels, oysters and fish, - all off-loaded daily by local fishermen. Venison, pheasant, rabbit, wild duck and various game birds are stalked locally and also feature on the menu. The Royal's owners, Roger and Bea McKie, have recently completely redecorated and refurbished the interior of the hotel, and the bedrooms have all been individually furnished. Each of them enjoys breathtaking views of Argyll's rugged coastline and the Island of Bute. There is plenty to do in the area: golfing, bird-watching, walking, wind surfing, fishing and sailing, (the hotel has its own private moorings and slip way), or you may just want to relax and unwind in these peaceful surroundings.

On reaching the seafront at Tighnabruaich, turn left through the village, and only 200 yards on the left you will come across **Susy's Tearoom and Giftshop**. This purpose-built establishment is perfectly sited with magnificent views down the west Kyles of Bute to Ardlamont Point and, in the distance, the Isle of Arran. The tearoom is open from 9.00 am to 5.00 pm from April to October, with extended hours till 9.00 pm during July and August serving morning coffee or afternoon tea with a range of delicious home-baked snacks, cooked meals for lunch or dinner, and light snacks are also available throughout the day. A wide selection of Scottish crafts and gifts are available in the gift-shop and there are ample free parking facilities for cars and coaches adjacent to the tearoom.

Susy's Tearoom, Tighnabruaich, Argyll PA21 2DX
Tel: 01700 811452

ISLE OF BUTE

ETTRICK BAY

Map 1 ref G13

6 miles W of Rothesay on minor road off the B875

A short ferry crossing from Colintraive will take you to the Island of Bute, an island which displays something of a split personality. Its sheltered east coast has been a popular holiday venue for Clydesiders since Victorian times; the west coast, however, never more than 5 miles distant, is sparsely populated, its most northerly minor road coming to a halt some 8 miles short of the northern tip of the island. Fortunately, there's no difficulty in getting to the mile-long sands of Ettrick Bay, regarded by many as the most beautiful place on the island.

Overlooking the sandy beach, the **Ettrick Bay Tearoom** enjoys fabulous views across the Sound of Bute to the mountains of Arran. This modern, purpose-built tearoom is owned and personally run by Margaret Rose Lyle who offers visitors a tempting array of cakes, pastries, light snacks, sandwiches and drinks. In addition to its lovely location fronting the beach,

Ettrick Bay Tearoom, Ettrick Bay, Bute PA20 0QX
Tel: 01700 504410

the tearoom is also close to woodland walks, and the surrounding area is rich in bird life. The Ettrick Bay Tearoom is open all day during the week and there is ample parking. The island's one and only town, Rothesay, is just a few miles away and well worth visiting for the famous Victorian toilets on the pier installed by Twyfords in 1899, and its 12th century castle. If you are looking for refreshment after visiting the castle, Margaret recommends "The Coffee Stop" just across the way in the High Street.

The largest community on Bute is Rothesay, an attractive small town which displays its legacy as a popular Victorian resort for Clydesiders in its tall colour-washed houses, trim public gardens, and pedestrianised esplanade. Long before the paddle-steamers brought 19th century holiday-makers here, Rothesay was a favourite refuge for Scottish kings in need of rest and recuperation. They would lodge at **Rothesay Castle** (Historic Scotland), built in the early 1200s and generally regarded as one of the finest medieval castles in the country. A picturesque moat surrounds the huge circular walls, (unique in Scotland), which in turn enclose the well-preserved Great Hall built by James IV. The Argylls sacked the castle in 1685 but did a less thorough job than usual, leaving much of it intact. Some 200 years later, the castle's hereditary guardians, the Marquesses of Bute, tidied the place up, opened it to the public, and Rothesay Castle has been one of the region's major tourist attractions ever since.

Rothesay has a definite taste for festivals. On the last weekend in August it hosts its own Highland Games, when the guest of honour may well be the Duke of Rothesay, a distinguished personage much better-known as heir to the throne, Prince Charles. During the third weekend in July, there's an International Folk Festival, and on May Day Bank Holiday the town resounds to the upbeat rhythms of a Jazz Festival.

For a comprehensive insight into the island's history, archaeology and natural history, a visit to the **Bute Museum** across from the Castle in Stuart Street, is essential and very rewarding. The museum houses exhibits from every period of Bute's history, from early stone tools to Clyde steamers. Extensive displays are dedicated to the island's birds and wildlife, with a colourful wild flower display throughout the summer. Special displays for children include a touch table, toddler's case, and small aquarium. A Museum Quiz is available free of charge. Other exhibits include nostalgic

Bute Museum, Stuart Street, Rothesay PA20 0BR
Tel: 01700 505067

paintings and photographs of old Rothesay, and the Museum shop stocks an interesting range of souvenirs, gifts and books. Bute Museum is open from April to September, weekdays from 10.30am to 4.30pm, Sundays from 2.30pm to 4.30pm. From October to March, the Museum is open Tuesday to Saturday, afternoons only, from 2.30pm to 4.30pm.

THE ISLE OF ARRAN

With some justification, Arran is often referred to as "Scotland in Miniature". Twenty miles long and ten miles wide, the island unfolds dramatically from the Highland scenery of the north, capped by Goat Fell (2866ft), to the typically Lowland landscape of farmlands and rolling moors in the south. The island has suffered a turbulent history, having been overrun by the Dalriada Scots who invaded from northern Ireland, then by the Vikings whose links with Arran are still celebrated, and finally by the Scottish Crown. Robert the Bruce stayed here in 1307 before leaving for the mainland to continue his struggle for Scottish independence, a mission he would finally achieve seven years later at the Battle of Bannockburn.

The island is almost entirely owned by the Duke of Hamilton and the National Trust of Scotland. Together they have successfully resisted any inappropriate development, ensuring that Arran is almost completely unspoilt. In addition, the island offers visitors a comprehensive range of recreational possibilities, from a choice of 7 golf courses, to fishing, watersports, pony-trekking, walking and climbing, as well as medieval castles and a wealth of prehistoric and Iron Age sites.

BRODICK

Map 1 ref G14

East Coast of the Island of Arran on the A841

The comings and goings of the ferries which link Brodick to the mainland at Ardrossan provide constant activity in this large village overlooking a broad, sandy bay and backed by granite mountains. Brodick's development as a tourist resort was obstructed for many years by the Dukes of Hamilton who owned the village and much of the surrounding land. Their ancestral home, **Brodick Castle** (National Trust for Scotland), stands to the north of the village crowning a steep bank. The oldest parts date back to the 13th century, with extensions added in 1652 and 1844, the latter in the familiar Scottish baronial style. The interior contains some fine period furniture, notable paintings (by Watteau, Turner and Richardson amongst others), and important collections of silver and porcelain. The castle grounds are particularly attractive. There's a formal walled garden which was first laid out in 1710, and a woodland garden covering some 60 acres, which was established in 1923 by the Duchess of Montrose, daughter of the 12th

Duke of Hamilton. The magnificent collection of rhododendrons is widely regarded as one of the finest in Britain. The two gardens form part of Brodick Country Park which also includes the mountain of Goat Fell (2618ft): a popular walk is the path leading to its summit where the views are quite staggering. The castle is open daily from Easter to October; the grounds are open daily throughout the year, from 10 a.m. to dusk.

Brodick Castle

In Brodick itself, the **Arran Heritage Museum** is housed in an 18th century crofter's farm and among its exhibits are a working smithy, an Arran cottage and a wide range of agricultural tools. The museum is open weekdays from Easter to October.

LAMLASH

MAP 1 REF G14

3 miles S of Brodick on the A841

The second largest village on the island after Brodick, Lamlash enjoys an unusually mild climate and its mainly Edwardian architecture bestows a pleasing kind of period charm. The village's curious name is actually a corruption of Eilean Mo-Laise, or St Molaise's Island, and originally the name applied to what is now called Holy Island, where the 6th century saint lived in a cave. The island, 2 miles from Lamlash, is currently owned by a group of Scottish Buddhists who have established a meditation centre there, but visitors are welcome to the island and there are regular ferries during the season.

Occupying a superb position by the beach, **The Drift Inn** enjoys fabulous views over Lamlash Bay to Holy Island. A family-run business, this spacious inn was originally built as a tearoom providing refreshments for passengers disembarking from the mainland ferry. (The old Clock Tower next door served as the ticket office). Although the ferry now sails into Brodick, the Drift Inn still offers locals and visitors alike a wide choice of drinks, including tea and coffee.

The Drift Inn, Lamlash, Isle of Arran KA27 8JN
Tel: 01770 600656

Inside, the decor is warm and relaxing, yet with a traditional feel and an open fire for those cooler days. Outside, the large beer garden runs down to the sea, with picnic tables overlooking the beach and bay. The inn specialises in freshly prepared, home-cooked food, including vegetarian options. Families are warmly welcomed, and there's a special menu for kiddies. If you fancy visiting Holy Isle, or just a trip around the bay, you'll find a boat hire centre close by. Brodick is just three miles away; and Brodick Castle, with its famous rhododendron gardens, a couple of miles further.

6 Northwest Highlands and Western Isles

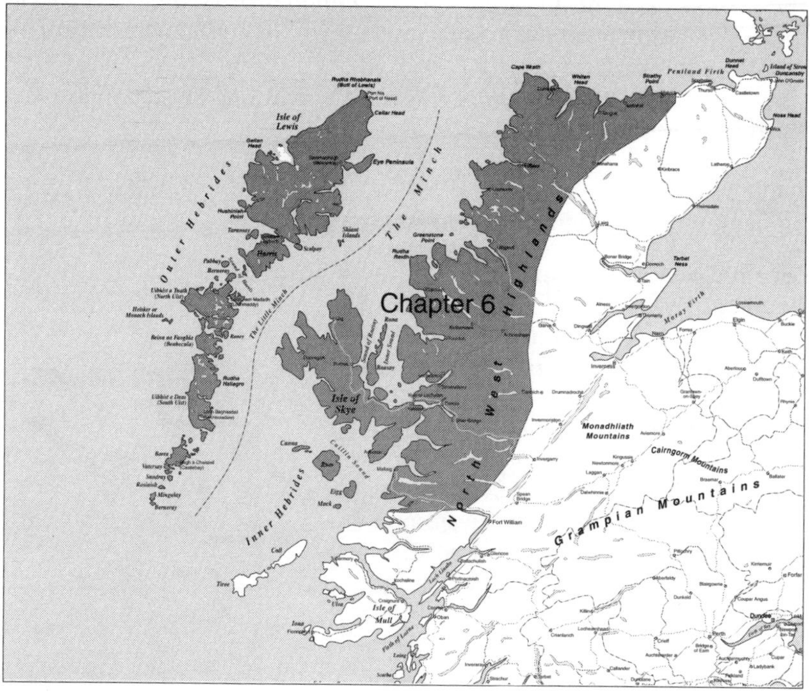

A land where in summer there is virtually no night; a region whose total population could be comfortably rehoused in a city the size of, say, Leeds; a landscape of mighty mountains and broad sea lochs; Scotland's "Empty Quarter", - it is this vast tract of country, lying to the north and west of Fort William, that we explore in this chapter.

The itinerary includes the romantic Isle of Skye, so closely associated with the dramatic story of Bonnie Prince Charles, and then travels north through a terrain whose inhospitable character seems to generate a compensating warmth of hospitality amongst the people who live there amidst scenery whose uncompromising grandeur is unmatched anywhere else in Britain.

The chapter concludes in west Sutherland where "in parts you have as much chance of coming across a golden eagle as you do a petrol station". This is magnificent wilderness country with no towns and with its few villages often many miles apart. "There is a sense of vastness" wrote Matthew Arnold more than a century ago, "miles and miles of mere heather and peat and rocks, and not a soul". Little has changed since then. The majestic mountains and the sea lochs biting deep inland have reminded many travellers of the Norwegian fjords, an appropriate comparison since the Vikings ruled the area for some two hundred years, their occupation recalled in many place names such as Gruinard Bay, originally "Grunna's Bay".

We begin our exploration of this huge area at one of Scotland's most historic locations, Glenfinnan.

GLENFINNAN

MAP 2 REF F9

18 miles W of Fort William on the A830

Set amid superb Highland scenery at the head of Loch Shiel, the striking **Glenfinnan Monument** (NTS) commemorates a poignant moment in Scottish history. Here, on August 19th, 1745, Bonnie Prince Charlie raised his standard and proclaimed his father as King James VIII of Scotland and III of England, thus setting in train the Jacobite Rebellion which would end so disastrously at the Battle of Culloden, eight months later. The tower, crowned by a fine statue of a clansman in full battle dress, was erected in 1815 by Macdonald of Glenaladale, a descendant of the Macdonald who was an early and enthusiastic supporter of the Prince. There's an internal stairway to the top of the tower where the views are, if possible, even more stunning than from the ground. The Trust's Visitor Centre has an exhibition which tells the story of the '45 and traces the Prince's wanderings after the battle.

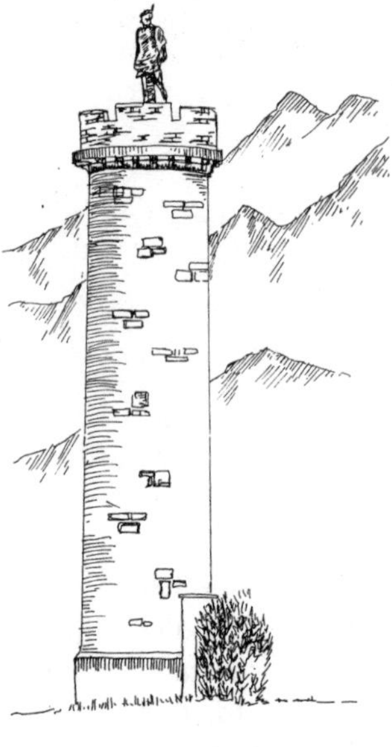

Glenfinnan Monument

A unique dining experience awaits visitors to the **Glenfinnan Dining Car**, next door to the Museum at Glenfinnan Station. In this restored 1950s carriage, Paul and Donna Peacock serve lunches and cream teas during the day and a restaurant menu in the evening. Favourite home-made specialities include the bread, soups and ice-creams. There's also a selection of Scottish ales and whiskies available to complement any occasion. Bookings are strongly recommended. The balcony offers breathtaking views of

Glenfinnan Railway Carriage, Glenfinnan
Nr Fort William PH37 4LT Tel: 01397 722400

Loch Shiel and the rugged mountain ranges beyond, a haven for many bird species. During the summer months, guests can sit back and take in the atmosphere as the Jacobite Steam Train regularly travels through the station. Paul and Donna can also offer unusual accommodation for visitors to the area, - the Glenfinnan Sleeping Car, built in 1958. The sleeper has been brought up to date with central heating and all modern facilities installed and is a popular novelty for families with an atmosphere children love. The carriage can accommodate ten people in four bedrooms and is fully equipped for self-catering although you may well prefer to take advantage of the excellent food available in the Dining Car.

ARISAIG

MAP 2 REF E8

35 miles NW of Fort William on the A830

The peaceful little village of Arisaig stands in a sheltered position at the head of Loch nan Cealt, a broad sandy bay protected from the open sea by a barrier of rocks and small islands. It was at the neighbouring bay of Loch nan Uamh that Bonnie Prince Charlie arrived on the mainland at the start of the 1745 rising and it was from there, fourteen months later, evading government bounty of £30,000 on his head, that he left Scotland for ever.

Set on the hillside above Arisaig, **Kinloid Farm Cottages** enjoy outstanding views across the surrounding countryside to sandy beaches and sea, with the islands of Eigg, Rhum, and the mountains of Skye spectacularly dominating the skyline. There are two cottages, "Pine" and "Birch", both identical in appearance and both particularly well-equipped. And each cottage has a veranda where you can sit and watch the wonderful sunsets over the islands. The cottages sit in over 1000 acres of hills and fields and further up in the hills there are small trout lochs where you can enjoy casting a line. A 20-minute walk will take you to the beach at Keppoch, or by driving just a couple of miles you will come to the larger beaches at Traigh, which also has a 9 hole golf course. Arisaig village with its shops and eating-places is only a mile distant, and the busy fishing town of Mallaig is about 5 miles away. At Mallaig you really shouldn't miss taking the ferry across to the scenic Isle of Skye, and during the summer season there are also ferries to Eigg and Rhum. **Kinloid Farm Cottages, Kinloid Farm, Arisaig PH39 4NJ Tel: 01687 450366.**

CAMUSDARACH — MAP 2 REF E8

37 miles N of Fort William off the A830

Just a mile or so around the bay from Arisaig and situated in an area of outstanding natural beauty, is **Camusdarach**, located on the "Road to the Isles", opposite the Isle of Skye and the Inner Hebrides. Here Angela Simpson offers holiday-makers an excellent choice of accommodation, including self-catering flats, a holiday cottage, bed & breakfast rooms, as well as a 42-pitch caravan and camp site. Bed and breakfast is available in the lovely old Victorian stone Lodge and there are two self-catering flats in the Estate Farmhouse across the courtyard. Millburn Cottage is a secluded 150-year-old stone shepherd's cottage, just 30 yards from the high water line on a bay in Loch nan Ceall, facing the village of Arisaig. The caravan/camp site,

Camusdarach, Arisaig, Inverness-shire PH39 4NT
Tel/Fax: 01687 450221

just a 5 minute stroll from sandy beaches, is served by immaculate modern toilet and shower facilities, laundry and drying machines, washing-up areas and facilities for the disabled and babies. This is "Bonnie Prince Charlie" country with superb scenery that includes the beach at Camusdarach, featured in the film *Local Hero,* the Silver Sands of Morar, and the beautiful, quiet surroundings of Loch Morar. There is easy access to the islands of Eigg, Rum and Muck, and historic Borrodale and Glenfinnan, Ardnish and the Ardnamurchan Peninsular are all within easy reach, providing a marvellous variety of walking opportunities at all levels.

MALLAIG

Map 2 ref E8

47 miles NW of Fort William on the A830

This compact little port is always busy with travellers arriving to catch one of the ferries to the Isle of Skye or to the smaller islands of Rum, Eigg, Canna and Muck. In addition there's a good choice of boat excursions, either guided or self-piloted. Mallaig is also the western terminus of the West Highland Line, a marvellously scenic route which provides a direct link to Glasgow. Tourism is obviously important to the town, but Mallaig is still a thriving fishing port and when the boats come in, the harbour is a scene of frantic activity. Architecturally, Mallaig has little of interest, but it does enjoy grand views of Skye and the islands of the Inner Hebrides. Two visitor attractions are worth a look: the **Mallaig Marine World** which is devoted to the town's fishing heritage and has tanks well-stocked with a variety of marine creatures; and the **Mallaig Heritage Centre** which tells the story of the town and the surrounding area through old photographs and films. To the north of the town, the Knoydart and Glenelg peninsulas are two of the last remaining wilderness areas in Britain: great empty, roadless stretches where the only possible access is on foot. Close to one of its few inhabited areas, near Glenelg, are the two **Glenelg Brochs**, Dun Telve and Dun Troddan (Historic Scotland). These circular stone towers, built by the Picts, are the best-preserved to be found on the mainland. They date back to the 1st century when they served as refuges from Viking attacks. Dun Telve is particularly striking, with walls 33ft high, a courtyard 30ft across, and spiral galleries within its double walls.

ISLE OF SKYE

Skye is the best known and, at 50 miles long and up to 25 miles wide, one of the largest of the islands of Scotland. The Skye Bridge (toll) now links the island to the mainland, although the vehicle ferry from Mallaig makes for a much more picturesque approach. The landscape of Skye is dramatic and beautiful whatever the season, but two areas deserve special mention. In the southwest, the spectacular peaks of the Cuillins rise more than 3000ft and offer a serious challenge to climbers, but there are also many good walks of varying difficulty for which Sligachan is a good starting point. North of Portree, the lonely Trotternish Peninsula is remarkable for its bizarre rock formations and its associations with Flora Macdonald. Skye is flooded with visitors in the summer months but, as so often in the Highlands and Islands, once you are away from the main tourist centres it seems you have the Isle almost to yourself. We begin our survey of Skye in the southeast corner of the island.

BROADFORD

MAP 7 REF E7

8 miles SW of Kyle of Lochalsh on the A87

Broadford has the distinction of being Skye's largest crofting township. It's a long straggling village set beside the bay of the same name, and surrounded by dramatic hills, - Beinn na Cailleach (2403ft), the Red Hills, and Applecross. The village is well-placed for exploring south Skye and has a number of good shops selling gifts or souvenirs.

And what better memento could there be of a visit to this romantic island than one of the beautiful Celtic rings created at **Skye Jewellery** in Broadford by Antony and Cheryl Shepherd. Their stunning creations incorporate the interlacing knotwork patterns which, down the centuries, have symbolised eternity. For the stones, Antony uses the local Skye marble which is quarried just a few miles from his workshop. When cut, the stone produces an amazing natural landscape, with startling effects of shading and shape and is ideal for paperweights and jewellery. Cheryl then uses her artistic talents to paint trees and birds on the stones, thus creating

Skye Jewellery, Shore Road, Broadford, Isle of Skye IV49 9AB
Tel: 01471 822100

solid pictures in tune with the landscape from which the stone has been unearthed after thousands of years. Every item, regardless of what particular form it takes, is unique and offers a truly original, hand-crafted gift to treasure. The Shepherds' unrivalled collection selection of gold and silver Celtic and Mackintosh jewellery and giftware is on display in their shop and a mail order catalogue is also available.

Millbrae House is a refurbished and extended crofthouse, originally built around 1860 and owned by Lord MacDonald until 1930. Situated in a quiet position, it looks across Broadford Bay to the islands of Scalpay and Raasay. The owners enjoy antiques. Philip restores furniture, makes Windsor chairs, writes, gardens, and works tapestries. Viera speaks many European languages, is fond of yoga, and both of them enjoy good conversation and bird watching. All four bedrooms at Millbrae House have private facilities and tea trays, and there is a comfortable guest lounge with books and TV. The house is centrally heated and has adequate parking. Close by is Elgol, with the superb Cuillin Hills, the Sleat peninsula,

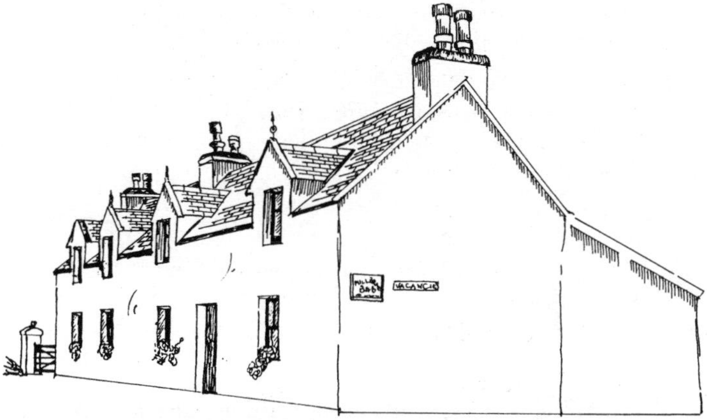

Philip and Viera Tordoff, Millbrae House, Broadford Isle of Skye IV49 9AE Tel/Fax: 01471 822310

the otter hide at Kylerhea, and Ashaig, with its early Christian associations. Excellent breakfasts are served; restaurants and shops are close by. Tariffs are very reasonable, and Millbrae is open from March to November. This is an exceptionally friendly, well-run, non-smoking house, with the warmest of welcomes.

PORTREE MAP 7 REF E6

34 miles NW of Kyle of Lochalsh on the A87

With a population of around 2000, Portree is the largest community on the island and its administrative centre. It's an attractive little town, enclosed by wooded hills with a deep, cliff-lined harbour busy with fishing boats and with whitewashed buildings all around. The harbour is well-protected by the bulk of the Isle of Raasay, easily reached by one of the regular boat trips available.

Right on the quay here is **The Lower Deck Seafood Restaurant**, an appropriate location for this outstanding restaurant which specialises in locally-caught seafish, salmon and white fish. It enjoys a fine view of the busy little harbour with the raucous cries of seagulls always in the background. Should you happen to be on the quay at the right time, you can watch your lunch or supper being landed, gleaming fresh fish the best of which will find their way to Dan Corrigall's kitchen at the Lower Deck. His restaurant is built in traditional style on the site of an earlier seafood restaurant called The Upper Deck. Inside, the Lower Deck is uniquely decorated in nautical style, featuring photographs of the old MacBrayne fleet of steamers and with ships' souvenirs and memorabilia all around. It's a suitable setting in which to enjoy the fruits of the sea, carefully prepared, attractively presented and complemented by a wine list which is both well-chosen and reasonably priced.

The Lower Deck Seafood Restaurant, The Harbour
Portree IV51 9DD Tel: 01478 613611

In Gaelic, Port an Righ (now Portree) means Port of the King, a name the town assumed after James V came here in 1540 to settle a feud between the Macleod and Macdonald clans. A more melancholy royal visitor to Portree was Bonnie Prince Charlie preparing to leave for France and life-long exile. Taking his leave of Flora Macdonald, the Prince rather optimistically remarked "For all that has happened, I hope Madam that we shall meet in St James' yet". The room at McNab's Inn where he bade her farewell is now part of the Royal Hotel.

One of the oldest buildings in Portree is **Meall House**, the former jail and courthouse. Until fairly recently it housed the Tourist Information Centre with the manager's office located in what used to be the condemned cell. From here, those sentenced to death would be taken to The Lump, overlooking the harbour. On this steep peninsula a flagpole marks the site of the gallows to which as many as 5000 people would flock for the free entertainment of a public execution.

Much more pleasant entertainment, (albeit for a modest charge), can be found at the **Aros Heritage Centre**, about a mile south of the town, where a variety of dioramas and videos recount the turbulent history of the island. And just to the east, housed in a converted fever hospital, An Tuireann Arts Centre (which *is* free) puts on exhibitions and concerts.

A little further afield, some 6 miles north, is the extraordinary **Old Man of Storr**, a 160ft pinnacle of rock that looks as if one vigorous push would topple it. It's actually part of a massive landslip from the face of the Storr mountain (2358ft) which still occasionally sheds huge blocks of stone.

Old Man of Storr

The Old Man can be reached by an easy 30-minute walk from the car park on the A855. There are many other spectacular and eccentric rock formations to the north, most notably the Quiraing (pronounced Coor-ang) with its outlandish forest of huge pinnacles and tortured rocks.

From the Quiraing, the A855 continues around the Trotternish Peninsula, passing Flodigarry where Flora Macdonald lived. Her cottage has been restored, and is now part of Flodigarry House Hotel. About 4 miles further on, the road passes the dramatically sited but minimal remains of Duntulm Castle, and after another couple of miles arrives at the village of **Kilmuir.**

In the burial ground here, a tall Celtic cross stands above Flora Macdonald's Grave, and nearby is a well-preserved crusader's slab. Also in Kilmuir is the **Museum of Island Life**, housed in a group of old cottages and exhibiting an interesting collection of old documents and photographs. The A855 continues down the western side of the peninsula to the attractive little port of Uig which has vehicle ferries serving the islands of Harris and North Uist.

Self-catering holidays are increasingly popular throughout the area, although renting a holiday cottage can be a chancy business. However, if you book through **Islands and Highlands Cottages**, based in Portree, you can feel confident that all their properties, large or small, new or old, are furnished and equipped to the highest standard, are excellent value for money, and most importantly, provide a welcoming home from home atmosphere. Each property has been personally visited and the agency's informative full-colour brochure includes comprehensive details along with photographs of each location. The brochure lists scores of holiday homes chosen to suit all tastes and pockets. They range from grand old mansions to trim Alpine lodges, from shoreside cottages where you can enjoy your supper whilst watching otters and seals, to comfortable town centre apartments. On the magnificent island of South Uist, the agency can even offer you a choice of horse-drawn gypsy caravans, a wonderful way of experiencing an old fashioned "life on the open road" holiday. Islands and Highlands Cottages specialise in those places most people only dream about, surrounded by awesome scenery and offering breathtaking sunsets, miraculous dawns and an abundance of wildlife.

Islands & Highlands Cottages, Bridge Road, Portree, Isle of Skye IV51 9ER Tel: 01478 612123 email: heather@losea.demon.co.uk

SKEABOST BRIDGE

MAP 7 REF D6

4 miles N of Portree on the A850

About 4 miles north of Portree, the road forks and if you take the left fork (the A850) you will soon come to a bridge across the River Snizort at Skeabost. On an island just below the bridge, reached by stepping stones, are the remains of a chapel reputedly connected with St Columba. A diligent search of the neglected cemetery will reveal memorials to three crusaders. Close by, on a minor road leading to the hamlet of Tote, stands Clach Ard, the "Stone on the Hill", which is engraved with Pictish symbols.

Occupying a superb position with glorious views over Loch Snizort, the **Skeabost House Hotel** is a comfortable, relaxing establishment run by the Stuart and McNab families. The core of this attractive, white-painted hotel is a grand 1870s mansion which still retains much of its original Scots pine panelling. Skeabost House stands in 12 acres of secluded woodland and landscaped gardens, amidst which is a rather tricky 9-hole golf course. The hotel's main dining-room has received a Rosette Award for the quality of its cuisine, with chef Angus McNab serving the best of Skye's and Scotland's larder, including locally-caught seafood and prime Scotch beef. The charming conservatory overlooking the loch serves excellent buffet luncheons, and in the evening offers a wide selection of light suppers. Skeabost House has 21 rooms, with an additional five in the modern Garden House in the grounds. All rooms are en suite and furnished and

Skeabost House Hotel, Skeabost Bridge, by Portree
Isle of Skye IV51 9NP Tel: 01470 532202 Fax: 532454

decorated to a very high standard. Another good reason for choosing the Skeabost House is that if you are staying for 3 days or more, both golf and fishing on the hotel's own 8 miles along the River Snizort are free.

GRESHORNISH

MAP 7 REF D6

18 miles NW of Portree, on minor road off the A850

Continue along the A850 for about 14 miles to the hamlet of Upperglen where a minor road to the right leads to the enchanting **Greshornish House Hotel**. The Isle of Skye provides all the ingredients for a perfect holiday: peace, tranquillity and some delightful places to stay like this historic hotel. Once an 18th century Scottish Highland mansion, Greshornish has been tastefully converted into a private country house hotel, secluded in its own 12 acres of picturesque grounds. This 3-Star Commended establishment offers its guests a real escape from the busy outside world. Immerse yourself in the gracious olde worlde charm that still lingers in these elegant surroundings. Each guest room has been individually tailored to meet your every need, complete with central heating and private facilities and there is even a 4-poster bedroom for those special occasions. Your hosts for your stay are Campbell and Sandra Dickson, a couple who offer their guests true Scottish hospitality, right down to Campbell's kilt and his tradition of piping all his visitors to dinner in the evening! All the food is freshly prepared using only the best local ingredients and is served in an elegant atmosphere with crystal glasses, mahogany tables, silver candelabra and silver tableware. The dining room is spacious

Greshornish House Hotel, Greshornish, Isle of Skye IV51 9PN
Tel: 01470 582266 Fax: 582345 Web Site: www.host.co.uk
email: campbell@greshornishhotel.demon.co.uk

and comes complete with open log fires that burn brightly in the colder months: they are also the main feature in the drawing room and attractive cocktail bar which is the perfect place to relax with a warming glass of whisky after that superb meal.

DUNVEGAN

MAP 7 REF D6

22 miles NW of Portree on the A850

Returning to the main road, the A850 leads to Dunvegan and the island's most imposing and historic building, **Dunvegan Castle**. For centuries the only way of reaching the castle was by sea, landing on the stony beach and entering beneath the portcullis of the sea-gate. Arriving by this route, friend and foe alike were presented with Dunvegan's most forbidding aspect, a daunting fortress surmounting a rocky crag. This spectacular site overlooking Loch Dunvegan has been fortified for more than a thousand years, for the last 750 of them as the stronghold of the Chiefs of Macleod. The present owner, John Macleod of Macleod, is the 29th chief in an uninterrupted line.

The oldest part of the castle is the Keep, built around 1340 by the 3rd Chief, Malcolm. The gruesome dungeon here, 16ft deep and just 6 feet wide, and covered by a heavy flagstone is a chilling memorial to medieval justice. Malcolm figures in one of the oldest of the Macleod legends. Returning from a clandestine visit to a neighbour's wife, he was confronted by a mad bull. Armed only with a dirk, he killed the beast and cut off one of its horns. Thereafter, the Macleod crest was emblazoned with a bull's head and the horn, rimmed with chased silver, was fashioned into a drink-

Dunvegan Castle

ing vessel. Clan tradition requires that the Chief's heir, on coming of age, must take a full horn of claret, - equivalent to a good bottle and a half, and drink it at one draught "without setting down or falling down". This traditional ceremony was last observed in 1965 when the present Chief drained the 10th century horn in 1 minute 57 seconds. The horn is on display at the castle, but even more treasured is the *Am Bratach Sith MhicLeoid*, the Fairy Flag. Experts agree that this tattered banner of faded yellow silk was made in the Middle East sometime between the 4th and 7th centuries AD, but its provenance remains a mystery. Tradition asserts that if the flag is waved on the battlefield, it will bring victory to the MacLeods; if spread on the marriage bed, the Chief will be blessed with a male child; and if unfurled at Dunvegan, will charm herring into the loch.

The tower in which the flag used to be housed was consequently named the Fairy Tower, a dainty name for a building with massive walls 10 feet thick in places, and still exactly as they were when built in 1500 by the 8th Chief, Alasdair "Crotach", or hunchback. The Chief's deformity resulted not from a birth defect, but from having an axe driven between his shoulder-blades in battle.

Little changed at Dunvegan over the next 300 years, but towards the end of the 18th century, the 23rd Chief, Gen. Norman MacLeod, began a thorough overhaul of the castle in order to make it more inviting for his young second wife, Sarah, fresh from the pampered life of colonial India. He remodelled the Great Hall into an elegant Georgian drawing-room, acquired some fine paintings by Ramsay and Raeburn, and generally transformed an uncompromising fortress into a gracious home. Half a century later, his grandson put the finishing touches to the castle as we see it today, adding battlements and the dummy pepperpot turrets that give this sprawling building its remarkable unity.

Dunvegan also offers visitors boat trips to the nearby seal colony, sea cruises, sea & loch fishing, a camp site and caravan park, craft shops, the "St Kilda Connection" woollens shop, a restaurant and a bistro. The castle is open daily from Easter to October; its lovely 18th century gardens are open daily all year. For more details, telephone 01470 521206.

In Dunvegan village itself is another major visitor attraction, the **Croft Studio**, founded by artist Daisy Budge. As a young art student, Daisy first saw the Isle of Skye from the deck of the steam-ship *Killarney* and fell in love with this enchanted island. In 1968, she opened her studio and craft shop in a former croft house at Dunvegan. Inspired by the magnificent scenery of Skye, Daisy began with watercolour paintings and hand-painted fabrics, but her interest in Celtic manuscripts such as the Book of Kells soon led her to develop her own designs for screen-printing. (This was at a time when Celtic art did not enjoy the recognition and respect it does today). In 1978, Daisy's son, Donald, returned to Skye to expand the screen-

The Croft Studio, Portree Road, Dunvegan, Isle of Skye IV55 8GT
Tel: 01470 521383

printing while his wife, Pamela, hand-painted Celtic designs and mythological subjects on wood. Pamela also continued the art of silk painting and extended the range of pressed-flower and seaweed lampshades. Today, the Croft Studio displays a wide range of original work, all of it produced here by members of the Budge family. You'll find watercolours, prints and cards from their own designs, wooden plaques hand-painted with Celtic motifs, wall-hangings, cushions, scarves and mirrors, and silver and pewter jewellery also inspired by Celtic imagery. The creativity and consummate craftsmanship of all these items make them pieces to be treasured.

STRUAN — Map 7 ref D6

12 miles E of Dunvegan on the A863

Elizabeth I never slept here, but that curiously-matched couple, Dr Samuel Johnson and his admiring biographer, James Boswell, certainly stayed at the **Ullinish Lodge Hotel**. They checked in, back in 1773, just at the time when a classical sensibility was beginning to appreciate such beautiful views. Their hotel overlooked Loch Bracadale, with a magnificent prospect across Loch Harport to the most romantic hills in Britain, the Cuillin Hills. The elegant 18th century building in which the Great Lexicographer and his sexually-rampant companion lodged has been tastefully converted by the resident owners, John and Claudia Mulford, to achieve the friendly and welcoming ambience of a family home, providing all the facilities which guests are now entitled to expect. The pleasant, intimate restaurant

Ullinish Lodge Hotel, Struan, by Dunvegan, Isle of Skye IV56 8FD
Tel: 01470 572214

offers an extensive choice of traditional Scottish Fayre, featuring fresh local fish, shellfish, meat and game. To complement cuisine of this quality, there is, of course, a fine selection of wines, malt whiskies and liqueurs. Standards of accommodation have changed dramatically for the better since Dr Johnson stayed at the Ullinish Lodge: all rooms now have private facilities, most of which are en suite, together with central heating, remote-control colour television, hair dryers and tea/coffee-making facilities.

THE WESTERN ISLES

Also known as the Outer Hebrides, the Western Isles stretch for 130 miles, a string of islands which in most places rise no more than a few hundred feet and are battered by the full force of the Atlantic. Westwards, the nearest landfall is Labrador, some 4000 miles away. It sounds desolate but there are miles upon miles of empty beaches with dazzling white sand, unbelievably clear water and breathtaking sunsets. There is also a fascinating range of flora and fauna here with most islands having at least one Nature Reserve. The islands have been inhabited for over 6000 years and there are numerous prehistoric remains, most notably the Callanish Standing Stones and the Carloway Broch. The area is a stronghold of Gaelic speech and culture melded with strong Scandinavian influences, - the Vikings ruled the islands from the 9th century until 1280 and many place-names are of Norse origin, especially in the north. Much more of a culture shock to visitors is the Sabbatarianism of the Free Church, the "Wee Frees", which imposes a strict observance of Sunday as a day of rest. Shops, pubs, garages, and public transport all close down and even the swings in the children's playgrounds are padlocked.

STORNOWAY (STEORNABHAGH) MAP 7 REF D3

Eastern coast of the Isle of Lewis on the A859

With around 8000 inhabitants, Stornoway is by far the largest community on the islands, the political and commercial centre of the Western Isles. Its harbour is no longer busy with the thousand or more fishing boats registered at Stornoway a century ago, but there are regular ferries to and from Ullapool and a small active fishing fleet whose catches are sold at the fish markets on Tuesday and Thursday evenings. The town's architecture is generally functional rather than attractive but there are two notable exceptions. One is **Lews Castle**, a mid-19th century mock Gothic pile, now part of the University of the Highlands and Islands, with attractive wooded grounds for which thousands of tons of soil had to be imported. The other is the former town hall, built in full-blooded Scottish Baronial style, which now houses the **An Lanntair Art Gallery**, a showcase for the work of local artists. Also worth a visit is the **Museum nan Eilean** (free) which has some interesting temporary exhibitions and a CD-ROM presenting the story of the famous Uig Chessmen, 12th century Viking chess pieces carved from walrus ivory which were unearthed in 1831 by a grazing cow near the village of Ardroil. The pieces themselves are occasionally on display here but otherwise divide their time between the Edinburgh Museum of Antiquities and the British Museum in London. And at the **Lewis Loom Centre** in Cromwell Street you can see how the islands' most famous export, Harris Tweed, is created.

TOLSTA CHAOLAIS MAP 7 REF E2

15 miles NE of Stornoway on the B895

The old white croft house known as **The Willows Vegetarian Guest House** sits alone by a loch where otters play in the early dawn amongst flocks of Whooper swans. This could be the smallest vegetarian guest house in Britain, offering just one suite comprising a comfortable twin room, bathroom

The Willows Vegetarian Guest House, 19 Tolsta Chaolais
Isle of Lewis HS2 9DW Tel: 01851 621321

and living/dining room. The perfect retreat, The Willows is also a wonderful base for those questing for history and mystery, being within a couple of miles of the Callanish stone circles and many other historical sites, some of them actually on the miles of golden sands of the island. There are no fanatical beansprout-eaters here! Debbie Nash, the owner, is known for her sumptuous cooking and has never been beaten by a special diet yet. Non-vegetarians are also welcome, - it's just that The Willows doesn't serve anything that would prefer to be walking or swimming around to being on your plate. Debbie and her husband David are interesting folks, - sometimes musicians, artists and craftspeople. Their guests are made to feel genuinely welcome and they always have time for a chat and a glass of the *uisge beatha.*

CARLOWAY MAP 7 REF D3
13 miles W of Stornoway on the A858

An outstanding location for a holiday with a difference is **The Gearrannan Blackhouse Village**, on the west coast of the island. Built of drystone masonry, the thatched blackhouses of Gearrannan are the last group of traditional Hebridean dwellings unspoilt by modern features to survive in Lewis. The Gearrannan Trust, a local charitable Trust, was set up in 1989 to restore the blackhouses and bring life back to them. This continuing project has already transformed the village. Houses are being restored using traditional methods in a way which beautifully combines the old with the new. Situated in a prime position within the village, directly next to the rocky shore overlooking the Atlantic Ocean, the residential blackhouse

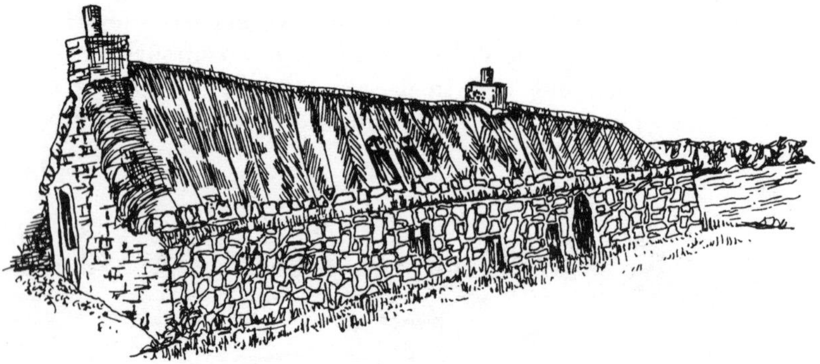

Urras Nan Gearrannan, Gearrannan, Carloway, Isle of Lewis HS2 9AL
Tel: 01851 643416 Fax: 643488. E-mail: Seanabheinn@sol.co.uk.
Web: http://www.hebrides.com/gearrannan

creates a perfect base for groups of up to 16 people. The blackhouse has been refurbished as a self-catering facility and is designed specifically for the needs of larger groups or families. The amenities include 4 bunk-style bedrooms, a solid fuel stove, showers, fridge freezer, microwave, washer/ dryer, and additional off peak heating. The area provides excellent opportunities for birdwatching, fishing and watersports, as well as participation in traditional rural activities such as crofting and weaving. Gearrannan is also close to numerous sites of interest, including Dun Charlabhaigh Broch and the Calanais (or Callanish) Stones. As one visitor remarked, "This place represents the best level of high quality accommodation and original culture in Scotland".

Located within a short drive of the magnificent sands of Dalbeg Bay, the **Doune Braes Hotel** offers its visitors comfortable accommodation and fine food. The hotel occupies a spectacular lochside position and most of the well-appointed bedrooms, (all equipped with TV and beverage-making facilities), enjoy lovely views. A former schoolhouse, Doune Braes is owned and run by Eileen Macdonald who offers her guests a mouth-watering menu of the best of Scottish cuisine, including delicious seafood dishes using local produce wherever possible. After a meal in the comfortable dining room visitors can relax with a fine single malt in the friendly bar or enjoy good conversation in the spacious lounge. The hotel is ideally placed for experiencing the fascinating history and atmosphere of this lovely island. Carloway Broch, a fine example of these ancient fortified circular buildings, lies close by and a few miles to the south the awe-inspiring standing stones of Callanish form an impressive prehistoric monument, - the Stonehenge of northern Britain.

Doune Braes Hotel, Carloway, Isle of Lewis HS2 9AA
Tel: 01851 643252 Fax: 01851 643435
e-mail user@doune-braes.dial.netmedia.co.uk

BALALLAN — MAP 7 REF D3

16 miles SW of Stornoway on the A859

If you are looking for self-catering accommodation in this peaceful area, Mrs Macdonald at **27 Balallan** can offer you the choice of either a self-contained first floor flat, suitable for a couple or two people sharing, or a four-bedroomed cottage located in a small village. Both are fully equipped,

Mrs M.A. Macdonald, 27 Balallan, Lochs, Isle of Lewis HS2 9PN
Tel: 01851 830328

have their own garden areas, and enjoy lovely views from the front windows. They are both also near the sea with many beautiful beaches within easy reach. The area is specially suitable for walkers, cyclists, and others who like a quiet country atmosphere. A brochure providing further information is available from:

BALIVANICH — MAP 6 REF B6

4 miles W of Gramsdale on the B892

For first class budget accommodation, you can't do better than seek out the **Taigh-na-Cille Bunkhouse** in the rural village of Balivanich on the west coast of Benbecula. This purpose built modern house stands on a site overlooking the historic ruins of the first church in the Western Isles, erected around the time of St Columba of Iona, and the accommodation also includes an Interpretive Centre which will help put you in touch with the history of those times. Taigh-na-Cille's airy open-plan design offers the convenience of self-catering with the comfort of home. The excellent facilities include bunks for eight people, hot & cold showers, a modern kitchen

**Taigh-na-Cille Bunkhouse, 22, Balivanich, Benbecula
Western Isles HS7 5LA Tel: 01870 602522**

with microwave and fridge, and a spacious, versatile dining area. And if you want a change from self-catering, there's a restaurant and café/bar close by as well as hotels which often lay on displays of Scottish dancing. The surrounding countryside is full of wild-life, especially birds, and plenty of fishing is also available.

ISLE OF BARRA

Despite its small area, just 4 miles wide and 8 miles long, Barra has been described as being the "Western Isles in miniature". There are sandy beaches and mountain peaks which rise to 1260ft, prehistoric relics and even a ruined medieval fortress, Kisimul Castle. It stands on a small island in the bay and is the ancestral home of the MacNeils, once notorious for their piracy and vanity. After years of neglect, the 45th Chief of the MacNeil clan bought back the castle in 1937 and it has since been restored to its original appearance. The castle is reached by ferry from Castlebay, the only settlement of any size on the island and the proud possessor of the only airfield in Britain that disappears under water twice a day, - scheduled flights to the tiny island land on the beach here.

Barra is popular with those who enjoy outdoor pursuits such as hill-walking, bird-watching or just wandering around this attractive island. Whatever your preference, you'll find a good base for exploring the island at **Meadowbank Self-Catering** in Northbay. Meadowbank offers quality accommodation in a comfortable modern cottage, (built in 1990), fully furnished with fitted carpets, double-glazed windows, all mod. cons. and with linen provided. There are 2 bedrooms, a living room, kitchen/dining area and a bathroom with shower. If you get tired of cooking for yourself, the cottage is only 500 yards from a hotel which serves bar lunches and suppers. At weekends hotels usually provides entertainment which you'll find advertised in shop windows during the previous week.

WESTER ROSS

Mrs M.T. Macneil, Meadowbank Self-Catering, 1 Bogach, Northbay
Isle of Barra, Western Isles HS9 5UX Tel/Fax: 01871 890286

The area known as Wester Ross provides the quintessence of Highland scenery, a vast tract of remote mountains and lochs which Dr Johnson described as "awful", using the word in its old meaning of inspiring awe. Huge areas of the wilderness here are now designated National Nature Reserves and virtually the whole of Wester Ross is officially classed as a National Scenic Area. The only community of any size is the little ferry port of Ullapool and there are few conventional tourist attractions such as historic houses or castles. But Wester Ross can boast one of Scotland's most popular visitor destinations, the famous **Inverewe Gardens** near Poolewe. Basking in the balmy Gulf Stream climate, the 2000 acres of woodland and gardens are home to a huge variety of exotic trees, shrub and flowers, all delightfully laid out and with grand views over Loch Ewe.

ACHINTRAID MAP 7 REF F6

30 miles NE from Kyle of Lochalsh on the A896

In a country where one begins to take spectacular views for granted, the vistas from the **Loch Kishorn Hotel** still strike the visitor as something special. This stylish modern hotel, designed and built by Margaretta and

Ian Beaton, sits high on the hillside enjoying fabulous views across Loch Kishorn to the mountains of Wester Ross. The hotel stands in 3 acres of its own grounds, open fields shared with long-haired Highland cattle which seem to have a natural knack for providing memorable "photo-opportunities". The conservatory restaurant shares those wonderful views across the loch and also offers a tempting à la carte menu which specialises in fresh-from-the-sea shell-fish caught by Ian and other local fishermen. And if you are planning to stay in the area, the hotel has 6 well-appointed bedrooms, all of them en suite. Because of its modern design, the hotel is disabled-friendly, offers ample parking space and every up-to-date amenity. Please note that the Loch Kishorn Hotel has a no-smoking policy. **Loch Kishorn Hotel, Achintraid, Strathcarron, N54 8XB. Tel: 01520 733212**

TALLADALE

MAP 7 REF F5

10 miles SE of Gairloch on the A832

From Gairloch the A832 passes through the glorious scenery of Wester Ross to Loch Maree, one of the most picturesque of the western lochs, and the village of Talladale. Queen Victoria stayed here for a few days in September 1877 and much enjoyed a trip in a rowing boat to Eilan Maree, or Isle of Maree. There, in accordance with immemorial custom, she hammered a copper penny into a tree "as a sort of offering" to Saint Maolruabh who lived there as a hermit in the 8th century. The tree has since succumbed to the effects of being poisoned by so much copper. The Queen also visited the waterfalls in Slattadale Forest which were re-named Victoria Falls in her honour. They can be reached by a short walk through the ancient Caledonian pines.

If you would like to bide a while in this enchanted area, **The Shieling** is an attractive timbered bungalow offering self-catering accommodation for up to 5 people. It is set in a beautiful and secluded position, about halfway between Gairloch and Kinlochewe, in the heart of Wester Ross. This is a breathtaking landscape of tranquil lakes, such as the lovely Loch Maree nearby, and majestic mountains like Ben Eighe, Slioch and Torridon. The bungalow is fully equipped to the highest standards and includes the attractive feature of a coal fire in the lounge. Lighting and linen are supplied free of charge; other electricity is provided by pound coin meters. The Shieling is an ideal base for fishing, hillwalking, or for just getting away from it all and relaxing. There are leisure facilities at Gairloch and Poolewe, the famous Inverewe Gardens (NTS) just beyond Poolewe, while the Visitor Centre near Kinlochewe will guide you to many other attractions and events in this spectacular corner of the Highlands. **For further information contact Alister Allan on 01463 772208 Fax:772308**

From Talladale, the A832 hugs the shore of Loch Maree for most of the

10-mile drive to Kinlochewe, with the huge bulk of Slioch (3260ft) dominating the view to the north. The road passes through the **Beinn Eighe Nature Reserve**, named after the towering Beinn Eighe, 3,188ft high, which stands at its heart. This 10,000 acres of pine forest and high moorland is part of the ancient Caledonian forest which once covered the whole of the country. The Reserve has the distinction of being the first to be so designated, in 1951, and is home to a remarkable variety of wild-life (wildcats, buzzards and golden eagles, for example) and dazzling natural alpine rock gardens on the upper slopes. The Visitor Centre has details of the rare species to be seen and also sells pamphlets describing two walks through the reserve.

GAIRLOCH

MAP 7 REF F5

57 miles SW of Ullapool via the A835 & A832

The busy little fishing port of Gairloch has been one of the main resorts of the north-west since Victorian times, with visitors of those days greatly appreciating its superb location, fine sandy beaches and scenic coastal walks. The village faces west, enjoying stunning views to distant Skye and the Torridon mountains and wonderful sunsets. There are facilities for almost every kind of outdoor activity from golfing to windsurfing and should the weather be inclement, the **Gairloch Heritage Museum** provides plenty of interest. Amongst the many fascinating items on display at the Museum are two sturdy fishing-boats constructed locally around the turn of the century; the huge lantern from Rudha Reidh lighthouse just up the coast; and an illicit still. This appealing museum, housed in a former farm steading, was established by local volunteers in 1977 and since then has garnered no fewer than seven National Awards. Since virtually all the exhibits have

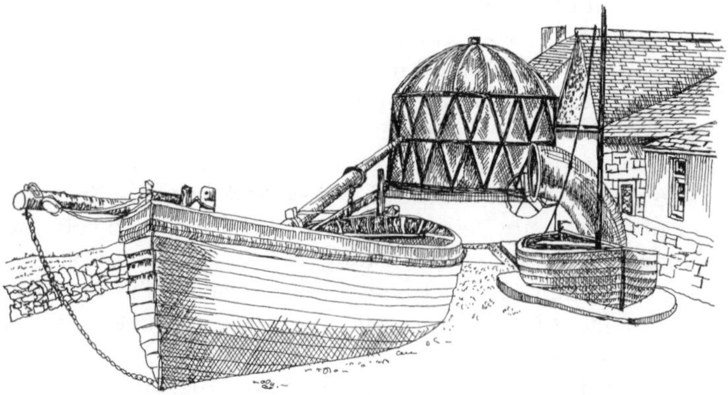

Gairloch Heritage Museum, Achtercairn, Gairloch
Ross-shire IV21 2BJ Tel: 01445 712287

been collected in Gairloch parish, a visit to the Museum is an excellent way of finding out what life was like in a typical West Highland parish in the past. In the same set of farm buildings, The Steading Restaurant occupies what used to be the cow byre. Converted so as to maintain a restful atmosphere in keeping with its surroundings, the licensed restaurant serves coffees, teas and meals throughout the day, with home baking, salad lunches and sea-food dishes as its very tasty specialities. Even if you are not visiting the museum, The Steading is so conveniently situated at the road junction in the middle of Gairloch that it is an ideal place for a meal when you are in the area.

Beautifully situated in its own grounds amidst mature woodland and enjoying magnificent vistas towards Old Gairloch Harbour and across to Skye, **Birchwood** is a welcoming guest house personally run by Ruth and Bill Swann, and which enjoys an AA 5-Q premier selected rating. The accommodation has recently been refurbished to a very high standard, with all six of the comfortable bedrooms en suite. Tea and coffee making facilities are also provided. Located close to Inverewe Gardens, and lovely Loch Maree, with sandy beaches and a 9-hole golf course within walking distance, Birchwood provides the perfect base from which to explore the many and varied points of interest in the Gairloch area. A set dinner is also available and Birchwood is a member of the "Taste of Scotland" scheme.

Birchwood, Charleston, Gairloch, Ross-shire IV21 2AH
Tel: 01445 712011

Set in a delightful riverside location, **The Old Inn** at Gairloch is a charming traditional coaching halt. Here, David and Ann Carruthers have created a friendly and relaxed atmosphere in which to unwind and savour the excellent cuisine, based on freshly-prepared Scottish produce. The inn is also well-known for its large selection of real ales which David and Ann

The Old Inn, Gairloch, Ross-shire IV21 2BD
Tel: 01445 712006

believe offers the most extensive choice in the Highland area and which has won The Old Inn the accolade of an entry in the Good Beer Guide. Or you could treat yourself to one (or more) of the many fine Highland Malt Whiskies available either in the cheerful horsebrass-decorated Lounge Bar or in the Riverside Room which overlooks the Flowerdale River and the restored old footbridge. In the bedrooms, the emphasis is on comfort and all rooms have either an en suite bath or shower, and most have a choice of both. From this lovely old inn, a gentle stroll will take you to the nearby harbour where, on most evenings, you can watch the day's catch being unloaded from the fishing boats.

NORTH ERRADALE — MAP 7 REF F5

64 miles SW of Ullapool on the B8021, off the A832

About 6 miles north-west of Gairloch is a Hidden Place that should definitely be sought out. A winner of The Macallan Taste of Scotland Special Merit Award for Hospitality, **Little Lodge** stands alone on the heather-wrapped peninsula above Gairloch, a white-washed former crofthouse with wonderful views of the Torridon Mountains and across the sea to Skye.

Little Lodge, North Erradale, Gairloch, Wester Ross IV21 2DS
Tel: 01445 771237

Little Lodge's owners, Di Johnson and Inge Ford, have created what one guide-book describes as "an idyllic retreat with superb cuisine". The 3-course Taste of Scotland dinner is planned and freshly prepared each day according to guests' preferences, and is based on the excellent seasonal local produce with freshly-landed fish from Gairloch a particular speciality. Breakfast, too, is made rather special with Inge's home-made bread, oatcakes, yoghurt, and preserves, along with eggs from the free-roaming hens outside. Great care is also given to the presentation of the dining-room itself. Tables are prettily laid with white cotton, silver, Wedgwood china, and flowers from the garden. The bedrooms, too, are attractively decorated and furnished with old pine and each has an en suite shower/WC room. Please note that the accommodation at Little Lodge is not suitable for children or pets, and is a totally non-smoking establishment.

MELVAIG MAP 7 REF F5

10 miles NW of Ullapool on minor road off the A832

From Gairloch a single track road leads to Melvaig, crossing five miles of moorland with some splendid views. After Melvaig the no through road leads to the northern tip of the promontory and a rather unusual place to stay. For accommodation with a unique flavour you really should try **The Lighthouse Hostel**. Formerly the keeper's house, it stands next to the still-operational Rua Reidh light tower which sits perched on the cliff tops looking out over the sea to Skye and the Outer Hebrides. The hostel is some 12 miles from Gairloch and 3 miles from its nearest neighbours in Melvaig, giving a truly "away from it all" location. Recently refurbished and upgraded, the house is comfortable, warm and homely, providing a wide range of rooms from 4 or 6-bedded hostel rooms, 4-person family rooms, doubles and twin rooms, some with private facilities. There's a self-catering kitchen, or you can opt to have meals in the dining-room. Fran

Rua Reidh Lighthouse, Melvaig, Gairloch IV21 2EA
Tel/Fax: 01445 771263

Cree and Chris Barrett, who own the hostel, also provide all-inclusive walking and other activity holidays, guided or independent. "Wilderness Walking", their standard guided walking programme, runs every week, Saturday to Saturday, from Easter to October, but there are many other options, and Fran and Chris will even arrange "bespoke" holidays to meet your particular requirements.

POOLEWE MAP 7 REF F5

8 miles NE of Gairloch on the A832

In this part of the country one comes to expect stunning views to open up at almost every turn, but the vistas of Loch Maree and the Isle of Skye from the viewpoint on the A832 just south of Poolewe are quite unforgettable. Poolewe itself is a picturesque crofting village set around the pool formed where the River Ewe tumbles into the loch of the same name. Loch Ewe is as pretty as any in Scotland but blemished in parts by a litter of bunkers, pill-boxes and gun sites, an unlovely legacy of World War II when the loch was a loading base for convoys to Russia. These scars are fairly localised but it seems extraordinary that they should still be in place more than half a century after the end of that conflict.

Fortunately, nothing mars the attractiveness of **Waterside of Poolewe** where even the names of the two cottages have a magic ring to them: Dóbhran and Corra-bhàn, - the Gaelic names for Otter and Heron. The owners, Dee and Derek Murton, can't guarantee that you will see a wild otter with its family, but on a good day between October and April you might see as many as five at once. And on most days you should see at least a couple of seals hunting right below your cottage. If you take time for a leisurely stroll along the shore to Inverewe Gardens, you will almost certainly catch sight of oystercatchers, herons, cormorants, mallards, Great Northern Divers, eider ducks, and if you're reasonably lucky, white-tailed sea eagles, wild deer, and even Golden Eagles. One of the cottages sleeps 4

Waterside, Poolewe, Achnasheen IV22 2JX Tel: 01445 781482

people, the other up to 6, and both are comprehensively equipped with a fridge, microwave, toaster, auto washer, tumble dryer and electric coffee maker, and the bathrooms have power showers, and also a bath for those long, lazy soaks. Staying at these cottages you can revel in the utter peace and quiet of unspoilt wilderness as you relish the thought of lunch or dinner either in your own home or at one of the excellent licensed restaurants in Poolewe. Children over 12 are welcome at Waterside, as are pets.

Few hotels in the world enjoy such a stunningly beautiful location as the **Pool House Hotel**. With a backdrop of soaring mountains, it faces lovely Loch Ewe and looks across to the world-famous Inverewe Gardens.

Pool House Hotel, Poolewe, by Achnasheen, Wester Ross IV22 2LE
Tel: 01445 781272 Fax: 781403

The view has a special significance since the hotel was once the home of Osgood Mackenzie, the man who, from the 1860s until his death in 1922, spent a fortune creating that sub-tropical "Oasis of the North". Pool House Hotel is particularly noted for its fine cuisine and has won several awards in recognition of its excellent cooking. The lochside restaurant is the ideal place to enjoy fresh local seafood, (Loch Ewe langoustine, perhaps); lamb, or venison from the hill. Alternatively, you can enjoy a more informal meal in the hotel's cosy bar/bistro. (Please note that Pool House is non-smoking, with the exception of the bar/bistro). In the summer months, the seaside patio provides a tranquil area for eating alfresco, perhaps sampling a traditional Highland cream scone tea. There are very special occasions at Christmas and Hogmanay when the hotel hosts gourmet occasions recapturing the splendid Dickensian feasts of bygone times.

Just to the north of Poolewe, **Inverewe Gardens** (NTS) are one of the "must-not-miss" attractions of the Highlands. In 1862, young Osgood Mackenzie inherited a huge, 12,000 acre estate from his stepfather, the Laird of Gairloch. The legacy wasn't as valuable as it sounds since almost all of those sprawling acres were barren, covered with beach gravel and sea grass. A dedicated botanist, Osgood made it his life's work to make this desert bloom. He purchased tons of the rich soil which Irish ships carried as ballast to Gairloch and smothered his arid domain with inches-deep layers of this unusual import. He planted a protective break of trees and began his project by filling a walled garden, which is still the centrepiece of the gardens, with plants from all over the world. Over the course of more than half a century until his death in 1922, he transformed this infertile peninsula into one of the great gardens of the world. Thanks to the mild influence of the Gulf Stream, the gardens are ablaze with exotic plants from the Far East, South America, Australasia and the Himalayas. Mid-May to mid-June is the time to see the rhododendrons and azaleas in their full glory; during July and August the herbaceous garden is at its most colourful. There's a mighty eucalyptus tree, the largest in the northern hemisphere and, close by, a Ghost Tree, so-called because it's an example of the earliest species of flowering trees. The Visitor Centre (open mid-March to October, daily) has an informative display about the history of the gardens, and is the starting point for guided walks which leave here every weekday at 1.30pm.

LAIDE

Map 7 ref F4

15 miles N of Gairloch on the A832

It was marauding Norsemen who, exhausted by their rape and pillage of the western Highlands, settled here and gave Gruinard Bay its name, "Grunna Fjord", meaning shallow fjord. The Bay lies in one of the most beautiful areas of the Highlands, and the **Gruinard Bay Caravan Park** occupies a superb seafront location just a few yards from the sandy beach. There are grand views across the bay to the mountains of Coigach and the Summer Isles. Bathing from the beach is safe, and sea fishing provides excellent sport in the bay. The Park offers 34 touring caravan and camping pitches on level grassland with surfaced internal roads. There are male and female toilets, and hot showers are provided free of charge. The Park also has a small shop where essential provisions are available. Eight Park-owned static caravans are available to rent, each one fully serviced and equipped. Gas, electricity, duvet covers and bed linen are all included in the rental.

Gruinard Bay Caravan Park, Laide, nr Gairloch
Wester Ross IV22 2ND Tel: 01445 731225

The surrounding area abounds in wild-life: you may well see an otter scrabbling along the beach, Eider Ducks and Northern Divers are frequent visitors, and if you enjoy fishing, the Park can provide you with permits to fish in the nearby lochs for a modest daily fee.

During World War II, the little island in Gruinard Bay was used for biological warfare experiments and for years afterwards public access was prohibited. It was not until 1987 that the Ministry of Defence at last began a programme of decontaminating the island, a process that included neutralising anthrax spores which can survive in the soil for up to a thousand years. The island, with its prime pasture and excellent beaches, was finally declared safe in 1990.

ULLAPOOL — Map 4 ref G4

59 miles NW of Inverness on the A835

The most northerly settlement of any size on the northwest coast is Ullapool, embarkation point for ferries to Stornaway. This appealing little town was purpose-built in 1788, to a design by Thomas Telford, by the British Fisheries Society which hoped to capitalise on the herring boom of the time. Ullapool's streets are laid out in a grid design, their regularity enlivened by brightly-painted houses and a wonderful variety of busy little shops. Despite its smallness, the town has the feeling of a cosmopolitan port: your next-table neighbours in one of its cosy pubs may well be speaking in strange tongues, - fishermen from eastern European countries as likely as not, celebrating their catch of Atlantic fish. Wildlife flourishes around Ullapool.

The only inhabitants of the **Summer Isles**, (to which there are frequent boat trips during the summer season), are colonies of sea-birds, and in the surrounding waters, dolphins and porpoises can be seen larking about, there are seals greedy for travellers' tit-bits, and if you are really lucky, you may get a sighting of an elusive otter. The town's comparatively short history, a mere two centuries, is amply recorded in the Ullapool Museum, housed in the old parish church, which has exhibits on crofting, fishing, and a more unsettling display chronicling the devastating effects of the 18th century Clearances when thousands of evicted crofters passed through the town on their way to a dubious future in the remote territories of Canada, Australia and New Zealand.

South of the town, **Corrieshalloch Gorge** is one of the most spectacular, and accessible, sights in the Highlands. A mile long and 200ft deep, this awesome ravine is additionally watered by the Falls of Measach which plunge 150ft down the hillside. The best view of the Falls is from the Victorian suspension bridge strung across the gorge, but do take note of its prominent warning that no more than two people at a time should stand on its vertigo-inducing boards.

LOCHINVER

MAP 4 REF G3

39 miles N of Ullapool on the A837

This busy little port is at its most active in the evenings when the fishing boats off-load their catch on to the pier. The scenery around Lochinver is spectacular even for the Highlands and there are many splendid walks around the village, either along the coast or to the summit of Suilven (2,399ft), a distinctive "sugar-loaf" mountain which dominates the area. Advice on walking routes can be obtained from the countryside ranger at the Visitor Centre which also has interesting displays on the region's history, geology and wildlife. And if you are travelling north from here, it's useful to know that Lochinver boasts the last cash machine until you reach Thurso.

In the heart of this sizeable village and close to the tourist information centre, **Polcraig Guest House** offers extremely comfortable bed & breakfast accommodation. This modern house is set on a hillside overlooking the bay and harbour, enjoying lovely views from the residents' lounge and dining room across to the Western Isles. All the rooms are en suite, (apart from one which has its own private bathroom), centrally heated, attractively furnished and provided with all the usual amenities such as television and a welcome tray. Polcraig has an added attraction for anglers. Excellent wild brown trout fishing on more than 100 hill lochs can be arranged by your host, Cathel Macleod, and the necessary permits obtained. Boats are available on many of the lochs and Polcraig has deep freeze facilities where you can store your catch as well as laundry facilities where you can wash and dry your wet clothes. Polcraig is also an ideal centre for anyone who

**Polcraig Guest House, Polcraig, Cruamer, Lochinver
Sutherland IV27 4LD Tel: 01571 844429**

enjoys the outdoor life or is just looking for a peaceful place to relax and enjoy some of the most magnificent scenery in Scotland.

RHICONICH MAP 4 REF H2

54 miles N of Ullapool on the A838

Set in the heart of northwest Sutherland, the only remaining true wilderness in the British Isles, the **Rhiconich Hotel** stands beside the River Rhiconich as it flows down from between Arkle and Foinaven to meet the sea at Loch Inchard. For anyone who enjoys the outdoor life, this is an exhilarating location, especially for bird-watchers. Over the years, guests at the Rhiconich Hotel have spotted no fewer than 108 different species, so pack your camera and binoculars and see if you can match, or even add, to that incredible tally. Anglers will also be happy here: in addition to its own fishing, the hotel has access to salmon and sea trout loch fishing in neighbouring estates. Following your day's activities, (or inactivity, if you prefer), you can enjoy a relaxing evening meal in the hotel's dining-room with its panoramic views over Loch Inchard. The menu offers a wide selection of dishes making full use of the very best fresh Scottish produce. Whether shell fish or white fish from the local port of Kinlochbervie, prime Scottish beef, lamb, and venison, or local salmon is your choice, you can be assured of a hearty meal. Bar lunches and suppers are also available, and all your meals can be complemented with a selection of wines. After dinner, coffee or a fine Malt Whisky can be enjoyed in the lounge, in front

The Rhiconich Hotel, Rhiconich, Sutherland IV27 4RN
Tel: 01971 521224

of an open fire, as you vie for telling the most convincing story of the size of "the one that got away". If you prefer a self-catering holiday, the Rhiconich Hotel can offer you two attractive choices, one within the hotel itself, another a couple of miles north of Kinlochbervie.

A few miles southwest of Rhiconich is **Handa Isle**, a Scottish Wildlife Trust bird sanctuary reached by a short ferry ride from the picturesque hamlet of Tarbet. There are breeding colonies of puffins, kittiwakes, fulmars, Great and Arctic skuas, and guillemots, who use every nook and cranny of the sea cliffs to make nests for their eggs. The Laxford sea cruise, sailing out of Fanagmore daily, displays this magnificent sight from another angle out at sea, where the knowledgeable boatman knows all the best spots for photographs. And about 15 miles drive from the Rhiconich hotel you can join another boat trip on a vessel called the *Statesman*. This will take you out to the seal colonies and can usually be relied on to include a sighting of a Golden Eagle. The boat also sails up to the highest waterfall in the British Isles, Eas-an-Coul, a spectacular sight when in full flow.

North of Rhiconich, the A838 cuts across to **Durness**, the most northwesterly village on the British mainland, a crofting village which was originally settled by the Picts around 400 BC. It's a popular base for walkers preparing to tackle the daunting hike to Cape Wrath, a huge craggy bulkhead jutting out into the Atlantic Ocean. Less energetic visitors can take a ferry and bus for the 12-mile journey to the Cape and its sturdy lighthouse which was built in 1828. Also well worth visiting while in Durness is Balnakiel Bay with its white sandy beach, and the astounding **Smoo Cave**, a vast limestone cavern easily reached by a path from the car park. Eastwards from Durness the A838 skirts scenic Loch Eriboll for some 12 miles to the Kyle of Tongue where a minor road to the left leads to Melness.

MELNESS — MAP 4 REF I2

41 miles N of Lairg on minor road off the A838

Melness is a pretty crofting village nestling above the bay on Melness Sands, with a small harbour and a community of resident seals. Located on the edge of the village, **The Craggan Hotel** has been owned and personally managed by the MacKay family for almost 30 years and they provide a warm and friendly welcome to all their guests. The Craggan offers excellent accommodation and a wealth of good home cooking based on recipes handed down through three generations. In the restaurant, with its cosy open fire, breakfast is available from 7am until 11am and thereafter you can choose from the All Day menu until late evening. The hotel has delightful views overlooking Rabbit Island and Eilean an Ron (Island of Seals) and the scenic splendours of northwest Sutherland are all within easy reach.

There's a good sandy beach within walking distance, two more a short drive away, and the attractive little town of Tongue with its ruined castle is just across the Kyle of Tongue. **The Craggan Hotel, Melness, by Lairg, Sutherland, IV27 4YR. Tel: 01847 601278**

BETTYHILL

MAP 4 REF I2

31 miles W of Thurso on the A836

One of north Sutherland's largest villages, Bettyhill was named after Elizabeth, 1st Duchess of Sutherland whose husband built it to house some of the crofters he had displaced from his land during the Clearances. Tragic though the circumstances were, it has to be said that the Duke chose a picturesque site for his new village which is set beside two magnificent beaches of white sand stretching in an arc between the Rivers Naver and Borgie. Part of the beaches lies within the Invernaver Nature Reserve, popular in the summer with Arctic terns who nest here, and where there's a very good chance of seeing an otter or two.

In the village itself, housed in what was St Columba's Parish Church, **Strathnaver Museum** boasts a large and interesting collection which ranges from a beaker of around 1800 BC, found in a burial kist close to the River Naver, to exhibits depicting the working and domestic life of local people right up until the present day. A major display is devoted to the Strathnaver Clearances, a tragic story brought vividly to life with the help of graphics, artefacts and models. Local schoolchildren have contributed by writing the story on display, as well as providing paintings and models, plus a

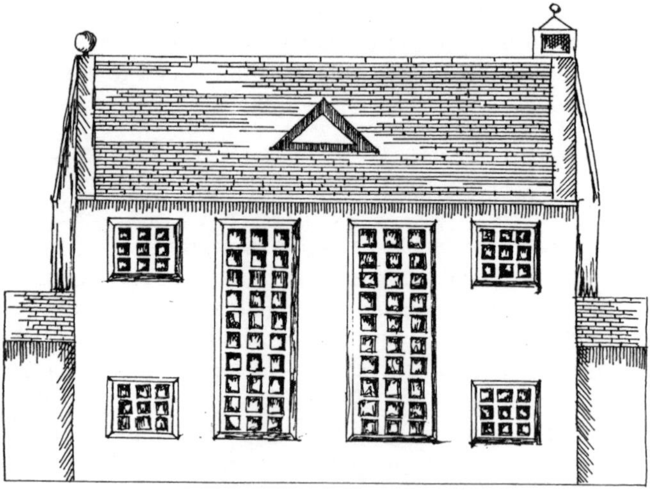

Strathnaver Museum, Clachan, Bettyhill, by Thurso Sutherland KW14 7SS Tel: 01641 521418

great deal of enthusiasm! On the upper floor of the building, the Clan Mackay Room explores the history of this clan which at one time dominated large expanses of north and west Sutherland. Several Clan Mackay Societies, scattered across the world, have contributed most of the exhibits and information on show. The museum also has a useful selection of books and fact-sheets about the area on sale. Nearby, opposite the west door of the museum, and situated within the graveyard, lies the remarkable **Farr Stone**, a carved Christian stone slab dating back to the 8th or 9th century.

Beyond Bettyhill, the A836 follows the coast, passing en route the unappealing complex of domes and chimney stacks housing the Dounreay Nuclear Power Station, (where there's a Visitor Centre open from Easter to September), and on to Thurso, the largest town in Sutherland, which is described in the next chapter.

7 From Inverness to John O'Groats

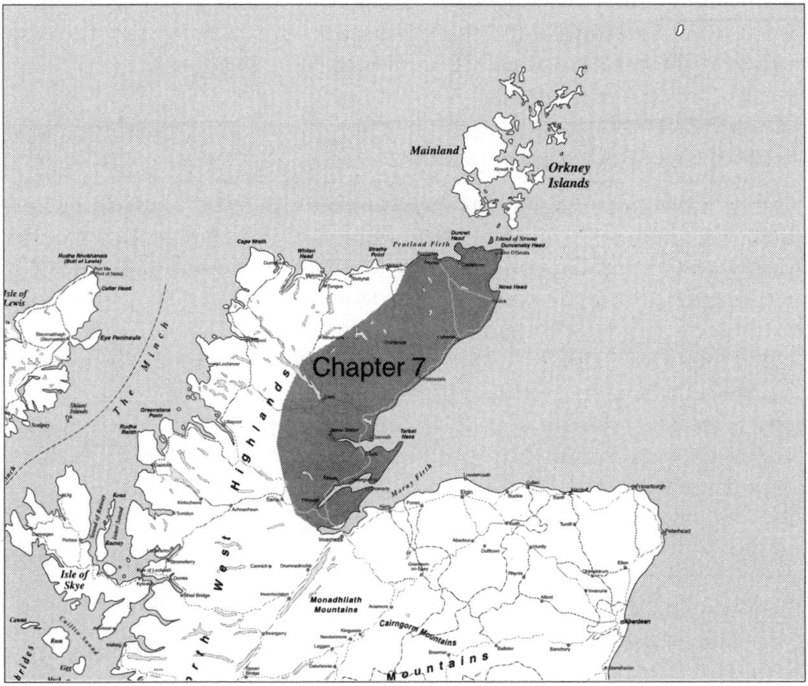

© MAPS IN MINUTES ™ (1998)

The scenery of the far northeast of Scotland is quite different from the rest of the Highlands. In place of majestic mountains towering over picturesque lochs is a landscape of softly undulating moors, fertile coastal strips and a scattering of small fishing villages. The area is rich in prehistoric remains, most notably the Grey Cairns of Camster and the Hill o'many Stanes, all near the village of Lybster. Of the Norsemen who dominated the region from the 9th century, the only legacy is in scores of place names such as Lybster itself, Wick ("Vik", a bay), and Sutherland, the "land south of Caithness". Sparsely populated, Caithness and east Sutherland nevertheless offers some outstanding attractions. There are resorts such as Dornoch, famed for its genial climate, tiny Cathedral, splendid beach and golfing facilities; dramatic natural features like the Black Rock Ravine near Evanton; Britain's grandest Youth Hostel, Carbisdale Castle; and one of the most sumptuous stately homes in the country, Dunrobin Castle. This classical example of High Victorian opulence was built by the Duke of Sutherland, reviled throughout the north as the initiator of the infamous Clearances which have poisoned Scottish history for generations. The tour concludes at John O'Groats, generally and incorrectly believed to be the most northerly point of mainland Britain, a distinction which properly belongs to Dunnet Head about 20 miles away. Our survey begins just to the north of Inverness at the charming spa town of Strathpeffer: the environs of Inverness have already been described in Chapter 1.

CROMARTY

MAP 4 REF I5

25 miles NE of Inverness on the A832

No-one travelling in these parts should miss a visit to the enchanting little town of Cromarty, an almost perfect example of an 18th century seaport. Narrow streets and old cottages are intermixed with handsome Georgian houses built during the period of prosperity from the 1770s to the 1840s. In 1772, the Laird of Cromarty, George Ross, founded a hemp mill here in which imported Baltic hemp was spun into cloth and rope. The business was spectacularly successful and the profits helped build some of Scotland's finest Georgian houses. Also dating from those affluent days is the elegant **Cromarty Courthouse** of 1782. It's now a museum which tells the story of the town with the help of an audio guide, films and animated figures. Visitors also receive a complimentary map of the town with suggested walks. One of the places it will lead you to is Hugh Miller's Cottage (N.T.S.), a charming thatched building of 1711 where the celebrated geologist and prolific man of letters was born in 1802. Apprenticed as a stonemason at the age of 16, he became fascinated by the fossils he came across. He read voraciously any book on geology he could lay his hands on and then wrote his own pioneering works of popular science. Amongst his many other writings, - poems, topographical accounts, and anti-Darwinian tracts, the most revealing is *My Schools and*

Cromarty Courthouse

Schoolmasters which makes it clear that even as a child Hugh was an obstreperous character. Later in life, Miller became embroiled in the virulent ecclesiastical controversy which split the Church of Scotland. Exhausted by illness and overwork, he shot himself at the cottage on Christmas Eve, 1856. The cottage has been restored to its early Victorian character and gives a good sense of what life in Cromarty at that time was like. Three years after Miller's death, a statue was erected adjoining the chapel and in the churchyard there are tombstones carved by him.

If you are travelling north from Cromarty, there's a quaint, two-car ferry service during the summer which will take you the mile or so across the mouth of Cromarty Firth to Balnapaling on the Nigg Peninsula.

STRATHPEFFER

MAP 4 REF H6

24 miles NW of Inverness on the A834

In its heyday as a spa town during the 19th century, Strathpeffer attracted visitors from all over Europe. They would stroll along the wide streets of the "Harrogate of the North", past elegant villas and hotels to the **Pump Room** where the sulphurous waters on offer were deemed so disgusting that they must surely be doing one some good. Legend has it that the hot springs that abound in this once-volcanic area were caused by the Devil taking a bath. Wherever the sulphurous waters mingled with those rich in iron, they turned black, a phenomenon attributed to the fact that the Devil was washing his filthy clothes. The Pump Room in the main square has been restored as the Water Sampling Pavilion where you may, if you wish, sample the evil-smelling liquid. Good health to you!

Other attractions in the town include the restored Victorian railway station where there are no trains but an interesting collection of craft shops, and a superb museum, the **Highland Museum of Childhood**. It tells the story of childhood in the Scottish Highlands through a series of well-presented displays each exploring a different theme, - education, health, home-life, folklore, and recreation. Items on show include toys, games, puppets, cradles, a school desk, slate and strap, as well as a number of rare dolls from the Angela Kellie Collection. Hands-on exhibits include a dressing-up box and a toy train for children of all ages. Particularly engrossing are the historic photographs of Highland children at work and play from late-Victorian times to the recent past. There's also an attractive café where, in good weather, tables are set out on the old railway platform, and a shop selling traditional toys, games, and children's books.

Eagle Stone

A curious tale is attached to the **Eagle Stone** which stands at the end of a lane off the main road. It is carved with an eagle, the crest of the Clan Munro and commemorates their victory over the Macdonalds in 1411. A local visionary, the Seer of Brahan, said that "ships would anchor here" if the stone fell three times. It has fallen twice, so it is now protected. The precaution seems wise, since many other of the Seer's prophecies have come to pass since his death in 1660. He is credited with fore-seeing the building of the Caledonian Canal, the Clearances, and World War II, as well as predicting that Strathpeffer "uninviting and disagreeable as it now is, the day will come when crowds of pleasure and health seekers shall be seen thronging its portals".

"No country - no place was ever for a moment so delightful to my soul" wrote Robert Louis Stevenson of his visit to Strathpeffer in 1880. It's not known whether the great novelist stayed in this charming little town but if he did the **Strathpeffer Hotel** would surely have made his visit even more enjoyable. A listed building of architectural interest, this well-equipped hotel, run under the personal supervision of the resident proprietor, Sean Kennedy, has 42 bedrooms, all en suite, centrally heated and with all mod-

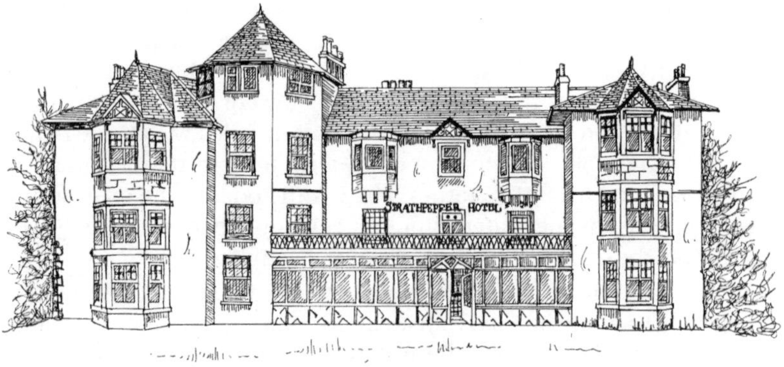

Strathpeffer Hotel, Strathpeffer, Ross-shire IV14 9DF
Tel: 01997 421200 Fax: 01997 421110

ern amenities. Residents have the use of a sauna, a spacious lounge and, a recent addition, a conservatory with a dance floor. The dining room, which seats 100 people, serves traditional Scottish fare, and several nights a week, the Strathpeffer features live entertainment. Adjacent to the hotel, Clisham House offers the same standard of first-rate accommodation and has the additional advantage of 6 ground floor bedrooms, one of which has facilities for the disabled. From either Clisham House or the, Strathpeffer, there's a wealth of choice for day trips: the Isle of Skye, Inverewe Gardens, Cape Wrath, Loch Ness cruises, to name just a few.

If you are thinking of staying in this idyllic Victorian spa town, then the **Richmond Highland House Hotel** also makes an ideal base for ex-

Richmond Highland House Hotel, Church Brae, Strathpeffer Ross-shire IV14 9AW Tel: 01997 421300 Fax: 421640

ploring both the town and the spectacular Highland countryside around. This small, family-run hotel, owned by Malcolm and Lesley Campbell, is an imposing stone building, fully licensed with separate smoking and non-smoking lounges, and a dining area. Restaurant facilities and bar meals are always available. Open all year, the hotel has six luxury en suite bedrooms, amongst them a family suite and a 4-poster bedroom overlooking the village. All rooms are fully equipped with colour television, radio, hair dryer and tea/coffee making facilities. Nearby there are facilities for fishing, shooting, pony trekking, many scenic walks and, of course, plenty of golf courses, one of which is a mere 300 yards away, - or the length of a good drive with the wind behind you! Only a little further away are the Falls of Rogie and in Strathpeffer itself a pipe band plays and children dance every Thursday and Sunday evening in the Square at 8.30 p.m.

DINGWALL

MAP 4 REF I6

15 miles NW of Inverness on the A862/A834

A traditional bustling market town set at the head of the Cromarty Firth, Dingwall's name is derived from the Norse "Thing Volle", place of the council, and for centuries Dingwall was the administrative centre for the large area of Ross and Cromarty. From being a southern outpost of the great Norse Earldom of Orkney, Dingwall became a strategic fortress of the Celtic Kings. The town's most famous, or notorious, son was born here around 1005 AD: Macbeth. His family lived in the Castle of which only a few stones remain. A more honourable, if less well-known, son of Dingwall is commemorated by the Sir Hector MacDonald Monument, a lofty square tower in the Mitchell Hill cemetery. Sir Hector (1853-1903) joined the army as a teenager, rose from the ranks and later led the Gordon Highlanders with distinction at the Battle of Omdurman. His colourful career is further celebrated in the Town House Museum with a collection of memorabilia.

Collectors of curiosities will want to seek out the Obelisk which stands on a mound behind the Town House. A worn inscription states that it was "Erected by George, Ist Earl of Cromartie, who died 1714 and is buried 3ft 6in southward hereof". The Earl himself chose this odd arrangement in order to thwart his wife's declared intention of dancing on his grave. The present obelisk is in fact a small replica of the 50ft high original.

EVANTON — Map 4 ref I5

16 miles N of Inverness on B817, off the A9

Evanton village lies at the foot of a remarkable natural feature, the **Black Rock Ravine**. This is a huge gash through the countryside, some 2 miles long but less than 12ft wide and in places 200ft deep, with the River Glass racing along its length. Just outside the village, atop Knock Fyrish (1483ft), stands a curious folly known as the Indian Temple. It was erected by Gen. Sir Hector Munro, who lived at nearby Novar House, with the twin objectives of providing work for the local unemployed and as a self-congratulatory way of commemorating his capture of Negapatam in India in 1781. The Temple was apparently modelled on that town's gateway.

"It's not so far to the Novar" says the brochure for the **Novar Arms Hotel**, adding the welcome words: "where your delight is our concern". Robin Murray has brought a very individual style of management to this attractive hotel and his philosophy can be summed up in six crisp words: "The answer's YES, what's the question?" He firmly believes that the customer is king and that staff, as well as management, should be able to

The Novar Arms Hotel, Evanton, Ross-shire IV16 9UN
Tel: 01349 830210 Fax: 830739 e-mail: novar@globalnet.co.uk.

respond positively to customers' needs. Most of those requirements will already have been very well taken care of, a fact recognised by the Scottish Tourist Board which, after its incognito inspection, awarded the hotel a 3-star rating. Food: The Novar Arms specialises in fresh Scottish food, simply prepared, - expect to find on the menu Venison, West Coast scallops, Dornoch Firth Mussels and locally-caught wild salmon, all fresh and deliciously prepared and presented. Drink: you'll find an excellent selection of best beers and lagers available along with many famous (and local) Scottish malt and grain whiskies. Accommodation: modernised in 1997/98, the hotel's bedrooms are all en suite with comfortable beds, remote control televisions, hair-dryers, direct dial telephones, and tea/coffee-making facilities. One wonders how many other hotels exist whose declared aim is "to anticipate and exceed customer expectations".

ALNESS

Map 4 ref I5

19 miles N of Inverness via the A9 and B9176

This small town, now by-passed by the A9, has grown rapidly over the past few years, with several industries starting up in the area. A more historic industry can be seen at work at the **Dalmore Distillery**, on the B817 to Invergordon, which offers guided tours by appointment on Tuesday and Thursday afternoons. Curiously, the distillery is usually closed during July and August.

With its turrets and castellated walls, **Teaninich Guest House** has the attractive appearance of a domesticated castle. The grand old house, overlooking the "moody" Cromarty Firth, was built in 1784 by Captain Hugh Munro on the site of its 15th century predecessor. As a young man on the

Teaninich Guest House, Alness, Ross-shire Tel: 01349 883231

crest of a brilliant military career, the Captain had been engaged to Jane, daughter of Sir Hector Munro of Novar, with her father's full permission. Hugh then left to join the Duke of York in Holland where he distinguished himself at the Battle of Neimeguen but, at the tender age of 24, lost his sight from a musket ball wound. On his return, Sir Hector withdrew his permission for the marriage. The blind Captain was said to have been extremely handsome, courteous and good-tempered, but he never married. The estate remained in Munro hands until the end of World War I when it passed to an American, Charles Harrison, who, it was believed, was the young man on whom the book *Little Lord Fauntleroy* was based. Teaninich House is now owned by the Ross family who take great pride and pleasure in making sure that their house guests are comfortable and happy. Evening meals can be taken in the beautiful dining-room in The Station Hotel in the village High Street.

TAIN

Map 4 ref I5

34 miles NE of Inverness off the A9

The most distinctive building in Tain is the **Tolbooth**, built in the 1500s and restored in 1707. It's an attractive sight with its conical spire and corner turrets but at the time of the Clearances this "sharp-pointed house" struck fear into the hearts of local crofters. It was then the administrative centre from which notices of dispossession were issued, and also the jail for anyone who tried to resist the order.

Tain Tolbooth

Tain's history stretches back to Viking times when it was the administrative centre for the area, its name a corruption of the Norse word "Thing", meaning a Council. St Duthus was born here around 1000AD, and sixty-six years later Tain became a Royal Burgh. The 900 Roses Garden commemorates the town's nine centuries of existence.

For a riveting insight into its history during that time, a visit to **Tain Through Time** is absolutely essential. This fascinating complex includes a Museum with a range of displays illustrating Tain's rich and varied past, the ruins of a Chapel destroyed by fire in 1428, and the 14th century St Duthus Church, one of Scotland's most important medieval shrines. This lovely

Tain Through Time, Tower Street, Tain, Ross-shire IV19 1DY
Tel: 01862 894089

building once housed the relics of St Duthus whose bones, enclosed in reliquaries of gold and silver, were believed to possess miraculous curative powers. (They mysteriously disappeared in 1560 and have never been seen since). King James IV made an annual pilgrimage here every year between 1492 and 1513, combining this pious act with a visit to his mistress, Janet Kennedy, whom he had installed in nearby Moray. Other attractions at this inventive centre include a dramatic sound and light show telling the story of some of St Duthus' miracles; the opportunity for children to dress up as a King's jester or learn the mysterious Ogam alphabet; and a gift shop selling a wide range of unusual gifts and souvenirs.

Just to the north of the town, off the A9, is the **Glenmorangie Distillery** which operated illegally for many years before acquiring a licence in 1843. Tours are available, and there's also a Visitor Centre and Shop. Tel: 01862 892477.

DORNOCH

Map 4 ref I4

41 miles NE of Inverness via the A9/A949

With miles of sandy beaches, and near the top of Scotland's listings for hours of sunshine, Dornoch is a trim holiday resort with flowers everywhere and a celebrated championship golf course. The town overlooks the Dornoch Firth with fine views across the estuary to the Tain peninsula. In the spacious main square, **Dornoch Cathedral**, dating back to 1224, dominates the town. The building suffered extensive damage in 1570 when a clan feud led to the Mackays of Strathnaver pillaging the town and setting fire to the Cathedral. Only the tower and its spire were left unscathed. The roofless choir, transept and nave were restored in the 1600s but it wasn't until 1924 that restoration work undertaken as part of the Cathedral's 700th anniversary celebrations revealed the beautiful 13th century stonework that had lain behind plaster for centuries. No fewer than 16 Earls of Sutherland were laid to rest here, and at the west end the 1st Duke, who died in 1833, is commemorated by a fine statue sculpted by Francis Chantrey.

Two other ancient buildings have acquired new roles: the tower of the 16th century Bishop's Palace is now part of Dornoch Castle Hotel, while the Old Jail currently houses a craft shop and a re-creation of a 19th century prison cell.

Incongruously, this attractive little town witnessed the last burning of a witch in Scotland. The year was 1722 when a misfortunate old woman named Janet Horne was accused of transforming her daughter into a pony, riding her to a witches' coven and having her shod there by the Devil. During her trial, Janet was judged to have confirmed her guilt of these improbable crimes by incorrectly quoting the Gaelic version of the Lord's Prayer. She was sentenced to be roasted alive in a barrel of boiling tar. This gruesome event is commemorated by the Witch's Stone, just south of the Square on Carnaig Street.

A mere 30-second walk from the town centre brings you to the **Burnside Guest House** where Kerry and Dave provide excellent bed and breakfast accommodation. Their Victorian house enjoys a quiet location despite being

Burnside Guest House, Shore Road, Dornoch, Sutherland IV25 3LS
Tel: 01862 810919 e-mail: burnsideguesthouse@msn.com

so conveniently close to the town centre and the venerable Cathedral. Also within walking distance are Dornoch's extensive beaches which have been accorded Blue Flag status and the Royal Dornoch Golf Course which is ranked 11th in the world and is also the most northerly first-class golf course in the world. Burnside has five comfortable and well-appointed letting rooms, 2 of them en suite. There are 2 family rooms, a double with a 4-poster bed, a twin and a single. Breakfast is included in the tariff and also available are evening meals when you can take advantage of the fact that Burnside is licensed. If you are thinking of staying in this appealing seaside town, the Burnside Guest House should be your first call.

Just a few minutes from the town centre and Dornoch's superb white sandy beach is **Achandean**, an attractive stone-built bungalow offering first-class bed and breakfast accommodation. The house is set back from the road in half an acre of sheltered, mature garden. Achandean is the home of Audrey and Basil Hellier who make every effort to ensure that visitors have a happy and enjoyable stay here. There are two attractive, good-sized en suite bedrooms, both fully equipped with colour television, clock radios, tea/coffee-making facilities and, most important, comfortable beds. Other amenities include a large, relaxing sitting room and a separate dining-room where, if you wish, you can enjoy an evening meal. Achandean provides an ideal base for exploring the "Roof of Scotland", - the former counties of Sutherland and Caithness with their lochs and legends, colourful history, and a wealth of ancient castles and monuments bearing testimony to the past. If you are a golfing devotee, the Championship Dornoch Golf Course is a two-minute drive from Achandean, and for bird-watchers the Loch Fleet Nature reserve is just three miles away to the north.

Achandean, The Meadows, Dornoch, Sutherland IV25 3SF
Tel: 01862 810413 Fax: 01862 810413

Just north of Dornoch is **Skelbo Castle**, on the shore of Loch Fleet. Originally built in 1259, it is now a dangerous ruin best seen from the roadside. Loch Fleet itself is a massive salt-water basin at the mouth of the River Fleet, a Scottish Wildlife Trust Reserve and home to many seals, ducks and waders.

SPINNINGDALE

MAP 4 REF I4

38 miles N of Inverness via the A9 and A949

Some enterprising hotelier built **The Old Mill Inn** at Spinningdale around 1745 to provide over-night food and accommodation for the drovers hustling their cattle southwards to English markets hungry for prime Scottish beef. By chance or by intent, the unknown founder of The Old Mill Inn placed his hostelry at a location which enjoys superb views over Dornoch Firth to the Ross-shire hills, an ever-changing panorama of skyscapes. Lesley

The Old Mill Inn, Spinningdale, Sutherland IV24 3AD
Tel: 01862 881219

Elizabeth Phelps' welcoming and friendly inn also enjoys clear views of the dramatic ruins of Dempster's Cotton Mill, built in 1793 and the only one of its type in the Highlands. Open from dawn to dusk, The Mill as it is affectionately known to locals, offers a good choice of accommodation with some rooms providing en suite facilities. Meals are available all day from either the bar menu or in the restaurant where you can select the table d'hôte or the à la carte menus, both of which offer an excellent selection of traditional Scottish Fayre from local sources and include vegetarian options. Families are especially welcome at The Mill: there's a special menu for younger guests and a baby-listening service is also available. More than 250 years after it was founded, The Old Mill Inn is still maintaining the highest traditions of Highland hospitality.

BONAR BRIDGE

MAP 4 REF I4

38 miles NW of Inverness via the A9/A836

The original bridge at Bonar was designed by Thomas Telford to cross the channel which links Dornoch Firth and the Kyle of Sutherland. That bridge was brought down by a flood and rebuilt in 1892. Bonar developed in medieval times when there was an iron foundry here, its smelting fuelled by timber from nearby oak forests. When James IV passed through the area, he was appalled by the depredations of the forest and ordered saplings to be planted. The legacy of this early example of royally-inspired conservation is the ancient woodland east of the village.

Another royal visitor to Bonar Bridge was Queen Victoria who arrived here by train which, she was surprised to discover, had been driven by the area's millionaire land-owner, the Duke of Sutherland. The Duke had thought it appropriate since he owned all the land the train had passed through since it set off from Inverness. Alighting from the train the Queen was amused to note that "There was a most excited station-master who would not leave the crowd of poor country-people in quiet, but told them to cheer and 'cheer again', another 'cheer', etc., without ceasing".

In the village itself, don't let the unpretentious modern exterior of **The Chequered Flag** stop you from visiting this interesting establishment which has been owned and run by the Fraser family since 1967. Part of it houses Jacqui and Marion Fraser's outstanding restaurant which offers an extensive à la carte menu and wine list every day until 11 pm. They also serve nourishing snacks to eat on the premises or to take away. Another good

The Chequered Flag, Migdale Road, Bonar Bridge
Sutherland IV24 3EG Tel: 01863 766235

reason for visiting the Chequered Flag is the Art Centre and Retail Outlet next door to the restaurant. Jacqui is an accomplished potter who operates as Creich Ceramics, her striking pieces of thrwon and hand-built pottery in stoneware and earthenware can be seen and purchased in the gallery here. Or you may, if you wish, buy art and craft materials for your own works of art.

About 3 miles northwest of Bonar Bridge, the neo-Gothic bulk of **Carbisdale Castle** towers over the Kyle of Sutherland. Despite its medieval appearance, the castle was actually built between 1906 and 1917 for the dowager Duchess of Sutherland. The circumstances were curious. After the death of her husband, the Duke's children by his first marriage had contested his will which left most of his vast estate to her. There was a lengthy legal battle in the course of which the Duchess spent six weeks in Holloway prison for contempt of court. She had destroyed some important documents relating to the suit. When the case was finally resolved, her stepchildren built the castle for her as a token of reconciliation. It is designed in three different styles to give the impression that it had been gradually extended over the years. After the death of the Duchess, the castle was acquired by a Norwegian shipping millionaire in 1933. He in turn left the castle, its contents and the estate, to the Scottish Youth Hostel Association. Most of the stately furnishings have gone but Carbisdale must still be the grandest youth hostel in the country.

INVERSHIN — MAP 4 REF I4

50 miles NW of Inverness via the A9/A836

The village of Invershin is probably best known for the **Falls of Shin**, just to the north. There's a platform from which, from May to November, you can watch wild Atlantic salmon leaping upstream through the rushing water. The Visitor Centre here has a shop, restaurant and adventure playground, and can also provide information about walks in the area. The Falls make a pleasant excursion from the **Invershin Hotel** which occupies a glorious position overlooking the waters of the Kyle of Sutherland and radiates a friendly and inviting atmosphere which has earned it the enviable reputation of being "*the* place to be in Sutherland". The hotel, which was originally a drovers' inn, lies within an area of outstanding scenic beauty. The surroundings offer visitors peace and tranquillity amongst mountain and moor, glen and loch, and vast stretches of open countryside, - this is, after all, the least populated part of the British Isles. The proprietors of this family hotel, Alex and Brett Richards, have made it their aim to ensure that after their daily excursions into the wilds of Sutherland, guests will enjoy a truly Highland hospitality. Good cooking of the highest standard is a hallmark of the Invershin, and the same concern for guests' creature comforts is demonstrated in the attractively furnished bed-

Invershin Hotel, Invershin, Sutherland IV27 4ET
Tel: 01549 421202 Fax: 421212

rooms, all en suite and all equipped with television and tea/coffee making facilities.

LAIRG MAP 4 REF I4

60 miles NW of Inverness on the A836/A839

Situated at the southern end of Loch Shin, Lairg lies at the centre of the region's road system. There's little to see in Lairg itself, except on the third Saturday in August each year when the Lairg Crofters Show takes over the village. First held over 75 years ago, it is the last surviving crofters' show on the Scottish mainland. Just outside the village is the **Ferrycroft Countryside Centre** where you'll find everything you need to know about the history, geography and amenities of the area. There are a number of audio-visual and other displays, picnic facilities and a children's play area. The Centre can also provide permits for fishing in Loch Shin which is noted for its salmon, char, sea and brown trout. Boats are available for hire from the Lairg Angling Club, a quarter of a mile north of the main dam.

From Lairg, the single-track A836 to Tongue passes through the wonderful scenery of Strath Tirry to the 350 metre high Cnoc A'Guibhais and, a little further, on, **The Crask Inn**. This attractive white-painted building, standing in splendid isolation, is owned and run by Mike and Kai (pronounced Key) Geldard. The Crask was a drovers' inn for centuries, providing minimal comforts, but nowadays it offers comfortable accommodation, excellent food and full bar facilities. Kai is a gifted cook and as well as being served a hearty breakfast visitors can also join her and Mike for an evening meal of superb Scottish fare, - salmon, trout, venison or game. There are 3 beautifully furnished double or twin rooms to let, all en suite, and fully equipped. If you happen to play the piano, then you'll be pleased

The Crask Inn, by Lairg, Sutherland IV27 4AB
Tel: 01549 411241

to know that the guests' sitting-room is furnished with a grand piano. Mike is a shepherd and guests are welcome to visit his flock of North Country Cheviot sheep while he is working them with his three border collies. Mike will also gladly arrange fishing permits and shooting, and advise on the best locations for hill walking and bird watching.

GOLSPIE MAP 4 REF J4

58 miles SW of Wick on the A9

Returning to the coast, the A9 continues northwards to the straggling red-sandstone village of Golspie, the administrative centre for Sutherland and the "capital" of the Dukes of Sutherland who still own vast tracts of north-east Scotland. Above the village, atop Beinn a'Bragaidh (1293ft high, and also known as Ben Vraggie), stands a colossal Monument, 100ft high, to the 1st Duke. It was this Duke who evicted some 15,000 crofters from his land during the infamous Clearances of the early 19th century. However, the inscription on his monument, "erected by a mourning and grateful tenantry", refers only to "a judicious, kind and liberal landlord who would open his hands to the distress of the widow, the sick and the traveller". For several years, campaigners have been trying to have the monument destroyed and another erected in memory of the Duke's dispossessed tenants. (It's a stiff climb up the hill to the monument: allow about 50 minutes each way, plus time to admire the spectacular views).

The Sutherland presence is also clear in Golspie's 17th century church where the finely carved and panelled Sutherland Loft, complete with its own retiring room, was installed for the then Earl in 1739.

A mile or so along the A9 from Golspie is **Dunrobin Castle**, set beside the sea and surrounded by woodland. The hereditary home of the Earls and Dukes of Sutherland, Dunrobin has a late-13th century square Keep, but most of the castle was built in the 19th century to a design by Sir Charles Barry in the exuberantly mock-medieval Scottish baronial style so popular at the time. Queen Victoria described it very accurately as "a mixture of an old Scotch castle and a French château". The treasures on show

Dunrobin Castle

include paintings by Landseer, Allan Ramsay, Reynolds, and Canaletto; some exquisite Mortlake tapestries; Louis Quinze furniture; a wonderfully ornate ceiling in the drawing room; and a library lined with sycamore wood. The castle is the largest house in the Northern Highlands with no fewer than 189 furnished rooms in all, although visitors only get to see 17 of the grandest ones. In the grounds, there are magnificent formal gardens to explore, modelled on those at Versailles, and a museum housed in a gracious 18th century building. It contains an astonishing collection including archaeological remains and hunting trophies from all over the world, Pictish stones, one of John O'Groats' bones, a "picnic gong from the South Pacific", and mementoes of Queen Victoria who was a great chum of the 3rd Duke and Duchess. The castle also has a restaurant and Gift Shop, and is open from April to mid-October. For more details, telephone 01408 633177. Nearby, Dunrobin Castle Station is one of the most exclusive railway halts in Scotland. It was built as a private stop for the Duke and his guests and last used regularly in the 1960s.

BRORA

Map 4 ref J4

47 miles SW of Wick on the A9

Brora has been described as "the industrial capital of Sutherland", an epithet referring to the coal which was discovered and mined here from the 16th century. In the 19th century, the Duke of Sutherland sank a new, highly-productive shaft, and also set up a brick works, paid for the railway to be extended, and even established a locomotive works. The last didn't flourish and was soon transformed into a woollen mill. More recently, the local miners abandoned the pit in favour of better-paid jobs on North Sea oil rigs, but there is still a thriving industry spinning Shetland wool. The town itself is unremarkable, although it does have a good sandy beach, and a mile or so north of the town the **Clynelish Distillery** (free) will provide you with a guided tour and a complimentary dram (Monday to Friday). **Hunters Woollen Mill**, known throughout the world for its tweeds and woollens, also welcomes visitors. Three miles north, on the seaward side of the A9, **Kintradwell Broch** is an impressive example of these circular, prehistoric forts, with an interior measuring some 30ft in diameter. During excavations in 1880, a macabre memento of ancient ways of dealing with criminals was uncovered in the form of two headless skeletons. A little further north, in a lay-by near Lothbeg, **The Wolf Stone** marks the spot where the last wolf in Sutherland was killed, around 1700.

HELMSDALE

MAP 4 REF J4

37 miles SW of Wick on the A9

This small coastal town of grey stone was largely built during the Clearances to house the crofters evicted from Strath Kildonan. These unfortunates were much luckier than most since their enforced removal to a windswept seaside location co-incided with the great herring boom of the 19th century and, seizing the opportunity, they thrived off this harvest from the sea. The great shoals of the silvery fish have now disappeared but Helmsdale is still a working port, its harbour busy with fishermen off-loading their catches. And the River Helmsdale which runs into the sea here is famed as one of the most prolific of the northern salmon rivers.

There's a fine sandy beach here and a shoreline where semi-precious stones such as amethyst and jasper are often found. Thousands of visitors each year make their way to the outstanding **Timespan Heritage Centre** where state-of-the-art displays and a video presentation tells the story of Helmsdale and its environs from prehistoric times to the present. You will learn about the Castle that once stood here, Vikings, Picts, the Clearances and the Kildonan Gold Rush. In 1869, gold was found in Kildonan Burn, about 10 miles inland, and a few lucky prospectors did make respectable sums. Tiny amounts of gold are still found every year and if you want to try your hand at panning, you can pick up a free licence and the necessary equipment from the gift and fishing-tackle shop across the road from Timespan.

Situated in a quiet corner of the town, overlooking the River Helmsdale,

The Old Manse, Stittenham Road, Helmsdale, Sutherland KW8 6JG
Tel: 01431 821597

(one of the north's great salmon rivers), is **The Old Manse**. It was formerly the home of a Church of Scotland minister and is now a very "visitor-friendly" small guest house run by Peter and Pat Mucha. The Old Manse specialises in arranging tailor-made holidays for anglers and others wishing to enjoy the many sporting activities available in the area. Peter is a qualified angling instructor and will happily give advice on all aspects of the sport. He also offers an experienced ghillie service and transport, as well as providing equipment such as outboard motors or a float tube. An individual package might include a six night stay with B & B, packed lunch, a 5-course evening meal, and free fishing on numerous hill lochs with a ghillie and transport provided. Drying and freezing facilities are also available. Helmsdale is also close to the R.S.P.B. reserve at Forsinard which makes The Old Manse an ideal base for bird-watchers too, and indeed for anyone wishing to explore the spacious landscapes of Sutherland and Caithness.

The whole area around Helmsdale is a sportsman's paradise and an ideal base is **The Belgrave Arms**, a family run hotel offering comfortable accommodation, good food, and a welcoming atmosphere. It's owned and run by Kathleen and Callum Taylor who will be pleased to make arrangements for whichever activities interest you. Permits to fish the association waters of the River Helmsdale, one of the most prolific salmon rivers in Scotland, can be obtained from the hotel, either for the day or week. There are many lochs at the head of the River Helmsdale, all of which have an

The Belgrave Arms, Dunrobin Street, Helmsdale Sutherland KW8 6JX Tel: 01431 821242

abundance of wild brown trout and excellent bags can be obtained. Deer stalking, grouse and rough shooting can also be arranged for the appropriate season. Local fishing boat skippers will take fishing parties out for sea angling, and bird watchers will be delighted with the abundance of wild life in the area and the chance of seeing many rare birds. In addition, there are many unspoilt beaches, interesting hill walks of varying degrees of climb, and within easy reach of the hotel there are 4 golf courses, ranging from a 9-hole course to the world-renowned Dornoch Links.

North of Helmsdale, the A9 winds up the hill to a plateau which ends at the sea in a striking rock called the Ord of Caithness (1300ft). There are wonderful views along the coast. It's said that men of the Sinclair clan will never cross the Ord on a Monday because it was on that day, in 1513, that a large party of Sinclairs marched through here on their way to the Battle of Flodden. Not one of them returned.

A little further north, at **Ousdale**, a footpath leads from a lay-by to the ruined crofts of Badbea. This lonely coastal settlement was founded by tenants evicted from the inland straths during the Clearances. An old tradition asserts that the spot was so exposed that children and cattle had to be tethered to prevent them being blown over the cliffs.

About 17 miles north of Ousdale, just beyond Dunbeath, the **Laidhay Croft Museum** is housed in a traditional thatched longhouse dating from around 1842 and displays numerous artefacts, furniture and structural features typical of a croft. The cruck-framed winnowing barn is particularly well worth seeing.

Four miles north of the Laidhay Croft Museum, at Latheron, the **Clan Gunn Heritage Centre & Museum** is housed in the village's 18th century parish church. The Centre is the base of the Clan Gunn Society which maintains the traditions of the Clan throughout the world. An intriguing exhibit proposes the theory that Scotsmen had arrived in America almost a century before Columbus supposedly "discovered" the continent. In support of this claim, the museum adduces a 600-year-old portrait of a Scottish knight, marked out in stone, on a quiet roadside in Massachusetts, and the tell-tale architecture of a strange round tower in Newport, Rhode Island. The tale is well-told and raises some mystifying questions.

After another 6 miles or so along the A9, turn left on a minor road just past the village of Lybster, and in about 7 miles you will come to the **Grey Cairns of Camster**, generally regarded as amongst the finest prehistoric sites in Britain and definitely not to be missed. Dating back to around 4000BC, these two monumental chambered cairns are approached by way of passages so low that at some points you have to crawl. The Round Cairn is 55ft in diameter, and 12ft high: the Long Cairn 200ft long and 65ft wide.

Two miles north of Lybster, just off the A9, there are yet more ancient remains near East Clyth. From the village a path leads to the Hill O'Many Stanes, an early bronze age construction with some 200 standing stones arranged in 22 rows running north to south. Archaeologists haven't yet worked out what their purpose was, but they do know that originally there were 600 stones in place.

WICK

In Old Norse "Vik" means a bay, and Wick is indeed set around a bay although its spread of dull grey houses makes the setting far from picturesque. Robert Louis Stevenson was scathing about Wick, describing it as "the meanest of man's towns, situated on the baldest of God's bays". Like Budapest, Wick is really two towns, with the original settlement standing on the north bank of the Wick River, and Pulteneytown on the south. The latter was named after the president of the British Fisheries Society which in 1806 commissioned Thomas Telford to design a new town to house crofters who had been evicted during the Clearances. The Society was motivated by the humane intention of providing work for them as fishermen and the herring boom of the mid-1800s more than fulfilled their wish. Wick became the busiest herring port in Europe with more than 1,000 boats registered here, exporting tons of the silvery fish around the world. Today, the derelict net-mending sheds, store-houses, and cooperages of Pulteneytown provide a forlorn testimony to those years of prosperity. The town's chequered history is well-presented at the Wick

Heritage Centre which, amongst many other interesting exhibits, displays an excellent collection of photographs dating back to the 1880s. The town's major visitor attraction, though, is Caithness Glass where you can watch glassmakers demonstrating their skill in this most tricky of processes, and purchase the finished products.

If you are planning to stay in Wick then you can be assured of a friendly welcome, good service and superb food at the **Queen's Hotel** in Francis Street. This spacious, stone-built hotel is conveniently located just a few minute's walk from the busy harbour, the town centre amenities, the Wick Heritage Centre and the popular showrooms of Caithness Glass. The Queen's Hotel offers its guests a comprehensive menu to excite their tastebuds. Local seafood and pasta are the specialities of the house, but

Queen's Hotel, 16, Francis Street, Wick, Caithness KW1 5PZ
Tel: 01955 602992

you'll also find lamb, pork and venison, as well as steaks which are all cut on the premises and weigh at least 12oz. The à la carte menu can be enjoyed in the comfort of the refurbished, intimate and cosy dining room. The Queen's also offers an extensive bar meal and supper menu, High Teas, a children's menu and vegetarian options. There are 10 letting rooms, 8 of them en suite, with a choice of single, twin, double, triple and family rooms. Children, of course, are welcome, and so too are pets. Wick is an ideal location for sea and loch fishing, touring northern Scotland and the Orkney Islands, as well as for golfing and shooting parties, and the Queen's Hotel makes a perfect base.

About 3 miles north of the town, on a windswept promontory, stand the theatrical ruins of Sinclair and Girnigoe Castles, in medieval times the twin residences of the Earls of Caithness. It was at Girnigoe Castle that the 4th Earl, suspecting that his son was plotting against him, imprisoned him between 1570 and 1576, and then left him to die of starvation.

THURSO

Map 5 ref K2

21 miles NW of Wick on the A9/A836

Thurso, with its nearby harbour of Scrabster, was a favoured landing place of the Vikings and it was they who gave the settlement the name of "Thors-a", Thor's river. Later, the port became the main conduit for trade between Scotland and Scandinavia but nowadays, apart from some fishing, the main activity is provided by the daily vehicle ferries to and from Stromness in Orkney, and for surfers for whom Thurso is a popular destination. In the oldest part of the town, set around the long, narrow harbour, there's a pleasant promenade; the ruins of the 13th century Old St Peter's Kirk; and the Meadow Well. The well was the main source of water for the town and remained so until the mid-1800s. It is now covered by an unusual circular building. Nearby, the **Thurso Heritage Museum** has a fine Pictish cross inscribed with intricate symbols, a reconstruction of a crofter's kitchen, and a notable collection of plant and fossil specimens gifted to the museum by Robert Dick (1811-66), a local baker who became a self-taught botanist and geologist.

Inland, the wide streets are the legacy of the model town built in the 1790s by the local laird, Sir John Sinclair, and designed "according to the most regular plan that could be contrived and in a manner not only ornamental but also positively well adapted for preserving the health and promoting the convenience of the inhabitants". A statue of Sir John stands near the bridge over the River Thurso.

KEISS

Map 5 ref L2

8 miles N of Wick on the A99

About half-way between Wick and John O'Groats is the quaint little fishing port of Keiss, (pronounced Keese), the main centre in Caithness for crab fishing. Just a few minutes walk from its picturesque harbour where you can watch fishermen off-loading their catch of crabs, lobster and other shellfish is the **Sinclair Bay Hotel**. Visitors to this charming old coaching inn are assured of a warm welcome from its owners, John and Judith Mowat. They offer first-rate bar lunches and evening meals as well as comfortable

Sinclair Bay Hotel, Keiss, by Wick, Caithness KW1 4UY
Tel: 01955 631233

accommodation, all at reasonable prices. Most of the rooms have grand sea views over Sinclair Bay and children and pets are especially welcome. Close by stand the ruins of medieval Keiss Castle and all along the coastline here are glorious safe and sandy beaches. John will gladly arrange sea, river, or loch fishing, golf or shooting for you. And photographers and painters will be enchanted by the area with its breathtaking seascapes.

About 3 miles north of Keiss, the **Northlands Viking Centre** at Auckengill features displays on the archaeological history of Caithness, especially the brochs, and on John Nicolson, a Victorian antiquarian who lived in the village.

JOHN O'GROATS — MAP 5 REF L1

17 miles N of Wick on the A99/A836

It's a mystery why John O'Groats has become accepted as the northern starting-point for the innumerable journeys made by walkers, cyclists, and even people pushing baths, traversing the 874 miles southwards to Land's End. Dunnet Head, over to the west, is a clear 3 miles further north and the itinerary "Dunnet Head to Land's End" surely has just as good a ring to it as the more familiar "John O'Groats to Lands End". But it seems unlikely that a tradition that began in mid-Victorian times is going to change.

The village takes its name from a Dutchman, Jan de Groot, who in 1496 paid a handsome sum to James IV for the exclusive right to run a ferry from here to the Orkney Islands. The business prospered but Jan, it seems, was burdened with a dysfunctional family, - eight sons who constantly quarrelled over who should take precedence after his death. In an inspired attempt to secure domestic harmony, Jan built an octagonal house so that each of his fractious children could enter by his own door and sit at (his) head of the table. A much less appealing version of the story is that Jan erected an eight-sided shelter for his ferry customers to protect them from the North Sea's gusting winds, whatever their direction. Whichever interpretation is true, a mound with a flagstaff marks the supposed site of the house/shelter and nearby is a much-photographed signpole, its arms pointing in all directions, each inscribed with the number of miles from John O'Groats to far-flung places.

Living up to its name, most of the guest rooms at the **Seaview Hotel** do indeed have striking views across the turbulent Pentland Firth to the Island of Stroma and the southernmost of the Orkney Islands. This comfortable, family-run hotel is under the personal direction of Andrew Mowat who makes every effort to ensure that guests have a relaxing and comfortable stay. Open all year, the Seaview Hotel serves food all day with fresh,

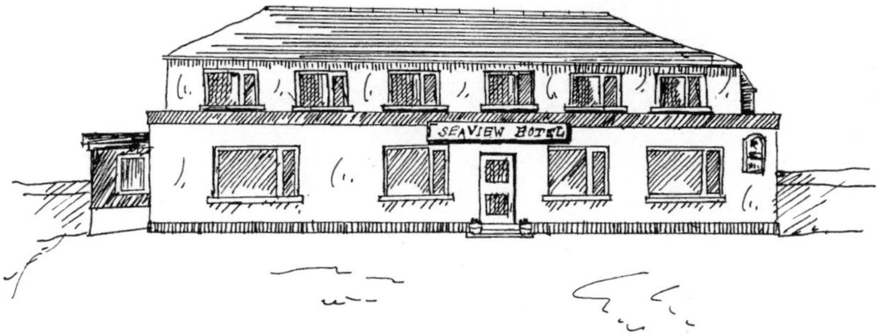

Seaview Hotel, John O'Groats KW1 4YR
Tel: 01955 611220

local seafood a speciality and another special attraction is its regular music evenings. The hotel is just a quarter of a mile from John O'Groats' modern harbour, built in the 1970s with the help of European funds, which has led to a revival in the traditional fishing for crabs and lobsters, one of the mainstays of the local economy and the basis of many an outstanding meal at the Seaview Hotel. And if you want to claim that you have visited the most north-easterly point, (not the most northerly), on mainland Britain, just travel the couple of miles to Duncansby Head where the headland is crowned by a 1920s lighthouse guarding the eastern end of the Pentland Firth.

In the sea to the east of John O'Groats stand **Duncansby Stacks**, a remarkable series of rocks sculpted by North Sea storms into stark pinnacles, arches and bridges, as well as two spectacular narrow inlets with perpendicular sides, known locally as "goes". This is a sea-bird haven, a veritable paradise for bird-watchers. Puffins, shags, fulmars, kittiwakes, all kinds of gulls and many more species nest on the rock ledges in their thousands, whilst off-shore stately gannets can often be seen diving on to an unwary fish.

About 20 miles northwest from John O'Groats, **Dunnet Head** is the most northerly point on the British mainland and actually nearer to the Arctic Circle than it is to London. Near the lighthouse, a viewfinder identifies the far distant mountains of Ben Loyal and Ben Hope, (visible on clear days), the Old Man of Hoy, off Orkney, and the other landmarks around. It's an excellent location to watch the ships in the busy shipping lanes of the Pentland Firth and an appropriate place to conclude this survey of the Scottish mainland.

8 Orkney and Shetland

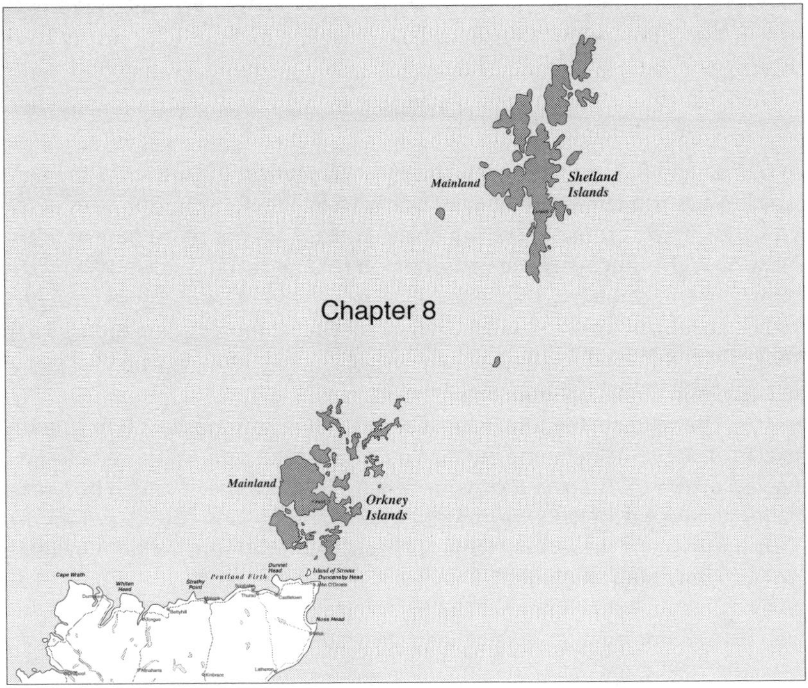

For more than 400 years, the Orkney and Shetland archipelagos were governed by Norsemen and the islands still have strong links with Scandinavia. Many of the place names are pure Norse and the ancient Norn language was still in use on Shetland until about one hundred years ago. Even today, the local accent is much closer to Scandinavian rhythms and inflections than it is to Scottish English.

Orkney has some 70 islands, although only 17 of them are inhabited. But they have been inhabited for more than 5000 years and can boast Northern Europe's greatest concentration of prehistoric monuments to prove it. Skara Brae on the Mainland (the largest island, some 20 miles long), is one of the best-preserved Stone Age settlements in Europe and across the islands there are literally hundreds of chambered tombs, stone circles and Iron Age brochs.

Sixty miles to the north, Shetland is closer to Bergen in Norway than it is to Edinburgh, the Arctic Circle nearer than Liverpool. In midsummer there is scarcely any night, just a dimming of the sky around midnight, a phenomenon known locally as "simmer dim". The islands' northerly location is rewarded with one of the most spectacular light shows on earth, - the Aurora Borealis, or Northern Lights, which shimmer across the night sky in September and October.

ORKNEY

Whaling and fishing have been the most important industries of the Orkney Islands and Orcadians at one time were the preferred employees of the Hudson's Bay Company. During both World Wars the naval base at Scapa Flow brought much-needed prosperity, a rôle performed nowadays by the North Sea oil industry. The generally flat and treeless but fertile land provides an abundance of wildflowers in the summer, and along with magnificent coastal scenery, the towering cliffs support a huge bird population during the breeding season.

On Orkney, says the local tourist board, "the commonplace is frequently extraordinary". Where else would you find a road sign asking you to give way to otters, or discover that your beach picnic has been raided by a seal? Killer whales patrol the surrounding waters and on Hoy colonies of mountain hares study passers-by with an inquisitive interest. As the Orcadian poet, Edwin Muir, recorded

> *"The Orkney I was born into was a place*
> *Where there was no great distinction between*
> *the ordinary and the fabulous; the lives of*
> *living men turned into legend".*

KIRKWALL — MAP 8 REF L23

Northeast Coast of Mainland

The most imposing building in Kirkwall, Orkney's capital, is the **Cathedral of St Magnus**, founded in 1127 in honour of Magnus, Earl of Orkney, who had been assassinated by his cousin in 1117. As Magnus was buried, a heavenly light irradiated the sky, divine confirmation it was thought of the Earl's sanctity. The Cathedral attracted pilgrims from across the extensive Earldom of Orkney, their donations helping to fund the building of this immensely impressive church with its pink, sandstone columns and arches of exposed brickwork. During restoration work back in 1911, a skull and some bones were found concealed in one of the pillars. The skull was cleft as if by an axe: exactly the way Magnus was said to have met his death. These relics are now on display in the Cathedral, along with a monument to the dead of the *Royal Oak* (torpedoed in Scapa Flow in 1939 with the loss of 833 men), and a collection of 16th and 17th century gravestones engraved with cheerful inscriptions such as *"Remember death waits us all, the hour none knows"*.

A mere 100 yards away is **Earl Patrick's Palace** which has been described as one of the finest pieces of Renaissance architecture to have survived in Scotland. Built around 1600 by the tyrannical Earl Patrick Stewart, the palace is now roofless but the superb central hall, the colossal fireplaces and the dismal dungeons evoke a powerful impression of upper-class Orcadian life in the early 17th century.

Standing in its own courtyard opposite the Cathedral with an ornamental garden behind, **Tankerness House** is a fine 16th century town house, considerably enlarged in the early 1700s, and now home to an interesting and wide-ranging museum celebrating some 5000 years of Orkney history. Look out for the Pictish board games, an Iron Age bone shovel, and antique bowls made from the vertebrae of whales. More specialised interests are catered for at the Orkney Wireless Museum, a tiny building chock-a-block with every conceivable kind of radio equipment, and the Highland Park Distillery where you can tour the lovely old buildings and enjoy a complimentary dram.

HOY — Map 8 ref K24

Southeast of Mainland

Hoy is the second largest of the Orkney Islands and scenically the most dramatic. Most of the north-west corner of the island lies within the RSPB North Hoy Reserve, home to a wide variety of birds amongst which are merlins, kestrels, peregrine falcons, and the largest colony of Great Black-backed Gulls in the world. The rest of the island is spectacularly under-populated with a mere 400 permanent residents.

RACKWICK — Map 8 ref K23

West Coast of Hoy

This tiny crofting community, flanked by towering sandstone cliffs, is reckoned to be one of the most beautiful places in Orkney, an ideal location for an "away from it all" holiday. At **The Glen**, Dorothy and Jack Rendall offer visitors a warm Orcadian welcome and excellent self-catering accommodation. The main cottage has attractive red-wood ceilings, deep wood-lined windows with flagstone sills and there are lovely views of the sea from the sitting room-cum-kitchen. The barn conversion also has red-wood ceilings and splendid views across the hills and moors. Outside, guests can enjoy the lawned garden with its patio and garden furniture and the

The Glen, Rackwick, Hoy, Orkney Isles KW16 3NJ
Tel: 01856 791262

wonderful open spaces all around. Walks radiate from the cottage in all directions: the beach is just half a mile away, the unique Dwarfie Stane, a 5000 year old rock tomb cut from an isolated block of red sandstone, about 3 miles distant, and a slightly shorter walk will take you to one of Orkney's most famous landmarks, the 450ft high sea stack known as the Old Man of Hoy.

SHETLAND

The sea is part of everyday life in Shetland, Britain's northernmost islands and such was the reputation of the Shetlanders' sea-faring skills that 3000 of them were serving with Nelson's fleet during the Napoleonic wars. Today, around 24,000 people live in the islands, but they are greatly outnumbered by some 30,000 gannets, 140,000 guillemots, 250,000 puffins, 300,000 fulmars and at least 330,000 sheep. Despite lying so far north, Shetland enjoys the benefit of the Gulf Stream which creates a temperate, oceanic climate. It doesn't however protect the islands from ferocious winter storms which have battered the coastline into a frazzled hem of caves, blow-holes and rock stacks. The best months to visit are from June to

September which are usually marked by long, dry sunny spells and, in June and July, almost continuous daylight making it possible for midnight golf tournaments to be held.

As in Orkney, the principal island is called Mainland, with Lerwick as the capital. The name Shetland is derived from the Norse word "Hjaltland", meaning high land, and for the most part the island is upland peat bog and grass or heath moor with countless small lochs of a brilliant blue. Some 50 miles long, Mainland is so indented that it varies in width from 20 miles to just a few yards and nowhere on the island is more than 3 miles from the sea.

Shetland is, of course, the home of the hardy ponies of that name, and the distinctive black and brown native sheep, said to be descended from a Siberian breed, are everywhere. Until the 1970s most Shetlanders were either fishermen or crofters but with the arrival of North Sea oil the economic pattern has changed dramatically. Most of the development though has been contained within the Sullom Voe area in the north of Mainland so those seeking unspoilt scenery, peace and quiet will not be disappointed.

LERWICK

Map 8 ref R34

East Coast of Mainland

The only town of any size in Shetland and the centre of all transport and communications, Lerwick, "da toon" to locals, where around one third of Shetlanders live. Its busy Harbour is always thronged with craft of all kinds: ferries, oil-rig supply boats, cruise liners, yachts, fishing and naval boats, even an occasional tall ship. (In 1999, the port is the venue for the Cutty Sark Tall Ships Race). There's also a replica Viking longship, "Dim Riv", which is available for visitors to row and sail.

Behind the harbour, the compact old town built in stone has some striking buildings, most notably the neo-Gothic **Town Hall** (free) with its stained glass windows depicting Shetland's history, and **Fort Charlotte** (free) originally built between 1665-67 during Charles II's war with the Dutch. The fort was attacked and burnt down by them in 1673 and not rebuilt until 1782 when it was named after George III's queen. There are some grand views from the battlements.

Also well worth a visit is the **Shetland Museum** (free) which documents the history of the islands from the earliest times to the present day. Amongst the treasures on display is the exquisite Gulberwick Brooch, a 9th century Viking cloak pin which, according to local legend, was about to be melted down by the young boy who found it when his father intervened.

Shetland's wealth of neolithic, Iron Age and Viking remains are too numerous to record in any detail but there are major sites at Jarlshof, where there's evidence of more than 4 millennia of continuous occupation, Clickimin Broch near Lerwick, and the Broch of Mousa near Sumburgh Head on the southern tip of Mainland.

Also pagan in origin is the boisterous event known as Up Helly Aa which takes over the town of Lerwick on the last Tuesday in January. Dressed in a bizarre motley of costumes and carrying flaming torches, up to one thousand islanders march through the town behind a replica Viking longship. In a field on the outskirts they toss their torches into the longship, creating a huge bonfire which marks the start of the evening celebrations.

UNST MAP 8 REF S32

Northeast of Mainland

Of Shetland's 15 inhabited islands, Unst is the most northerly and packed into an area just 12 miles long by 5 miles wide you'll find some of the most spectacular scenery in Shetland, - stupendous cliffs, sculpted sea stacks, sheltered inlets, golden beaches, heather-clad hills, freshwater lochs, fertile farmland, and even a unique, sub-arctic stony desert. Unst also offers standing stones, brochs, ruined Muness Castle (built in 1598), two important National Nature Reserves, Hermaness and Keen of Hamar, as well as an abundance of wild-life: free-roaming Shetland ponies, sea-birds, seals and porpoises, even, if you're lucky, sightings of otters or killer whales. It seems fitting somehow that in Robert Louis Stevenson's *Treasure Island* the map showing where the treasure is hidden closely resembles the shape of Unst. The author visited the island in 1869, following in the footsteps of his father, Thomas, who built the spectacularly-sited lighthouse on Muckle Flugga rocks in 1857-8.

The main settlement on Unst is Baltasound which has shops, a post office, marina, leisure centre with heated swimming pool and, nearby, the island's airport. It also boasts an excellent hotel occupying a lovely position overlooking the sea: the **Baltasound Hotel** which claims the distinction of being the most northerly hotel in Britain. Stone-built, with a Scandinavian-style wooden extension and pine log chalets in the garden, this welcoming hotel is family-owned and run by Jean Ritch, her son Geoffrey, and daughter Desley. They also have their own salmon farm, so fresh salmon is always on the menu along with free range organic eggs and other local produce whenever possible. The Ritchs are happy to cater for special diets, - vegan, gluten or sugar-free, just let them know. Drinks on offer include the local ale, "Auld Rock", brewed at the Valhalla Brewery on Unst which, of course, is the most northerly in Britain. The Baltasound has 25 guest rooms, (of which 22 are en suite), some in the main hotel building, others in the attractive chalets. There's a comfortable residents' lounge, lined with mellow pine and stocked with a selection of Shetland books and magazines. The hotel is just 2 minutes from the new pier in

Baltasound Hotel, Baltasound, Unst, Shetland ZE2 9DS
Tel: 01957 711334 Fax: 711358 E-mail: balta.hotel@zetnet.co.uk

Baltasound's harbour and a 5-minute walk will take you to the Keen of Hamar National Nature Reserve, a dramatic moonscape which nevertheless supports a number of rare plants, including Edmondston's Chickweed found nowhere else in the world. With free access all across the island, Unst is especially popular with walkers and all visitors appreciate the peace of an area which is crime free, where children are safe, and where residents happily leave their doors unlocked and the keys in their cars.

A couple of miles north of Baltasound, Haroldswick is home to Britain's most northerly Post Office, the fascinating **Unst Heritage Centre** (free) which has permanent displays on the island's geology, genealogy and Unst's famous fine lace knitting and spinning, and the Unst Boat Haven (free) which houses a unique collection of traditional Shetland fishing craft. A little further north, a walk through the Hermaness National Nature Reserve will bring you to a clifftop panorama overlooking the Muckle Flugga rocks and Out Stack, the very last speck of northern Britain.

TOURIST INFORMATION CENTRES

Centres in **bold** are open all the year around.

Aviemore
Grampian Road, Aviemore, PH22 1PP
Tel: 01479 810363 Fax: 01479 811063

Ballachulish
Albert Road, Ballachulish, Argyll, PA39 4JR
Tel: 01855 811296 Fax: 01855 811720

Bettyhill
Clachan, Bettyhill, by Thurso, Sutherland, KW14 7SS
Tel/Fax: 01641 521342

Broadford
The Car Park, Isle of Skye, IV49 9AB
Tel: 01471 822361 Fax: 01471 822141

Campbeltown
Mackinnon House, The Pier, Campbeltown, Argyll, PA28 6EF
Tel: 01586 552056

Carrbridge
Main Street, Carrbridge, Inverness-shire, PH32 3AS
Tel/Fax: 01479 841630

Craignure
Isle of Mull
Tel: 01680 812377

Daviot Wood
Picnic Area (A9), by Inverness, IV1 2ER
Tel: 01463 772203 Fax: 01463 772022

Dornoch
The Square, Dornoch, Sutherland, IV25 3SD
Tel: 01862 810400 Fax: 01862 810644

Dufftown

Clock Tower, The Square, Dufftown, Moray
Tel: 01340 820501

Dunoon

7, Alexandra Parade, Dunoon, Argyll, PA23 8AB
Tel: 01369 703785

Durness

Sango, Durness, by Lairg, Sutherland, IV27 4PN
Tel: 01971 511259 Fax: 01971 511368

Elgin

17, High Street, Elgin, Moray, IV30 1EG
Tel: 01343 542666

Forres

40, East High Street, Forres, Moray
Tel: 01309 672938

Fort Augustus

Car Park, Fort Augustus, Inverness-shire, PH32 4DD
Tel: 01320 366367 Fax: 01320 366779

Fort William

Cameron Centre, Cameron Square, Fort William
Inverness-shire, PH33 6AJ Tel: 01397 703781 Fax: 01397 705184

Gairloch

Achtercairn, Gairloch, Ross-shire, IV22 2DN
Tel: 01445 712130 Fax: 01445 712071

Glenshiel

Shielbridge, Glenshiel, Ross-shire, IV40 8HW
Tel/Fax: 01599 511264

Grantown on Spey

54, High Street, Grantown on Spey, Morayshire, PH26 3EH
Tel/Fax: 01479 872773

Helmsdale

Coupar Park, Helmsdale, Sutherland, KW8 6HH
Tel/Fax: 01431 821640

Inveraray

Front Street, Inveraray, Argyll
Tel: 01499 302063

Inverness

Castle Wynd, Inverness, IV2 3BJ
Tel: 01463 234353 Fax: 01463 710609

John O'Groats
County Road, John O'Groats, Caithness, KW1 4YR
Tel: 01955 611373 Fax: 01955 611448

Kilchoan
Pier Road, Kilchoan, Acharacle, Argyll, PH36 4LH
Tel: 01972 510222

Kingussie
King Street, Kingussie, Inverness-shire, PH21 1HP
Tel: 01540 661297

Kyle of Lochalsh
Car Park, Kyle of Lochalsh, Ross-shire, IV40 8AQ
Tel: 01599 534276 Fax: 01599 534808

Lairg
Ferrycroft Countryside Centre, Lairg, Sutherland, IV27 4AZ
Tel/Fax: 01549 402160

Lochcarron
Main Street, Lochcarron, Ross-shire, IV54 8YD
Tel: 01520 722357 Fax: 01520 722324

Lochgilphead
Lochnell Street, Lochgilphead, Argyll
Tel: 01546 602344

Lochinver
Kirk Lane, Lochinver, by Lairg, Sutherland, IV27 4LT
Tel: 01571 844330 Fax: 01571 844373

Mallaig
TIC, Mallaig, Inverness-shire, PH41 4SQ
Tel: 01687 462170 Fax: 01687 462064

Nairn
62, King Street, Nairn, Nairnshire, IV12 4DN
Tel/Fax: 01667 453753

North Kessock
Picnic Site, North Kessock, Ross-shire, IV1 1XB
Tel: 01463 731505 Fax: 01463 731701

Oban
Argyll Square, Oban, Argyll, PA34 4AR
Tel: 01631 563122

Portree
Bayfield House, Bayfield Road, Portree, Isle of Skye, IV51 9EL
Tel: 01478 612137 Fax: 01478 612141

Ralia

A9 North, by Newtonmore, Inverness-shire, PH20 1BD
Tel/Fax: 01540 673253

Spean Bridge

TIC, Spean Bridge, Inverness-shire, PH34 4EP
Tel: 01397 712576 Fax: 01397 712576

Strathpeffer

The Square, Strathpeffer, Ross-shire, IV14 9DW
Tel: 01997 421415 Fax: 01997 421460

Strontian

TIC, Strontian, Argyll, PH36 4HZ
Tel/Fax: 01967 402131

Tarbert

Harbour Street, Tarbert, Argyll
Tel: 01880 820429

Tomintoul

The Square, Tomintoul, Morayshire
Tel: 01807 580285

Thurso

Riverside, Thurso, Caithness, KW14 8BU
Tel: 01847 892371 Fax: 01847 893155

Uig

Ferry Terminal, Uig, Isle of Skye, IV51 9XX
Tel/Fax: 01470 542404

Ullapool

Argyle Street, Ullapool, Ross-shire, IV26 2UB
Tel: 01854 612135 Fax: 01854 613031

Wick

Whitechapel Road, Wick, Caithness, KW1 4EA
Tel: 01955 602596 Fax: 01955 604940

INDEX OF TOWNS AND VILLAGES

A

B

C

D

M

N

O

P

R

S

T

U

W

INDEX OF PLACES TO STAY, EAT, DRINK & SHOP

Accommodation

Accommodation (Cont.)

Accommodation (Cont.)

Pubs, Inns and Wine Bars

Restaurants

Restaurants (Cont.)

Specialist Shops and Activities

Tea Rooms, Coffee Shops and Cafes

INDEX OF PLACES OF INTEREST

A

B

C

D

E

F

G

H

I

J

K

L

M

N

O

P

R

S

T

U

V

W

THE HIDDEN PLACES
Order Form

To order any of our publications just fill in the payment details below and complete the order form ***overleaf***. For orders of less than 4 copies please add £1 per book for postage and packing. Orders over 4 copies are P & P free.

Please Complete Either:

I enclose a cheque for £ .... made payable to Travel Publishing Ltd

Or:

Card No: | | | | | | | | | | | | | | | | |

Expiry Date: | | | | |

Signature: ....

NAME: ....

ADDRESS: ....

....

....

POSTCODE: ....

TEL NO: ....

Please send to: Travel Publishing Ltd
7a Apollo House
Calleva Park
Aldermaston
Berks, RG7 8TN

THE HIDDEN PLACES

Order Form

	Price	Quantity	Value
Regional Titles			
Cambridgeshire & Lincolnshire	£7.99	....	....
Channel Islands	£6.99	....	....
Cheshire	£7.99	....	....
Cornwall	£7.99	....	....
Devon	£7.99	....	....
Dorset, Hants & Isle of Wight	£4.95	....	....
Essex	£7.99	....	....
Gloucestershire	£6.99	....	....
Heart of England	£4.95	....	....
Highlands & Islands	£7.99	....	....
Kent	£7.99	....	....
Lake District & Cumbria	£7.99	....	....
Lancashire	£7.99	....	....
Norfolk	£7.99	....	....
Northeast Yorkshire	£6.99	....	....
Northumberland & Durham	£6.99	....	....
North Wales	£7.99	....	....
Nottinghamshire	£6.99	....	....
Peak District	£6.99	....	....
Potteries	£6.99	....	....
Somerset	£6.99	....	....
South Wales	£4.95	....	....
Suffolk	£7.99	....	....
Surrey	£6.99	....	....
Sussex	£6.99	....	....
Thames & Chilterns	£5.99	....	....
Warwickshire & West Midlands	£6.99	....	....
Welsh Borders	£5.99	....	....
Wiltshire	£6.99	....	....
Yorkshire Dales	£6.99	....	....
Set of any 5 Regional titles	**£25.00**	....	....
National Titles			
England	£9.99	....	....
Ireland	£8.99	....	....
Scotland	£8.99	....	....
Wales	£8.99	....	....
Set of all 4 National titles	**£28.00**	....	....
		______	______
		______	______

For orders of less than 4 copies please add £1 per book for postage & packing. Orders over 4 copies P & P free.

The Hidden Places

Reader Comment Form

The *Hidden Places* research team would like to receive reader's comments on any visitor attractions or places reviewed in the book and also recommendations for suitable entries to be included in the next edition. This will help ensure that the *Hidden Places* series continues to provide its readers with useful information on the more interesting, unusual or unique features of each attraction or place ensuring that their stay in the local area is an enjoyable and stimulating experience.

To provide your comments or recommendations would you please complete the forms below and overleaf as indicated and send to: The Research Department, Travel Publishing Ltd., 7a Apollo House, Calleva Park, Aldermaston, Reading, RG7 8TN.

Your Name:

Your Address:

Your Telephone Number:

Please tick as appropriate: Comments ☐ Recommendation ☐

Name of *"Hidden Place"*:

Address:

Telephone Number:

Name of Contact:

THE HIDDEN PLACES
Reader Comment Form

Comment or Reason for Recommendation:

....

....

....

....

....

....

....

....

....

....

....

....

....

The Hidden Places

Reader Comment Form

The *Hidden Places* research team would like to receive reader's comments on any visitor attractions or places reviewed in the book and also recommendations for suitable entries to be included in the next edition. This will help ensure that the *Hidden Places* series continues to provide its readers with useful information on the more interesting, unusual or unique features of each attraction or place ensuring that their stay in the local area is an enjoyable and stimulating experience.

To provide your comments or recommendations would you please complete the forms below and overleaf as indicated and send to: The Research Department, Travel Publishing Ltd., 7a Apollo House, Calleva Park, Aldermaston, Reading, RG7 8TN.

Your Name:

Your Address:

Your Telephone Number:

Please tick as appropriate: Comments ☐ Recommendation ☐

Name of *"Hidden Place"*:

Address:

Telephone Number:

Name of Contact:

THE HIDDEN PLACES

Reader Comment Form

Comment or Reason for Recommendation:

....

....

....

....

....

....

....

....

....

....

....

....

....

THE HIDDEN PLACES

Reader Comment Form

The *Hidden Places* research team would like to receive reader's comments on any visitor attractions or places reviewed in the book and also recommendations for suitable entries to be included in the next edition. This will help ensure that the *Hidden Places* series continues to provide its readers with useful information on the more interesting, unusual or unique features of each attraction or place ensuring that their stay in the local area is an enjoyable and stimulating experience.

To provide your comments or recommendations would you please complete the forms below and overleaf as indicated and send to: The Research Department, Travel Publishing Ltd., 7a Apollo House, Calleva Park, Aldermaston, Reading, RG7 8TN.

Your Name:

Your Address:

Your Telephone Number:

Please tick as appropriate: Comments ☐ Recommendation ☐

Name of *"Hidden Place"*:

Address:

Telephone Number:

Name of Contact:

THE HIDDEN PLACES

Reader Comment Form

Comment or Reason for Recommendation:

....

....

....

....

....

....

....

....

....

....

....

....

....

MAP SECTION

The following pages of maps encompass the main cities, towns and geographical features of the Highlands and Islands of Scotland, as well as many of the interesting places featured in the guide. Distances are indicated by the use of scale bars located below each of the maps

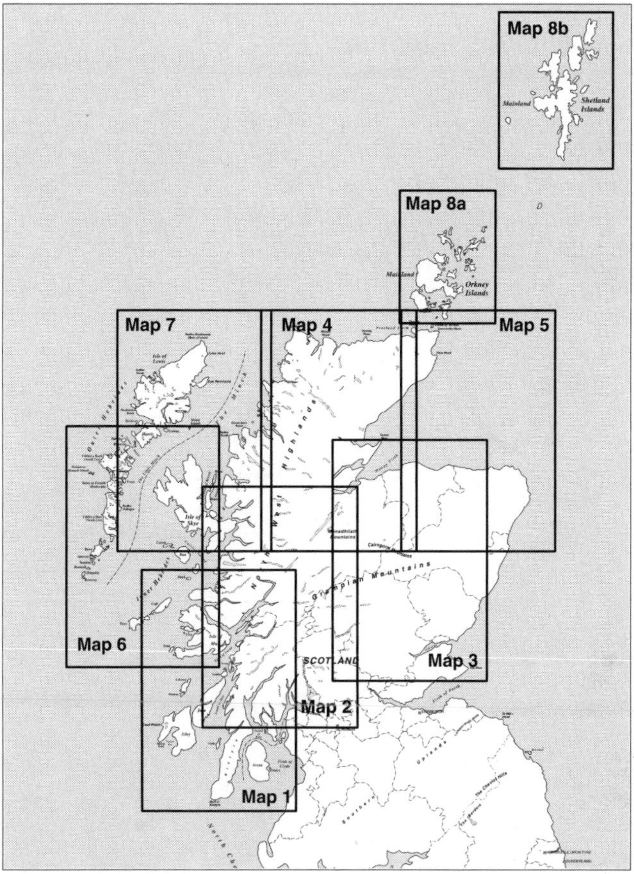

Map 1

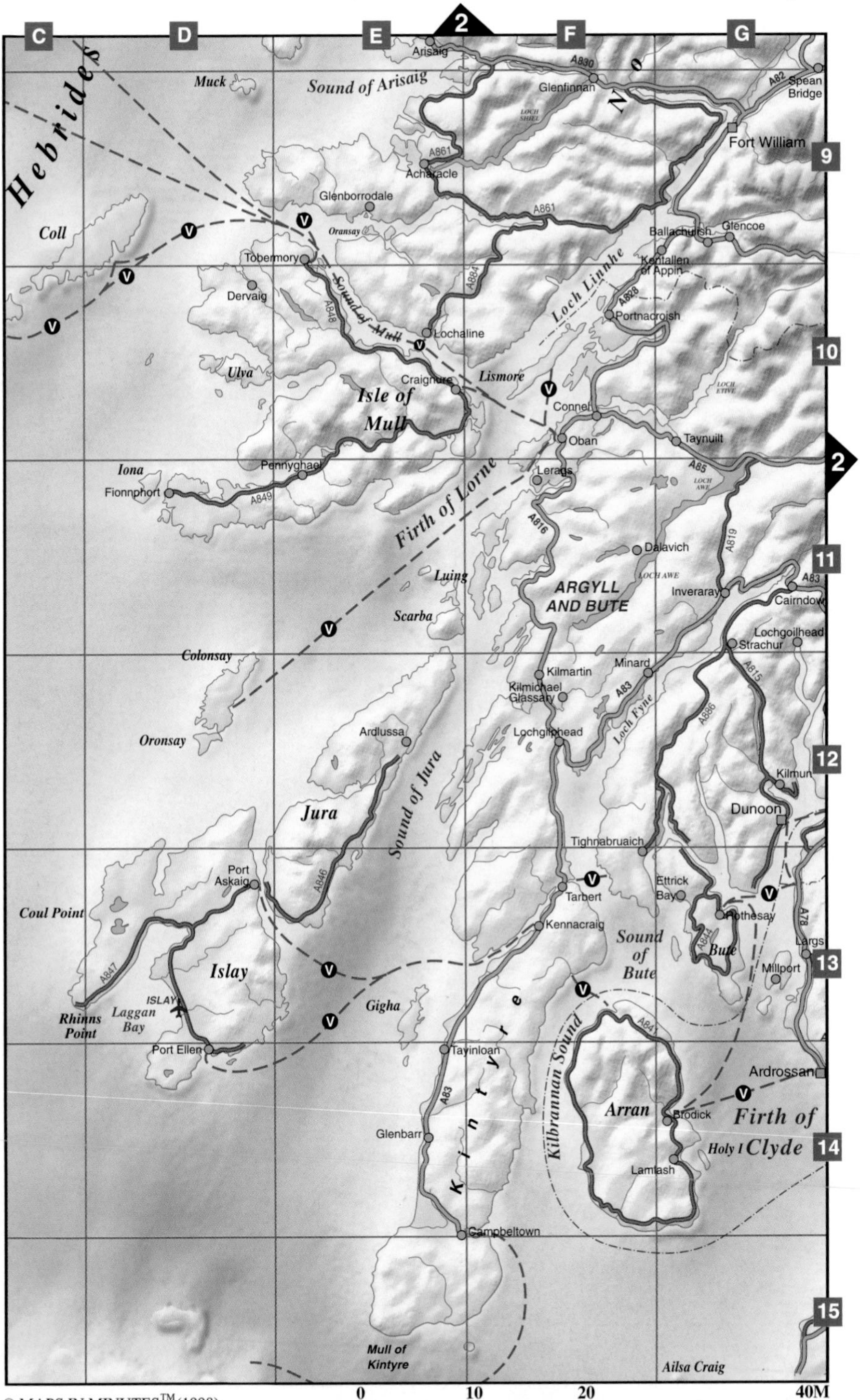
C
D
E
F
G
2
Hebrides
Muck
Sound of Arisaig
Arisaig
A830
Glenfinnan
A82
Spean Bridge
LOCH SHIEL
Fort William
9
A861
Acharacle
Glenborrodale
Oransay
Coll
A861
Ballachulish
Glencoe
Tobermory
Kentallen of Appin
Loch Linnhe
Dervaig
A848
Sound of Mull
A884
A828
Portnacroish
Lochaline
10
Ulva
Craignure
Lismore
LOCH ETIVE
Isle of Mull
Connel
Oban
Taynuilt
2
Iona
Pennyghael
Lerags
A85
LOCH AWE
Fionnphort
A849
Firth of Lorne
A816
Dalavich
A819
11
Luing
LOCH AWE
ARGYLL AND BUTE
Inveraray
A83
Cairndow
Scarba
Lochgoilhead
Strachur
Colonsay
Kilmartin
Minard
Kilmichael Glassary
A815
A83
A886
Loch Fyne
Ardlussa
Oronsay
Lochgilphead
12
Kilmun
Sound of Jura
Jura
Dunoon
Tighnabruaich
Port Askaig
A846
Ettrick Bay
Tarbert
Coul Point
Rothesay
Kennacraig
A78
A844
Sound of Bute
Bute
Largs
13
Islay
Millport
A847
ISLAY
Rhinns Point
Laggan Bay
Gigha
A841
Port Ellen
Tayinloan
Kintyre
Kilbrannan Sound
Ardrossan
A83
Arran
Brodick
Firth of Clyde
Holy I
Glenbarr
14
Lamlash
Campbeltown
15
Mull of Kintyre
Ailsa Craig
0
10
20
40M

Map 2

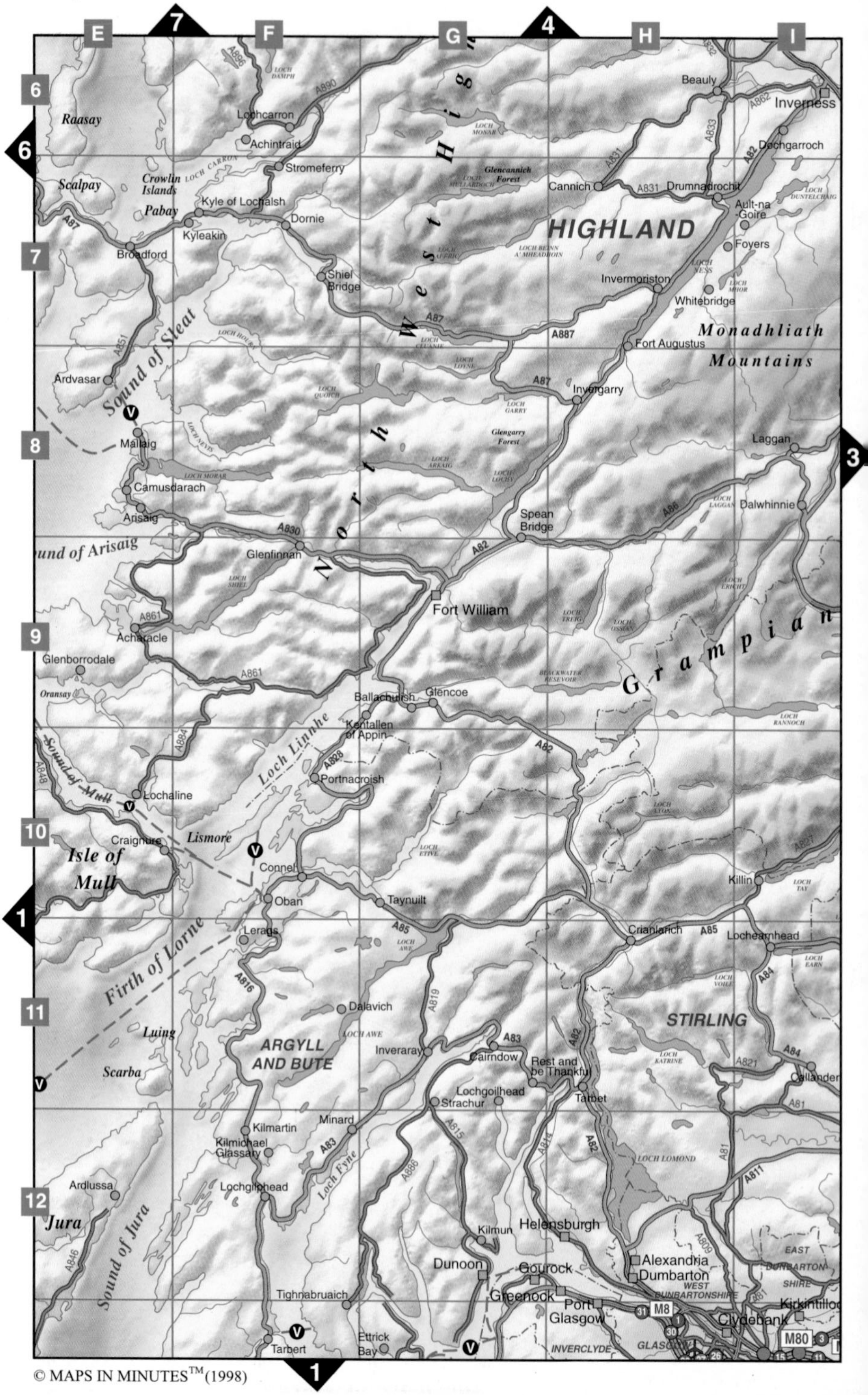

E
F
G
H
I
7
4
6
7
8
9
10
11
12
3
1
Raasay
Scalpay
Crowlin Islands
Pabay
Beauly
Inverness
Dochgarroch
Lochcarron
Achintraid
Stromeferry
Kyle of Lochalsh
Kyleakin
Dornie
Broadford
Shiel Bridge
Glencannich Forest
Cannich
Drumnadrochit
Ault-na Goire
Foyers
HIGHLAND
Invermoriston
Whitebridge
Monadhliath Mountains
Fort Augustus
North West Highlands
Sound of Sleat
Ardvasar
Mallaig
Invergarry
Glengarry Forest
Laggan
Camusdarach
Arisaig
Spean Bridge
Dalwhinnie
Sound of Arisaig
Glenfinnan
Fort William
Acharacle
Glenborrodale
Oransay
Grampian
Ballachulish
Glencoe
Kentallen of Appin
Loch Linnhe
Portnacroish
Sound of Mull
Lochaline
Craignure
Lismore
Isle of Mull
Connel
Oban
Taynuilt
Killin
Lerags
Crianlarich
Lochearnhead
Firth of Lorne
Dalavich
STIRLING
Luing
ARGYLL AND BUTE
Inveraray
Cairndow
Rest and be Thankful
Scarba
Lochgoilhead
Strachur
Tarbet
Callander
Minard
Kilmartin
Kilmichael Glassary
LOCH LOMOND
Ardlussa
Lochgilphead
Loch Fyne
Jura
Sound of Jura
Kilmun
Helensburgh
Alexandria
Dumbarton
EAST DUNBARTONSHIRE
WEST DUNBARTONSHIRE
Dunoon
Gourock
Greenock
Port Glasgow
Kirkintilloch
Clydebank
Tighnabruaich
Tarbert
Ettrick Bay
INVERCLYDE
A87
A851
A890
A831
A833
A82
A887
A830
A86
A861
A884
A828
A848
A85
A816
A819
A83
A815
A814
A886
A84
A821
A81
A811
A809
A846
A827
M8
M80

Map 3

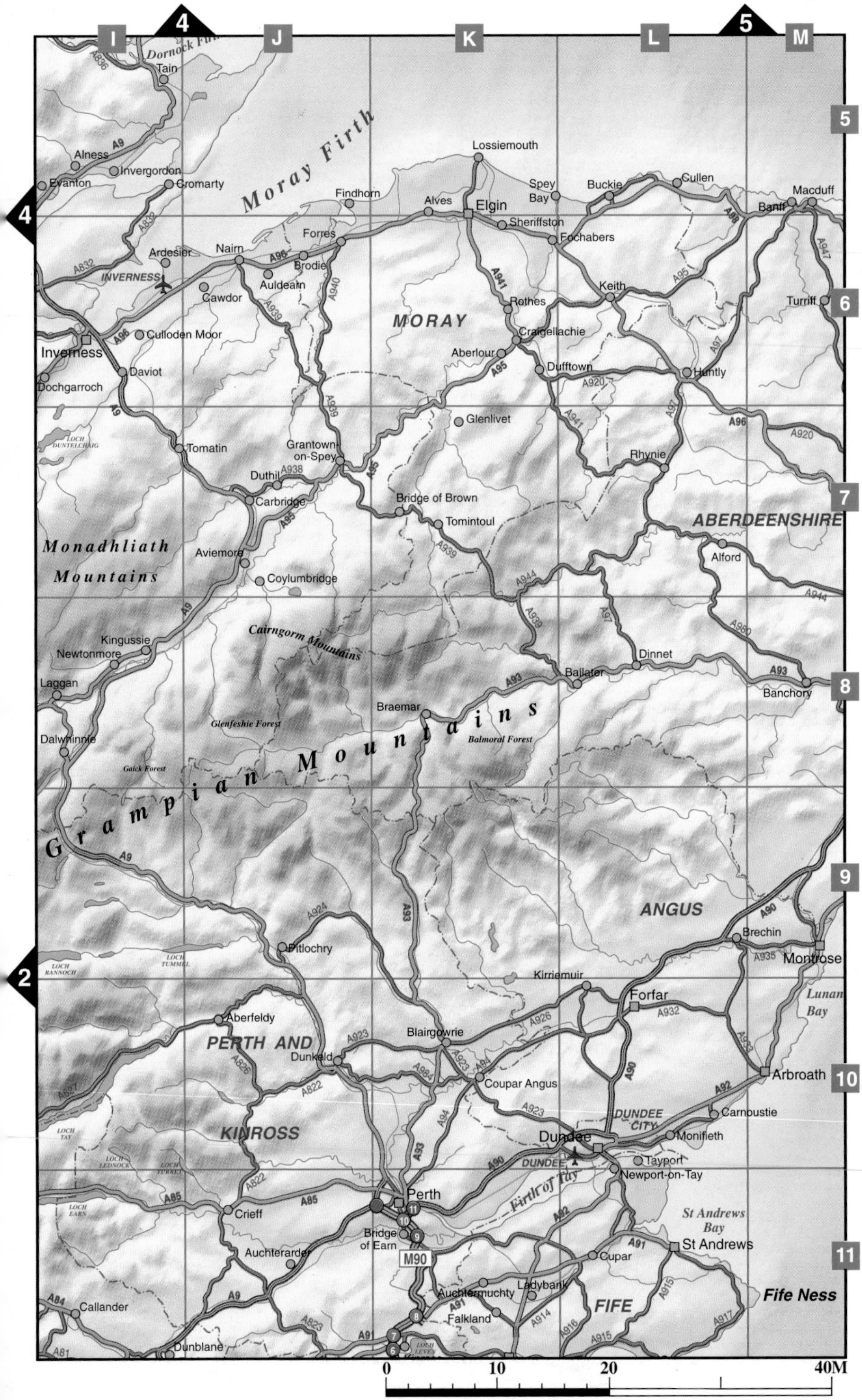

I
J
K
L
M
4
5
2
6
7
8
9
10
11
Dornock Firth
Tain
Moray Firth
Alness
Invergordon
Evanton
Cromarty
Lossiemouth
Findhorn
Alves
Elgin
Spey Bay
Buckie
Cullen
Macduff
Banff
Sheriffston
Fochabers
Forres
Nairn
Ardesier
Brodie
Auldearn
INVERNESS
Cawdor
Keith
Turriff
Rothes
MORAY
Craigellachie
Culloden Moor
Inverness
Aberlour
Dufftown
Daviot
Dochgarroch
Huntly
Glenlivet
Tomatin
Grantown-on-Spey
Rhynie
Loch Duntelchaig
Duthil
Carbridge
Bridge of Brown
Tomintoul
ABERDEENSHIRE
Alford
Monadhliath Mountains
Aviemore
Coylumbridge
Cairngorm Mountains
Kingussie
Newtonmore
Dinnet
Ballater
Banchory
Laggan
Braemar
Glenfeshie Forest
Balmoral Forest
Dalwhinnie
Gaick Forest
Grampian Mountains
ANGUS
Brechin
Montrose
Pitlochry
Loch Rannoch
Loch Tummel
Kirriemuir
Forfar
Lunan Bay
Aberfeldy
Blairgowrie
PERTH AND KINROSS
Dunkeld
Coupar Angus
Arbroath
Carnoustie
Loch Tay
DUNDEE CITY
Dundee
Monifieth
DUNDEE
Tayport
Newport-on-Tay
Loch Lednock
Loch Turret
Firth of Tay
Perth
Crieff
Loch Earn
St Andrews Bay
Bridge of Earn
St Andrews
Cupar
M90
Auchterarder
Ladybank
Auchtermuchty
Fife Ness
FIFE
Callander
Falkland
Dunblane
Loch Leven
A9
A836
A839
A832
A96
A939
A940
A941
A95
A98
A947
A97
A920
A938
A944
A980
A93
A924
A926
A932
A933
A935
A90
A923
A984
A94
A822
A826
A827
A85
A92
A91
A914
A916
A915
A917
A84
A81
A823
0
10
20
40M

Map 4

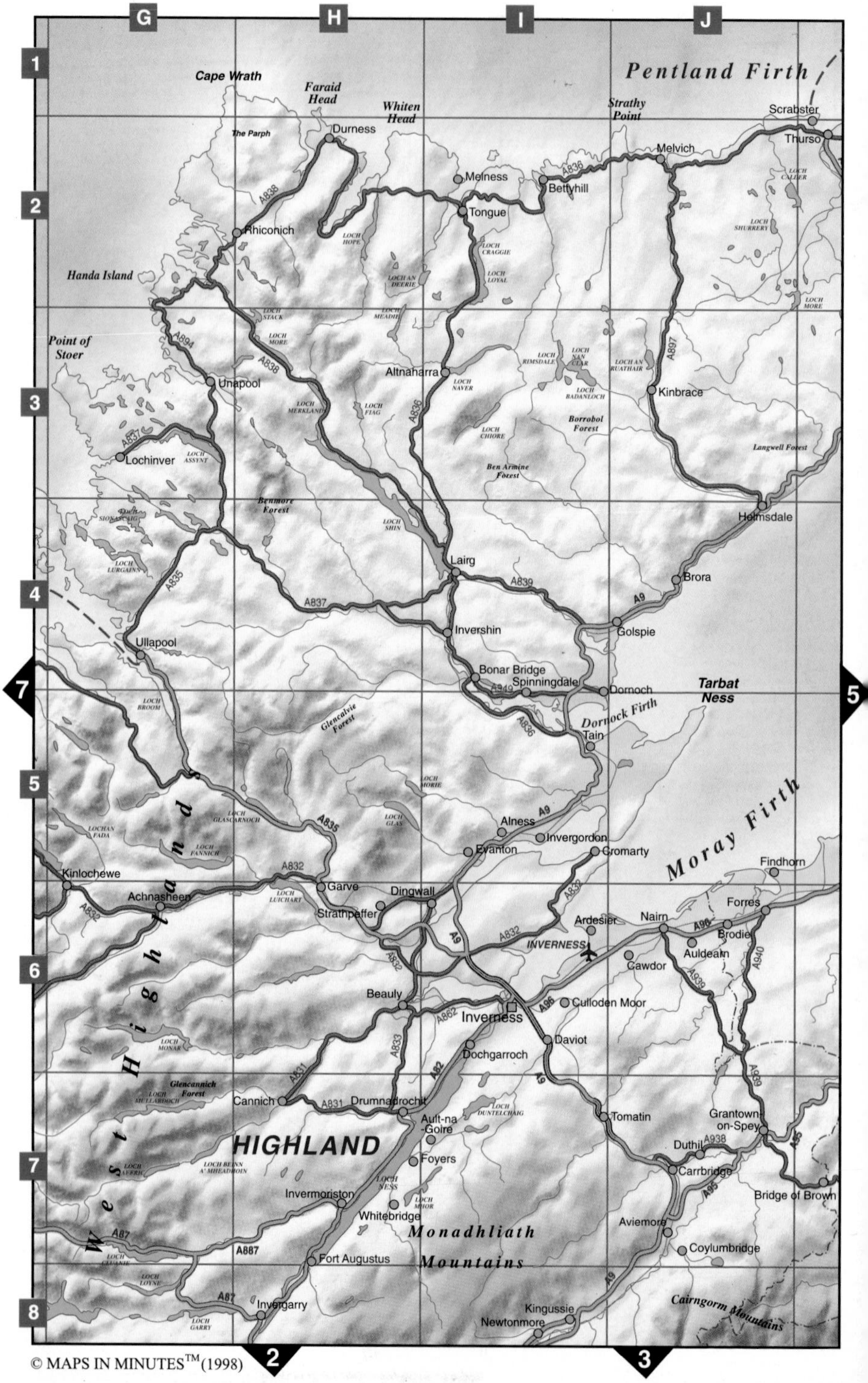

G
H
I
J
1
2
3
4
5
6
7
8
7
5
2
3
Pentland Firth
Cape Wrath
Faraid Head
Whiten Head
Strathy Point
Scrabster
Thurso
Durness
The Parph
Melvich
Melness
Bettyhill
Tongue
Rhiconich
Handa Island
Point of Stoer
Unapool
Altnaharra
Kinbrace
Borrobol Forest
Langwell Forest
Ben Armine Forest
Lochinver
Benmore Forest
Helmsdale
Lairg
Brora
Golspie
Inverhsin
Ullapool
Bonar Bridge
Spinningdale
Dornoch
Tarbat Ness
Dornock Firth
Tain
Glencalvie Forest
Moray Firth
Alness
Invergordon
Evanton
Cromarty
Findhorn
Kinlochewe
Garve
Achnasheen
Dingwall
Strathpeffer
Ardesier
Nairn
Forres
Brodie
Auldearn
INVERNESS
Cawdor
Beauly
Inverness
Culloden Moor
Daviot
Dochgarroch
Cannich
Drumnadrochit
Glencannich Forest
Ault-na-Goire
Tomatin
Grantown-on-Spey
HIGHLAND
Foyers
Duthil
Carrbridge
Invermoriston
Whitebridge
Bridge of Brown
Aviemore
Monadhliath Mountains
Coylumbridge
Fort Augustus
Invergarry
Kingussie
Newtonmore
Cairngorm Mountains
West Highlands
A838
A836
A897
A894
A837
A835
A839
A9
A949
A832
A96
A940
A939
A862
A833
A831
A82
A938
A95
A87
A887

Map 5

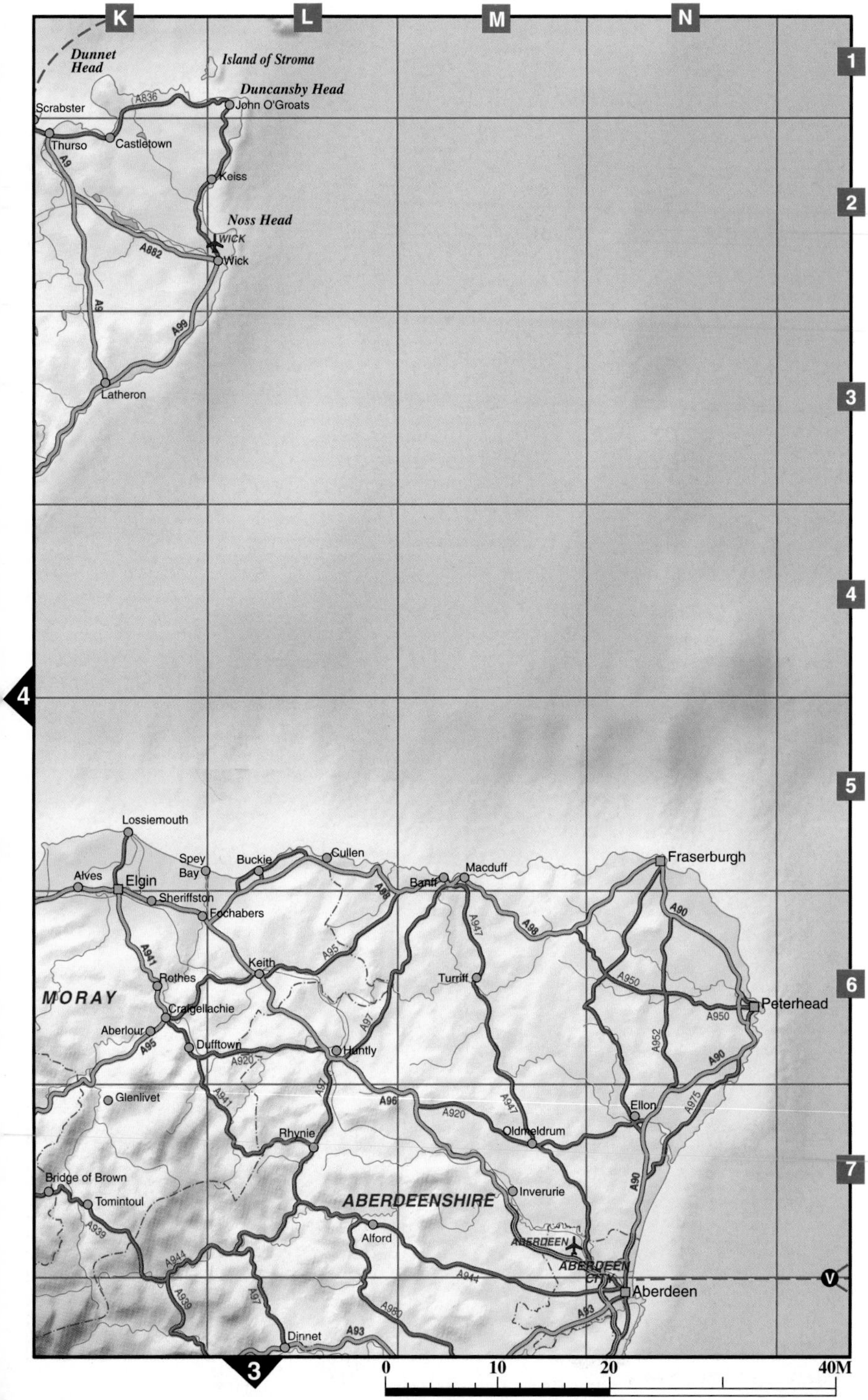
K
L
M
N
1
2
3
4
5
6
7
Dunnet Head
Island of Stroma
Duncansby Head
John O'Groats
Scrabster
A836
Thurso
Castletown
A9
Keiss
Noss Head
WICK
A882
Wick
A99
Latheron
Lossiemouth
Spey Bay
Buckie
Cullen
Alves
Elgin
Sheriffston
Fochabers
Banff
Macduff
A98
Fraserburgh
A90
A947
A95
Keith
A941
Rothes
MORAY
Craigellachie
Turriff
A950
Peterhead
Aberlour
A97
Dufftown
Huntly
A920
A952
Glenlivet
A96
Ellon
A975
Oldmeldrum
Rhynie
Inverurie
Bridge of Brown
Tomintoul
ABERDEENSHIRE
A939
Alford
ABERDEEN
A944
ABERDEEN CITY
V
Aberdeen
A980
A93
Dinnet
0
10
20
40M

Map 6

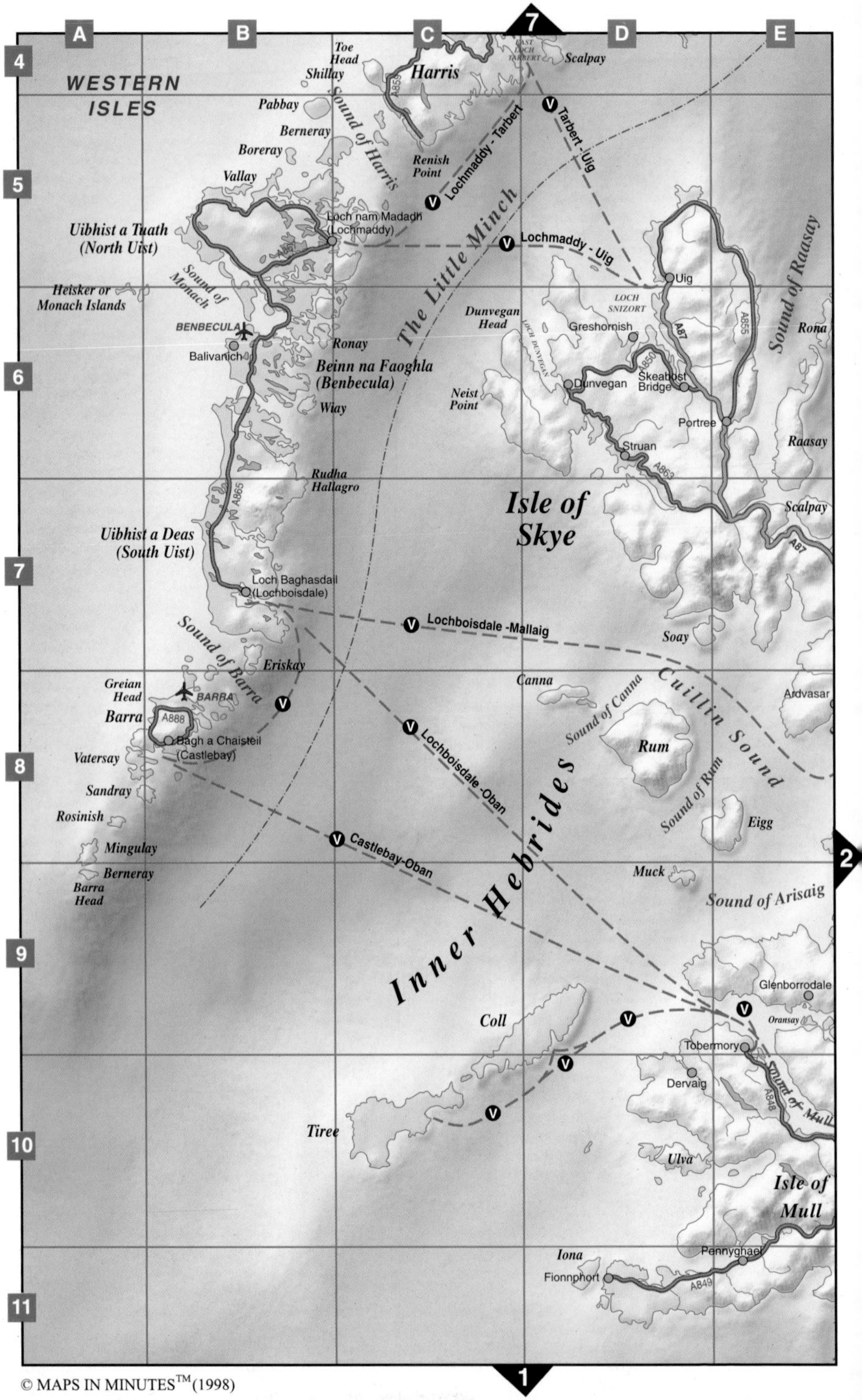
WESTERN ISLES
Harris
Toe Head
Shillay
Pabbay
Berneray
Boreray
Vallay
Sound of Harris
Renish Point
Scalpay
Lochmaddy - Tarbert
Tarbert - Uig
Loch nam Madadh (Lochmaddy)
Lochmaddy - Uig
Uibhist a Tuath (North Uist)
Sound of Monach
Heisker or Monach Islands
BENBECULA
Balivanich
Ronay
Beinn na Faoghla (Benbecula)
Wiay
The Little Minch
Dunvegan Head
Neist Point
Uig
LOCH SNIZORT
Greshornish
Dunvegan
Skeabost Bridge
Portree
Struan
Sound of Raasay
Rona
Raasay
Rudha Hallagro
Isle of Skye
Scalpay
Uibhist a Deas (South Uist)
Loch Baghasdail (Lochboisdale)
Lochboisdale -Mallaig
Soay
Sound of Barra
Eriskay
Greian Head
BARRA
Barra
Bagh a Chaisteil (Castlebay)
Vatersay
Sandray
Rosinish
Mingulay
Berneray
Barra Head
Canna
Sound of Canna
Cuillin Sound
Rum
Ardvasar
Lochboisdale -Oban
Castlebay-Oban
Sound of Rum
Eigg
Muck
Sound of Arisaig
Inner Hebrides
Glenborrodale
Coll
Oransay
Tobermory
Dervaig
Sound of Mull
Tiree
Ulva
Isle of Mull
Iona
Fionnphort
Pennyghael

Map 7

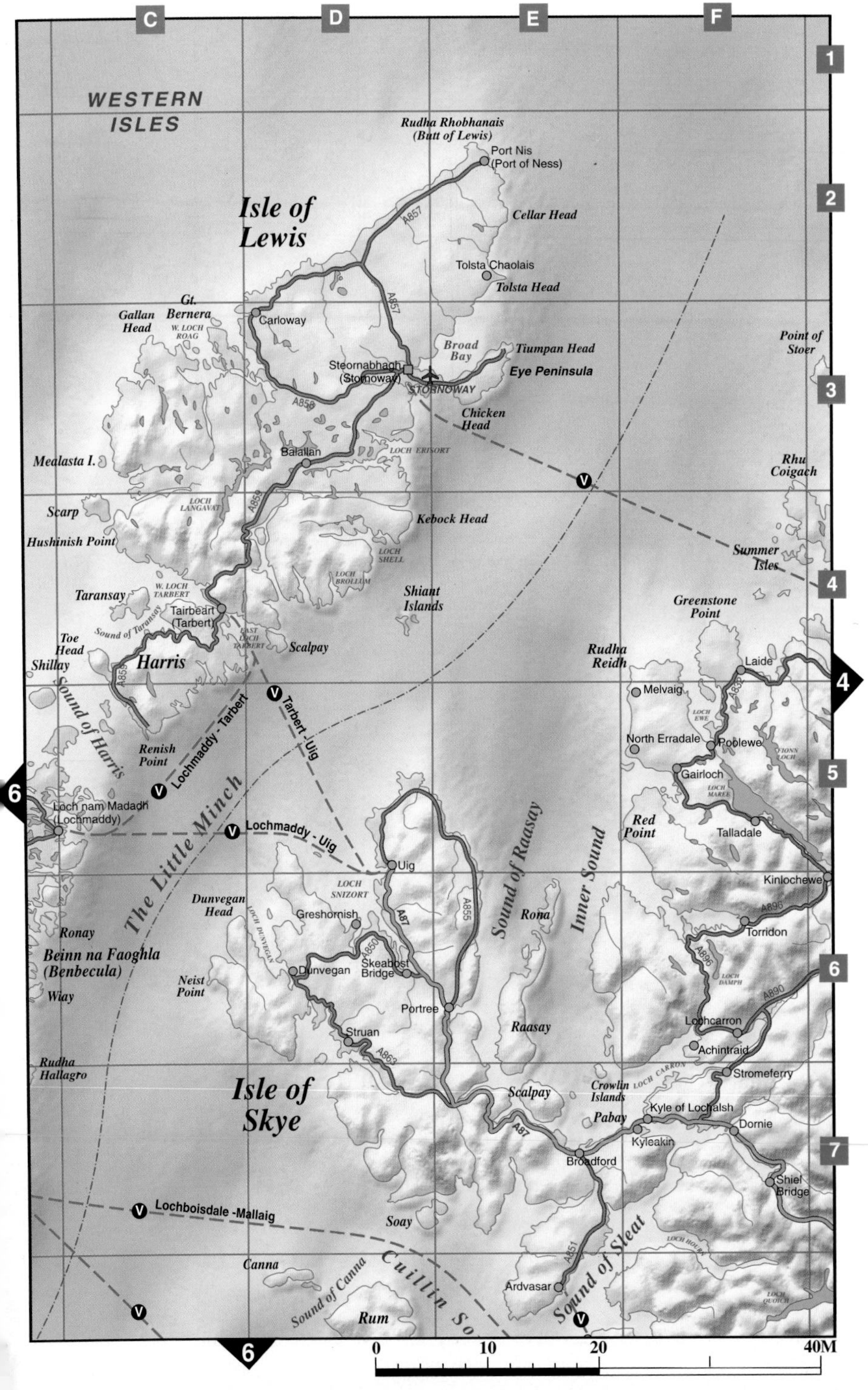

C
D
E
F
1
2
3
4
5
6
7
WESTERN ISLES
Rudha Rhobhanais (Butt of Lewis)
Port Nis (Port of Ness)
Isle of Lewis
A857
Cellar Head
Tolsta Chaolais
Tolsta Head
Gt. Bernera
Gallan Head
W. LOCH ROAG
Carloway
Broad Bay
Tiumpan Head
Eye Peninsula
Steornabhagh (Stornoway)
STORNOWAY
A858
Chicken Head
Point of Stoer
Balallan
LOCH ERISORT
Mealasta I.
Rhu Coigach
Scarp
LOCH LANGAVAT
A859
Kebock Head
Hushinish Point
LOCH SHELL
LOCH BROLLUM
Summer Isles
Taransay
W. LOCH TARBERT
Shiant Islands
Greenstone Point
Tairbeart (Tarbert)
Sound of Taransay
EAST LOCH TARBERT
Scalpay
Toe Head
Harris
Rudha Reidh
Shillay
Laide
Melvaig
Tarbert - Uig
Lochmaddy - Tarbert
Sound of Harris
LOCH EWE
A832
North Erradale
Poolewe
Renish Point
FIONN LOCH
Gairloch
LOCH MAREE
Loch nam Madadh (Lochmaddy)
Lochmaddy - Uig
The Little Minch
Sound of Raasay
Inner Sound
Red Point
Talladale
Uig
LOCH SNIZORT
A855
A87
Kinlochewe
Dunvegan Head
LOCH DUNVEGAN
Greshornish
Rona
A896
Torridon
Ronay
A850
Beinn na Faoghla (Benbecula)
Dunvegan
Skeabost Bridge
LOCH DAMPH
Neist Point
A890
Wiay
Portree
Raasay
Lochcarron
Struan
Achintraid
A863
Rudha Hallagro
LOCH CARRON
Stromeferry
Isle of Skye
Scalpay
Crowlin Islands
Pabay
Kyle of Lochalsh
Kyleakin
Dornie
Broadford
Shiel Bridge
Lochboisdale -Mallaig
Soay
Sound of Sleat
LOCH HOURN
A851
Canna
Cuillin So
Sound of Canna
Ardvasar
LOCH QUOICH
Rum
0
10
20
40M

Orkney

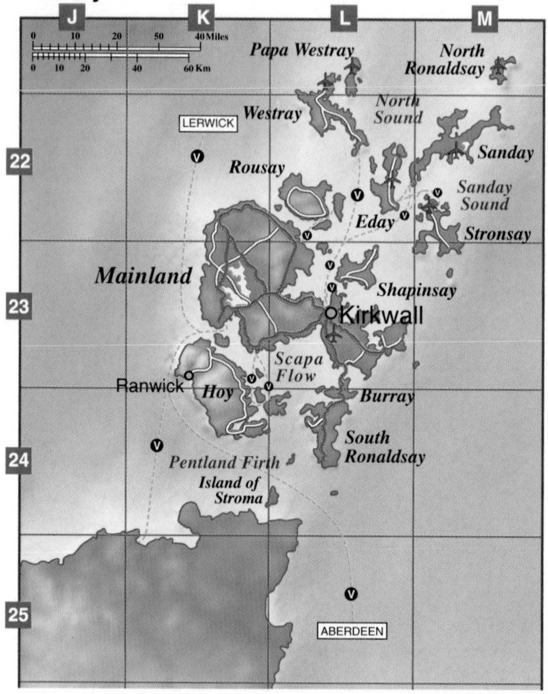
J
K
L
M
0 10 20 50 40 Miles
0 10 20 40 60 Km
22
23
24
25
Papa Westray
North Ronaldsay
Westray
North Sound
LERWICK
Sanday
Rousay
Sanday Sound
Eday
Stronsay
Mainland
Shapinsay
Kirkwall
Scapa Flow
Ranwick
Hoy
Burray
South Ronaldsay
Pentland Firth
Island of Stroma
ABERDEEN

Shetland

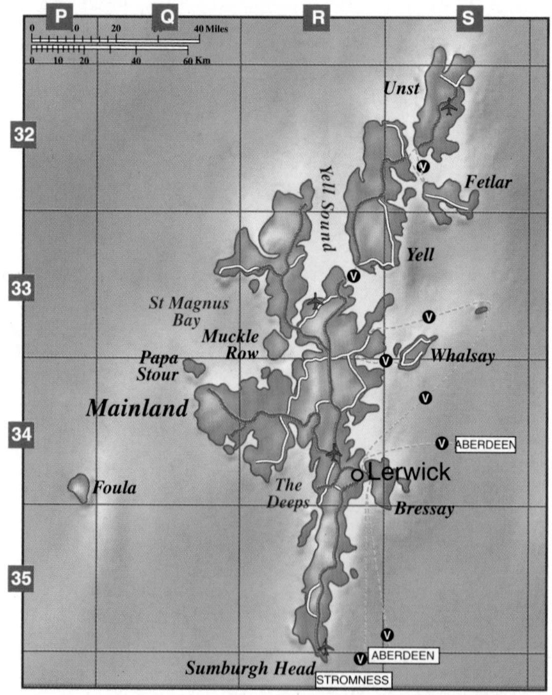
P
Q
R
S
0 10 20 40 Miles
0 10 20 40 60 Km
32
33
34
35
Unst
Yell Sound
Fetlar
Yell
St Magnus Bay
Muckle Row
Whalsay
Papa Stour
Mainland
ABERDEEN
Lerwick
Foula
The Deeps
Bressay
ABERDEEN
Sumburgh Head
STROMNESS